ISBN 978-1-331-85180-6
PIBN 10242162

English
Français
Deutsche
Italiano
Español
Português

www.forgottenbooks.com

Mythology Photography **Fiction**
Fishing Christianity **Art** Cooking
Essays Buddhism Freemasonry
Medicine **Biology** Music **Ancient
Egypt** Evolution Carpentry Physics
Dance Geology **Mathematics** Fitness
Shakespeare **Folklore** Yoga Marketing
Confidence Immortality Biographies
Poetry **Psychology** Witchcraft
Electronics Chemistry History **Law**
Accounting **Philosophy** Anthropology
Alchemy Drama Quantum Mechanics
Atheism Sexual Health **Ancient History**
Entrepreneurship Languages Sport
Paleontology Needlework Islam
Metaphysics Investment Archaeology
Parenting Statistics Criminology
Motivational

"I am the Light of the World."
—Jᴇsᴜs.

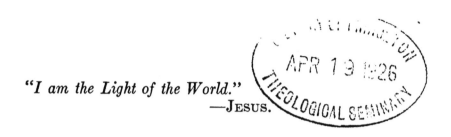

NINE
REAT PREACHERS

BY

ALBERT H. ᵛCURRIER, D.D.

THE RUMFORD PRESS
CONCORD · N · H · U · S · A

DEDICATION

To his former pupils, students of his classes in Oberlin Theological Seminary during the twenty-six years of his service in that institution as instructor in the art of preaching, whose careers he has followed with sympathetic interest ever since they went forth at graduation to the great work of preaching the Gospel, this volume is affectionately dedicated by

THE AUTHOR

PREFACE

The biographical studies contained in this volume have been culled from a delightful field of literature. For many years the author has roamed about this field with pleasure and profit. From the experience thus obtained he heartily concurs in the opinion of Professor Benjamin Jowett, the famous Master of Balliol College, Oxford University, that "Of great men it may be truly said that it does us good only to look at them. The lives of great and good men are the best sermons; and the preacher may do well sometimes to shield himself behind them and so to speak with greater authority than his own words could fairly claim." Professor Jowett's volume of "Biographical Sermons" affords a good illustration of the truth of his words.

If "history is philosophy teaching by example," as an eminent writer has said, biography of this kind is even more; it is both philosophy and Christianity exemplified in the most impressive object-lessons.

The author cherishes the hope that the studies given in this volume which relate to preachers of different denominations, will convince its readers that "All faiths afford the constant and the wise"— a better acquaintance with whom through its pages will be found stimulating and profitable. It is his belief that we do well as Christians to recognize the comprehensive character of Christianity and the essential agreement of its adherents of different names. Our hymnals contain, and we use in our public worship with hearty enjoyment and spiritual benefit, hymns composed by Catholics, Anglicans, Presbyterians, Methodists, Quakers, Unitarians and other religious hymn-writers. They assist the devotions and kindle to the adoration of God and faith in Christ all Christian believers. A similar effect is produced by the lives and sermons of the preachers of different denominations. They reveal "one faith, one hope, one baptism''; they inspire and nourish in us the same religious sentiments, and convey to us the essential truth of the Gospel of Jesus Christ.

Whatever, then, the religious denomination one may belong to, his attitude to other Christians should be one of brotherly kindness and tolerance instead of sectarian coldness. No good reason can be given why they should not heartily unite in the promotion and support of measures of approved value for the social and moral welfare of mankind, or for the establishment and support of whatever form of worship and Christian fellowship may seem best, or alone feasible, in the community where they live.

"I cannot," says Richard Baxter, "be so narrow in my principles of church communion as many are, that are so much for a liturgy, or so much against it; so much for ceremonies, or so much against them, that they can hold communion with no church that is not of their mind and way. I am not for narrowing the church more than Christ himself alloweth us, nor for robbing him of any of bis flock."

By scorning such narrowness and cordially fraternizing with all who sincerely profess to love and honor Christ we best honor his name and illustrate the harmony of feeling and practice existing among the Christians expressed in one of the best of our Christian hymns:

> "O Lord and Master of us all!
>   Whate'er our name or sign,
>   We own thy sway, we hear thy call.
>   We test our lives by thine."
>
> *Whittier.*

Of the biographical studies composing this volume, two, *Bossuet* and *John Bunyan*, have previously appeared in the *Bibliotheca Sacra*, and the author is indebted to the kindness of the publishers of that quarterly for the permission to insert them here. Of the rest, none have been published before.

Oberlin, O., January 25th, 1912.

TABLE OF CONTENTS

NINE GREAT PREACHERS

I
INTRODUCTION

INTRODUCTION

THE INTEREST AND VALUE OF MINISTERIAL BIOGRAPHIES

We desire to present to the consideration of our readers some special reasons that recommend this class of literature to them for their perusal and study. Before entering, however, upon the consideration of these reasons one or two objections sometimes made to such studies claim brief notice.

It may be said that the writers of these biographies are usually partial friends or blind hero-worshippers, and that they do not give a true and reliable account of the men whom they pretend to describe; they exaggerate their merits, and they hide or extenuate their faults to such a degree that the result is entirely untrustworthy and misleading. Such men as they describe, it may therefore be said, never really lived, and the admirable portraits of them which they present are largely creations of their own imaginations. So the admiration they excite in us is unwarranted and not likely to prove beneficial, as no good can be expected from what is false. To this objection it may be replied that it is easy to make all proper deductions for the possible partiality and hero-worship. We do this continually in our estimates of those whom the

3

fond partiality of relatives or friends clothes with unreal perfections. It is possible and easy to discern the shadow of truth underneath the exaggerations. They represent, we may say, what the clearer vision of love perceives—the soul of excellence in spite of every fault. They represent, if not what the persons portrayed really were as judged by an uncharitable world, yet what they aimed to be and often seemed to be. And it may be insisted that there is profit in the contemplation of this, though somewhat of hallucination is experienced. It is good for men to believe in the possibility of such excellence. The hallucination, if such there be, is similar to that which some celebrated piece of antique statuary like the Venus di Milo, or the Hermes of Praxiteles, recovered from the ruins of Olympia, exerts upon an admiring art student or susceptible spectator, who though he must own and regret the mutilations that mar its beauty, yet in spite of them discerns the glorious ideal that the artist had in mind and to a large extent expressed in his work, and which still survives the marring effect of its mutilation.

It may be also objected to such studies that they are likely to prove more injurious than beneficial by inducing a slavish imitation of the subjects of them to the loss of one's independence of mind. There is, perhaps, some danger of this. Phillips Brooks, who highly extols the value of biographical literature, candidly confesses the danger. "Here," he says, "is the only danger I know in the reading of biographies, lest he who reads should lose himself,

4

shall come to be not himself, but the feeble repetition of some other man." The same danger, however, attends our highest blessings; the blessings of friendship, of social intercourse, of study of the great masters of style, and of the inspiring authors of remarkable works of literature.

But we do not because of this danger refuse to form friendships, or decline the pleasure of intercourse with attractive people, or the benefit that comes from familiarity with the masters of literature. We guard against the danger by trying to get from these blessings their proper benefit. This, in every case, is not that of servile imitation, but of inspiration or suggestion. Instead of surrendering our personal independence and "swamping" ourselves or suppressing our own creative powers in the endeavor to imitate them, we are incited, if we use them aright, to improve ourselves and perfect our work by the suggestions they give. Their effect on the mind is that of a fertilizing agency, by which its natural powers are not dwarfed or extinguished but stimulated to answer the ends of its existence. It is like the influence of Milton on Burke, or of Tillotson on Dryden, by which these eminent writers became not copyists of the styles of Milton and Tillotson, but makers, each of them, of a better style of their own. The same thing is true of the ideas obtained from the study of the masterpieces of literature. The mind thus becomes not only a casket of pearls gathered from the writers studied, but a producer of pearls itself. The pearls of thought gathered are seed thoughts. Sown in the mind, they make it a fruitful bed of pearls, *i. e.*, they produce harvests of similar ideas, often expressed and shaped with similar felicity, but a felicity of their own.

Let us now consider some reasons that commend ministerial biographies to us as profitable for perusal and study.

I. *There is a strong presumption in favor of such books, as likely to afford profitable reading, from the fact that they belong to the same class of literature as the Gospels and the book of Acts.* The whole Bible, indeed, may be described as a collection of biographies rather than of religious dogmas and precepts. Its method of teaching is not so much didactic as illustrative. It instructs us in the nature and obligations of religion principally by examples and object-lessons rather than by doctrinal statements and definitions. How precious and impressive these sacred biographies of the Bible are, whether of the Old Testament or of the New! The longest of them is not a word too long; the shortest of them is so significant that an ocean of meaning seems to be contained in a drop of words. Take that of Enoch, for example. What is said of him is compressed in a few sentences. There is nothing here to satisfy vain curiosity, no elaborate narrative touching things private or public, but little more than is summed up in the declaration—"And Enoch walked with God, and he was not, for God took him." But how sublimely significant, nevertheless, this declaration is! It is like the enbalmed heart of a king, the rest of whose body has turned to indistinguishable dust. Nothing more

6

is needed to give us the assurance that here was one of earth's great men, and that he deserved a place in the roll of God's saints.

Still more may be said of the biographies of the New Testament. That of Christ in the Gospels is an inestimable treasure; that of the apostles an unfailing inspiration. By means of these sacred biographies of the Bible the knowledge of God and of the effect of his saving truth has been spread abroad and is kept alive in the world. Generation after generation feed upon them and derive spiritual life from them. By them our faith is firmly anchored in the teachings of our religion. By them the church of God continually renews its ideals of Christian character and duty. According to the study given them and the observance paid to their teachings is its standard of piety and endeavor. If they are neglected, its spiritual life declines; if they are thoughtfully read and pondered, this life is invigorated and it exerts a transforming influence over the world.

The influence of ministerial biographies is in the same line with the power of the sacred Scriptures. The subjects of them, almost without exception, fully believed in and loved the Bible. They were diligent students of its pages, they embraced its invitations, they relied upon its promises, they obeyed its precepts. Their religious faith was shaped by its instruction; from it they "fetched the sacred fire that kindled their sacrifices." They were, in short, Bible Christians; their ministry was a Bible ministry, and whatever success they had in the world they owed to this fact. It may, therefore, be truthfully said that the credit of their characters and work gives new luster and credit to the Bible, inasmuch as they are embodiments of its great ideas. Embodying its great ideas, they exhibit its best fruit—that of an earnest vital piety. And if the perusal of their biographies do nothing else but quicken the piety of their readers and give them a higher standard of piety, they receive from them the best thing they can get and what is most essential to their own welfare and the good of society.

These biographies, furthermore, illustrate and confirm the truth of the Scriptures; they stamp it as divine. Now that the attesting power of the early miracles, authenticating Christianity as from God, has become somewhat enfeebled by lapse of time, and the record of its mighty works in the beginning has by familiarity grown less impressive, and doubt and incredulity are beginning to rise in men's minds with palsying effect, this truth has received a fresh attestation of its divine origin and authority from these examples of its indestructible vitality. By reason of them the believing people of God can say: "Now we know that it is no transient superstition, nor cunningly devised fable, as the emboldened scepticism of the age asserts. In it there dwells a supernatural potency—an undecaying vitality. Like the Christ, whom it presents, it is "the same yesterday, today and forever." Age doth not wither it, nor the growth of knowledge discredit it. It is authenticated as the truth of God in the nineteenth and twentieth centuries by mighty works quite as marvelous as those which attested it in the first century. Its continual operation in the world has been, and is such as to create what Doctor Storrs called "a standing miracle"—"the standing miracle of Christendom," to bear constant and indubitable witness to its truth. The lives of eminent missionaries of the past century to the unchristian peoples of the world—of Judson, Coan, Williams, Paton, Thoburn, Hume and many others too numerous to mention, and the lives of humble city missionaries, such as Lord Shaftsbury speaks of as his helpers in the effort to evangelize and uplift the poor of London, and of such devoted lay-preachers and Christian toilers among the poor of New York as those described in "Down in Water Street," and in Dr. J. W. Chapman's "Life of S. H. Hadley": and the lives of devoted ministers and evangelists, as Edward Payson, C. L. Goodell, Charles G. Finney and Mr. Moody, are filled with wonderful works as great and marvelous as those of the apostles. Doctor Pierson cannot be accused of exaggeration in calling the story of their achievements "A New Acts of the Apostles." These "New Acts," equally with the Old, prove the Gospel "the power of God unto salvation." It is not an extinguished torch whose oil is entirely consumed and whose wick has burned to a cinder. It is on the contrary an inextinguishable torch whose flame is fed from inexhaustible sources and which burns without being consumed like the burning bush, which the Church of Scotland has made the symbol of its enduring faith and inextinguishable life.

9

II. *These ministerial biographies are very entertaining.* Nowhere in the whole range of literature, can we spend more delightful hours, or find more healthful mental recreation than among the published reminiscences of clergymen, such as Charles Kinglsey, F. W. Robertson and C. H. Spurgeon of England; and Lyman Beecher, Charles G. Finney, Henry Ward Beecher, Phillips Brooks and Edward Everett Hale, of our country. A good example was given the past year in *The Outlook* for Nov. 12th, in the "Reminiscences of Edward Everett Hale" by George S. Merriam. It seemed to us in reading it a charming and effective piece of portraiture, by which every trait of that admirable man was set forth with abundant wealth of illustration and felicity of style. He possessed a rare combination of qualities, mental, moral and social and he was largely endowed with each kind. His inventiveness and fertility of mind were apparent from the number of his writings. But numerous as these were—flowing seemingly from an inexhaustible spring—their excellence was as remarkable as their quantity. Mr. Merriam says: "He had wit, he had humor, and something more—a vein of fancy, a happy and merry make-believe. . . . His peculiar humor and fancy blossomed out in a fairy-story quality which he often threw into his writings. It gave sometimes a whimsical form to his inveterate optimism. He turned to it for his own and his friends' delectation as a child turns to its play. It tinges many of his stories of serious purpose like 'Ten Times One is Ten.' Truth to tell, the roseate hue sometimes is followed by a touch of disheartenment in the listeners. Real drunkards are not always so surely and swiftly reformed; the visible Kingdom of God does not seem to advance by a tenfold multiplication annually. . . . But his rainbows made the tramp along the dusty highway more cheerful even if you never found the pot of gold." His moral and social qualities made him a wise and sympathetic counsellor of people of every class—of those in perplexity and trouble, and those afflicted with sore bereavement. His "happy and merry make-believe" made him the welcome companion of children and imaginative young people, and his fancy with its bias to drollery mingled with wisdom wove wholesome fictions and extravagances that forced smiles and approval from both the fun-loving and the serious-minded. His religious creed and his preaching were marked by the broadest charity; and he sought to win men to his religious belief not by arguments and theological controversy, but by "the way of life which he taught and which he lived and which . . . generates an atmosphere in which scepticism withers." "Life—that," says Mr. Merriam, "was his characteristic word, and the motto on his church stationery was, 'I am come that they might have life and that they might have it more abundantly.'"

To meet this man on the street, and receive his greeting of "Good Morning," was a benediction that made the whole day good. Similar is the effect of perusing these "Reminiscences," in which his friend has embalmed his memory.

One rises from the perusal refreshed, morally invigorated and inspired with the purpose of fulfilling Mr. Hale's parting exhortation on one occasion to this friend: "Make good society where you are." Not all the reminiscences of clergymen, we admit, are equally interesting with this example, but generally, we repeat, ministerial biographies are entertaining. Our judgment is based upon quite a wide acquaintance with them; which experience, candidly weighed, leads us to recognize the truth of a witty remark once made in our hearing in regard to the ministry by the Rev. Daniel Butler, familiarly known as "Bible Butler," as representing the American Bible Society in Boston and the churches of New England. Witnessing their sparkling sallies of wit and racy wisdom before the meeting, as they gathered at the entrance of the church and upon the lawn, on an occasion that brought a large number of ministers together, Mr. Butler dryly said: "The hilarity of my ministerial brethren at these gatherings always reminds me of the words of the Psalmist: 'The trees of the Lord are full of sap!'"

III. *The biographies of eminent servants of God in the work of the ministry—whether ecclesiastically ordained thereto, or unordained—afford an effective cure for religious discouragement and depression.* Sometimes in their religious works and Christian activities good people are dismayed at the number and greatness of the obstacles opposed to them. Because of the infirmity of our human nature their zeal abates and their spirits flag. It seems to them, then, that their work is altogether vain; that they accomplish little or nothing by it, that their best efforts result only in weariness and disappointment. "Why attempt anything further?" "Why spend our strength for naught?" the discouraged heart then cries. These suggestions have a paralyzing effect. The strongest and most energetic and courageous men, like Elijah and John the Baptist and the great reformers, Luther, Knox, and the most heroic missionaries, have all felt the depressing spell and been almost overcome by it, so as to sink down into a state of dull apathy and despair. At such times a good biography—with its thrilling account of noble and beneficent achievement—is a wholesome spiritual tonic. It energizes and inspires the tired heart and jaded spirits with fresh life and renewed vigor. The subject of it encountered similar obstacles and felt similar discouragement— but roused by the voice and strengthened by the power of God, he rose up and renewed the fight and won at last. Its effect is like that of martial music upon soldiers weary with long marches and faint with hunger. The trumpet peal revives their courage—rekindles their ardor and nerves them to a conquering pitch of endeavor. It is a familiar story of classic literature that Themistocles, the leader of the Greeks at Salamis, was stimulated to those daring efforts which gave them the victory by the remembered example of Miltiades the Greek leader at Marathon. So the leaders of the Church have often been incited to triumphant effort by the examples of those who had wrought righteousness in the service of God. This is one of God's ways of inspiring man, a method of his providence. The coals from off his altar, by which his chosen ones have had their lips touched to eloquence and their sins of indolence and cowardice purged away, are the bright records of those who have laid themselves upon his altar and worked for his glory.

IV. *In the reading and study of ministerial biographies, we receive interesting and valuable suggestions as to the best methods of ministerial work, and the best means of attaining the highest success in the ministry.* Such knowledge is particularly valuable to ministers themselves, who more than any other class are likely to be readers of these biographies. The subjects of them were among the most eminent and successful in their sacred calling. But for their distinction in it, in some way or other, their biographies would not have been given to the world. The fact of a biography in every case implies that the subject of it was believed to be more than ordinary; that his life contained important lessons, or was marked by extraordinary achievements; or that he possessed a character of such beauty and moral excellence as make it deserving of general admiration and worthy of emulation. But his eminence and success may have been due as much to the wise methods he used as to his superior moral and mental qualities, or his genius. In respect to the latter, he may be—probably *is* —inimitable; in respect to the former, his example can be profitably studied and to some extent copied. We think it may be truly affirmed that ordinary abilities trained and directed by wise methods will often appear to better advantage and achieve more usefulness than extraordinary abilities ill-directed. This remark will be found true of the whole range of ministerial activity. Whether we consider his pulpit performances or his pastoral work, a good method counts for much. Such methods are often discovered or suggested in the biographies of eminent ministers. These methods were peculiar to the persons whose ministry they distinguished. There is wisdom in studying them and often great advantage in adopting them. By doing this, one is saved from mistakes and the loss of time and the toil involved in painfully and slowly groping for a way to success, when a clear and practicable way has been already discovered and its value well tested.

We venture to particularize some valuable accomplishments that may be thus acquired: Several things are involved in the art of effective preaching. Foremost among these are personal piety, a familiar acquaintance with the Bible, a good understanding of its teaching, the ability to reason soundly, and the skill to put one's thoughts logically and attractively together. Besides these, an opulent and forcible diction ready to the tongue, the power of apt illustration, of natural and easy gesture and a good voice, which the preacher knows how to manage so as impressively to express the varying shades of thought and feeling that occur in speaking; these are usual adjuncts of pulpit power.

As illustrating the value of a good voice, well managed, we quote what President Francis

Wayland, of Brown University, says of the preaching of Dr. Eliphalet Nott: "When settled in Albany, his reputation as a preacher was unparalleled. Those who heard his sermon on the death of Hamilton declared it was the most eloquent discourse they ever heard. So far as I can recall his manner, after the lapse of many years, the excellency which gave him so great power was in the tones of his voice. I would almost say they were so perfect that a man who did not understand English would, from his tones alone, have been able to form an idea of the train of thought he was pursuing. When he uttered a sentence, the emphasis, inflections and tones were so perfect that every part was distinctly connected with that to which it belonged and you never failed to comprehend his meaning precisely. When to this were joined the tones of emotion adapted to every range of human feeling, you may possibly perceive what must have been the effect." In the biography of Doctor Guthrie we have a similar testimony as to the power and charm of his voice: "He had a powerful, clear and musical voice, the intonations of which were varied and appropriate, managed with an actor's skill though there was not the least appearance of art."

This power of the voice, characteristic of almost all eminent preachers and orators, is almost never a natural gift. It is largely the result of elocutionary training. It was so with Guthrie and Nott. Whitefield and Beecher, and a study of their biographies will reveal their methods of improving it. Guthrie thus tells how it was with himself: "When a divinity student I paid more than ordinary attention to the art of elocution, knowing how much of the effect produced upon the audience depended on the *manner* as well as on the matter; that in point of fact the manner is to the matter as the powder is to the ball. I attended elocution classes winter after winter, walking across half the city and more after eight o'clock at night, fair night and foul, and not getting back to my lodgings until about 10:30 o'clock. There I learned to find out and correct many acquired and more or less awkward defects in gesture, to be in fact natural; to acquire a command over my voice so as to suit its force and emphasis to the sense, and to modulate it so as to express the feelings, whether of surprise or grief or indignation or pity. I had heard very indifferent discourses made forcible by a vigorous delivery, and able ones reduced to feebleness by a poor pithless delivery. I had read of the extraordinary pains Demosthenes and Cicero took to cultivate their manner of public speaking and become masters of the arts of elocution, and I knew how by a masterly and *natural* use of them Whitefield could sway the crowds that gathered to hear him at early morn on the commons of London.''

Guthrie likewise possessed to an eminent degree the power of apt, impressive illustration. Joined to the witchery of his voice, it amounted sometimes to a power of enchantment. His auditors were then spellbound by it. An amusing instance is presented in the conduct of a Highland cattledrover one day in Guthrie's congregation in Free

St. John's. The man stood throughout the service in one of the crowded aisles within a few yards of the pulpit. From the first he was riveted, a pinch of snuff every now and then evincing his satisfaction. Toward the end of the sermon and just as)the preacher was commencing a prolonged illustration the stranger applied to his horn mull. Arrested, however, he stood motionless, his hand raised with the snuff between his fingers, his head thrown back, his eyes and mouth wide open. The instant that the passage was finished and before the audience had time to recover their breath, the drover applied the snuff with gusto to his nostrils, and forgetting in his excitement alike the place and the occasion, turned his head to the crowd behind and exclaimed, "Na, Sirs, I *never* heard the like of that!"

Such a power of vivid illustration is invaluable to a preacher. It is characteristic of the greatest preachers. Chrysostom had it, and so bound his hearers as with a spell that pickpockets plied their trade without detection among them while he was preaching. Beecher had it to a remarkable degree, as the writer remembers well from having often sat spellbound when a young man under his preaching. To be sure, natural gifts of imagination and fancy are required, as a bird must have wings to fly. But these gifts must be exercised and suitably directed. The faculty of skilful and appropriate illustration is a product of diligent self-culture with a basis of native endowment. This was the case with Guthrie and Beecher. Both of these preachers developed it by painstaking effort, having early in their ministry discovered its effectiveness in addresses to popular audiences.

It gives me pleasure to be able to quote the following testimony of the late Dr. William M. Taylor, of New York, in support of my opinions. He says: "If I may speak from my own experience there is no faculty which is more susceptible of development by culture than that of discovering analogies. When I commenced my ministry, it was a rare thing with me to use an illustration. My style then was particularly argumentative, and my aim was to convince and satisfy the understanding, and then to make my appeal warmly to the heart. But shortly after my removal from my Scotch parsonage to Liverpool, Guthrie's "Gospel in Ezekiel" was published, and this was followed a few months later by Mr. Beecher's "Life Thoughts." These two books opened my eyes to see what was lying all around me. Under the inspiration which they communicated to me, I began to look for spiritual analogies in everything. The books I read; the places I visited; the incidents that passed under my observation; the discoveries of science with which I became acquainted—all were scanned by me for the purpose of finding in them, if possible, something that might be used in pulpit illustration. And so it came that when I sat down to my desk, appropriate analogies would rise to my pen, and the difficulty was not how to get illustrations, but which to choose out of the many that offered themselves for my purpose." (See "The Ministry of the Word," page 192.)

The autobiographic testimony of Doctor Taylor proves both that the illustrative faculty, when naturally small, may be greatly developed and improved, and that he learned the methods of its culture and effective use from Guthrie and Beecher to transmit them in turn to others in the ministry.

✓ Another important and essential requisite to effective preaching is a good style of oral address. We mean by this—as distinguished from a bookish or essay style—an easy, forcible, *talking* style, that shall give fit and orderly expression to one's flowing thought in the presence of a congregation of listeners. Mere fluency is not enough, nor imperturbable boldness of spirit, though self-possession is necessary. It implies a careful premeditation, so that one knows what he wants to say, and a command of language and of the mental faculties so complete and absolute that he can utter his thought with sure and ready tongue and full swing of personality, without hesitation and with natural appropriate feeling.

This style of utterance more than any other thing distinguishes a powerful preacher. There are various methods of acquiring it according as men are made. Some have acquired it by following the suggestions of Dr. R. S. Storrs in his valuable "Preaching without Notes," which is largely descriptive of his own interesting experience in the ministry; others like Fox and Pitt, the great English Parliamentary orators, as described by Goodrich's "British Orators," by the practice of translating aloud into idiomatic English the great orators of antiquity, combined with the resolute determination to speak whenever opportunity was given; still others, as Bunyan and Spurgeon, Newman Hall and Moody, did theirs by beginning early, with their hearts aflame to tell men of God's love and his salvation through faith in Christ, though they did it bunglingly and with many grammatical errors and ludicrous mistakes joined to confusion of mind and matter; but they would not wait to obtain more polish "nor stand shivering on the brink," but plunged boldly into the stream of talk, resolved to "sink or swim, survive or perish," in a brave endeavor to speak their message, with the result that they made themselves by persistent practice effective preachers, whose style was that of earnest men talking to other men of the way of salvation.

Bossuet, the greatest of the French pulpit orators, acquired his remarkable style, as Alexander Hamilton and Daniel Webster acquired theirs, by previous writing upon the topic of discourse. So much did Bossuet write, that he may be said to have written out his sermons entirely before he went into the pulpit. But "the written sermon," says his biographer, "was not written to be exactly repeated." This effort of memory while speaking he could not make; he would have lost much of his freedom and force and naturalness if he had attempted it. Handicapped by this burden laid upon his mind, the fire and force of his soul would have been sensibly affected. The purpose of previous writing was not to provide himself with the exact words needed to express his thought, but to develop his thought and to familiarize his mind with the ground to be gone over, that, with a clear foresight of the way and the goal, he might run forward with all his speed. Then he trusted to his powers of expression as determined by circumstances and the inspiration of the moment, and the sermon as preached was usually almost identical in language with the one written. The thing to be noticed is that this eloquent preacher, of such resources and gifts, took so much pains to prepare himself with his pen beforehand, as if he could not trust himself otherwise to speak well. With a fertile imagination and great readiness of speech, he left little to chance. Though he might have won admiration with slight toil by the mere exercise of his splendid gifts, for forty years he never ceased from toiling to satisfy his standard of excellence and make himself more perfect.

The biographies of these different men show their various methods of preparation. Wise and happy is he who by study of them finds a model best suited to himself for imitation and acquires a good style of oral address.

Another valuable acquirement which ministers, particularly those of non-liturgical denominations, may obtain from the study of ministerial biographies, is the ability to lead their congregations acceptably and happily in public worship. To give voice, in prayer, to the spiritual affections and religious longings of their congregations is not the least important function of such ministers. Bishop Vincent of the Methodist Episcopal Church once told the writer that he regarded it as the most difficult of their public duties, and one which, he thought, is seldom happily performed. When it is thus performed and gives fit expression to the conscious needs and aspirations of the worshippers, how acceptable it is! Then the minister is a true priest to his people, bringing them near to God and offering in their behalf appropriate sacrifices of praise and prayer in which they heartily concur. How shall one qualify himself to perform this important and difficult office? Ministers, and also devout laymen who occasionally lead the devotions of others, often wish they had the secret of success. There is no better way of acquiring it than by study of the biographies of those ministers who have been eminent for it, and ascertaining through these how they won their success. Such were Edward Payson and the late C. L. Goodsell of St. Louis. That which was most prized and distinctive in their public ministries was their pulpit prayers. These impressed and edified their congregations more than their sermons. "His prayers," says one who had the privilege of sitting under the ministry of Doctor Payson, "always took my spirit into the immediate presence of Christ amid the glories of the spiritual world. It was always a letting down to open my eyes when he had concluded and find myself still on the earth." His biography tells us the secret of his eminence in this service. In the first place, as a godly man he daily exercised his spirit in private prayer. His heart and his lips were *habituated* to it, because he felt it to be a religious duty and he found sincere delight in it. In addition to this, he made the subjcet of public prayer a matter of special study and much thought. He endeavored to form right conceptions of it, to determine what its true purpose is, what the conditions are of its right performance, and he wrote out his thoughts upon the subject in a valuable paper that is included in his biography. Thus his soul became so conversant with the theory and practice of prayer, private and public, that it easily winged its flight to the throne of God and delighted in communion with him, and also made others sharers of its spiritual rapture, as a practiced singer who delights in song lifts to heaven the souls of those that hear. In this way Dr. Payson made what is too often a cold and uninteresting part of the public worship of the sanctuary a means of grace and of spiritual joy to worshippers. If the ministerial reader of his biography is encouraged in the endeavor to impart a similar interest to this office of public prayer, he receives an inestimable benefit himself and communicates it to his fellow worshippers.

Methods of successful pastoral work as well as of pulpit ministration may be learned from ministerial biographies. No minister of the gospel can read those of Baxter, McChene, C. L. Goodsell and H. C. Trumbull without being made wiser for this work. They studied how to approach men easily and happily with the subject of religion until they acquired great skill and success in doing it. Their methods of introducing the subject by conversation, by letter, by friendly attentions of various kinds, are well worth study by any who wish to acquire somewhat of their skill and success.

V. *By the study of these biographies one acquires high ideals of character and achievement.* One man is superior to another, and accomplishes more in the world not merely because he is endowed with superior natural abilities but because he has a higher ideal of excellence. This he may have obtained from his parents and instructors, but more probably from his reading. A good biography perhaps has given it to him. Having it, how is he affected by it? Recall the influence of ideals in art and literature. Giotto, Fra Angelico, Raphael, Michael Angelo—these eminent artists had ideals of saintly beauty and physical perfection, which possessed their minds and gave shape to the work of their hands. Their ideals forbade contentment with commonplace achievements. They stimulated them to attempt higher and better things to the last.

So with the great masters in literature. Milton, for example, tells us of his studies of Plato, Xenophon, Dante, and Petrarch, and how through their influence he "was confirmed in this opinion, that he who would not be frustrate of his hope to write well in laudable things ought himself to be a true poem, a pattern of the best and honorablest things;" and how he himself indulged the hope that he "might perhaps leave something so written to aftertimes as they should not willingly let die. . . . These thoughts possessed me. For which cause . . . I applied myself . . . to fix all the industry and art I could unite to the adorning of my native tongue . . . to be an interpreter and relater of the best and sagest things among mine own citizens throughout this island in the mother dialect; that what the greatest and choicest wits of Athens, Rome or Modern Italy and those Hebrews of Old did for their country, I in my proportion might do for mine." These confessions reveal a mind that had received through its studies a high ideal, which attuned his heart to its work and shaped his thoughts to those forms of eloquent expression that came from his hand.

We suppose that he never quite attained his ideal, that his mind had glimpses of a perfection which his hand never achieved, but he was led by it to greater things than he otherwise would have reached. So of other writers whom we admire or fondly love. It was his ideal which inspired Whittier to attempt his highest verse, and which, after he had done his best, made him say to the friends who crowned him on his seventieth birthday with the laurel of their praise:

> "You do but read between the written lines
> The finer grace of unfulfilled designs."

Similar is the operation of high ideals in the work of the Christian ministry or of any other honorable calling. They keep the mind fixed upon a high mark; they refine and exalt its perceptions of duty and of excellence, until these result in a permanent moral elevation of character, and a remarkable power of achievement. Such moral elevation

of character and superiority in achievement shed
a dignity and beauty over all the actions of life.
What we mean is shown by Phillips Brooks in the
fine illustration which forms the conclusion of his
instructive essay upon Biography: "There are,"
he says, "some of the great old paintings in which
some common work of common men is going on,
the meeting of two friends, the fighting of a battle,
a marriage or a funeral, and all the background
of the picture is a mass of living faces, dim, misty,
evidently with a veil between them and the life
we live, yet evidently there, evidently watching
the sad or happy scene, and evidently creating
an atmosphere within which the action of the picture goes its way. Like such a picture is the life
of one who lives in a library of biographies, and
feels the lives which have been, always pouring in
their spirit and example on the lives which have
succeeded them upon the earth."

This elevating effect of biographies is due to the
spiritual converse had with those whose lives they
record. We know them and converse with them
in their best moments, for the things we read of
them comprise the best things they said and did.
We are in good society while turning over the pages
that report these. Our hearts thrill to their words
and narrated deeds as to those of some high company to which a rare good fortune has admitted
us. And they not only inspire us at the time,
but they linger long in our remembrance with sweet
and wholesome effect. They permanently influence
for good our characters and opinions; by familiar

converse with them we are able to catch somewhat of their spirit and tone.

James Russell Lowell truly says:

"As thrills of long-hushed tone
    Live in the viol, so our souls grow fine
    With keen vibrations from the touch divine
Of noble natures gone."

II
CHRYSOSTOM

II

CHRYSOSTOM

A. D. 347–407

Of the highest rank among the great preachers of Christianity in the past, "one of half a dozen at most," Dr. R. S. Storrs says, was the illustrious John of Antioch, best known by the name of Chrysostom, "of the golden mouth," given him on account of his great eloquence. He was born of noble parentage at Antioch, in 347 A. D. His father, Secundus, was an officer, *Magister Militum,* in the Imperial army of Syria. He, dying in the infancy of his son, left a young widow, Anthusa, twenty years of age, who, refusing to marry again, devoted herself to the care of her two little children, John and an older sister. She appears, from all that we can learn, to have been a remarkable woman, remarkable for her piety and for the mental and moral qualities displayed in the training of her children, and the management of the considerable estate left by her husband. Chrysostom himself informs us that when his teacher, the celebrated Libanius, heard of the manner in which she had acquitted herself of her parental task, he exclaimed: "Heavens! what women these Christians have!" She was to her son what Monica was to Augustine; it was her influence and her molding hand that had most to do with shaping his character. She jealously guarded him from the pollutions of the great and corrupt city of Antioch; she provided him with the best instructors; she fostered and stimulated the extraordinary mental gifts and aptitude for learning displayed by him in childhood; and, above all, she encouraged him in pious habits and an intimacy with pious companions.

Twofold Environment—Local and Imperial

Consider the impressive local environment amid which he grew up and lived until near the age of fifty, and the probable influence of it upon him.

Antioch was one of the most splendid cities of the Roman Empire. Situated on the southern bank of the Orontes within a few miles of the Mediterranean Sea, both Nature and Art had made it beautiful and imposing. Readers of "Ben Hur" will recall the description given in that celebrated work of the principal features of this great metropolis of Syria. The descriptions found there represent quite faithfully and truly what Antioch was in the days of its meridian splendor, which lasted to the time of Chrysostom and later. It had a population of 200,000 people, of a heterogeneous character, consisting of Asiatic, Syrian, Greek, Jewish and Roman elements. The river Orontes was the principal gateway through which it was connected with and enriched by the commerce of the world. All lands contributed of their resources to its wealth and pleasure and luxury. It was a magnificent city. Its streets were adorned with covered collonades of marble, on either side, beneath which its inhabitants walked protected from the scorching sun of summer and the rains of winter. From the mountains to the south, massive stone aqueducts, whose solid masonry remains to this day, brought copious streams of water to supply its numerous baths and fountains. Everywhere the cool refreshing spray and the soothing sounds of flowing water delighted the senses. Splendid villas in the midst of beautiful gardens adorned its suburbs; likewise pleasure groves and parks, which the people much frequented. Among the latter was the celebrated Grove of Daphne, described with such fullness by General Wallace in his famous work of fiction. It was dedicated to the worship of Apollo, was furnished with every enticement to the senses, and so rich in its enchantments that the saying arose concerning it: "Better be a worm and feed on the mulberries of Daphne than a King's guest." In the mixed population of this great city, "the impulsive oriental temperament was the most dominant. They abandoned themselves freely to those voluptuous recreations for which their city and climate afforded every facility and inducement. The bath, the circus, the chariot races and the theatre were their constant amusements, and pursued by them with the eagerness of a pleasure-loving nature."

In the time of Chrysostom, 100,000, or one half of the population, was nominally Christian. They embraced all degrees of strictness from the severest asceticism to almost pagan laxity.

Such was the local environment, outside his home, amid which Chrysostom grew up and lived there in Antioch.

There was still another environment outside of
this, which needs also to be considered if we would
clearly understand the character and the life of
Chrysostom. It was the environment which the
great Roman world afforded at that particular time.
In the pages of Gibbon we read what the conditions
of things then were. The Roman Empire was fast
declining under those influences that brought it to
its ultimate downfall. The stern virtue and discipline which had brought the world under its sway
having become relaxed, it was undergoing dissolu-
tion through the joint operation of internal corruption and external attack from the barbaric peoples
that lay outside its borders. There was decay of
every kind, decay of domestic virtue, decay of
patriotism, decay of faith in the old religion before
faith in the new Christianity was strong enough to
take its place, decay in the power of law, decay of
industry, decay of all the elements of security. We
get glimpses in the pages of the historian of "a large
mass of the population hovering midway between
Paganism and Christianity; we detect an oppressive
system of taxation; a widely spread venality in the
administration of public business; a general insecurity of life arising from the almost total absence
of what we understand by police regulations; a
depressed agriculture; a great slave population; a
vast turbulent army as dangerous to the peace of
society as the enemies from whom it was supposed
to defend it; the presence of barbarians in the
country as servants, soldiers or colonists; the constantly impending danger from other hordes ever

hovering on the frontier and like famished wolves gazing with hungry eyes on the plentiful prey which lay beyond it."

The imperial authority, dependent for its support upon the favor of the army, was a perilous and precarious possession. Those who held it enjoyed their dignity at a tremendous price for themselves and their families. Murder lurked for them on every hand, and they often fell victims to it. In one of the writings of Chrysostom, his treatise *de Virginitate*, there is an impressive passage reviewing the tragical events and misfortunes that overtook the wearers of the imperial purple during the fifty years from 330 to 380. There were nine emperors during that time. Two only, out of the nine, died natural deaths. Of the other seven, one had been killed by a usurper, two fallen in battle, one slain in a sedition of his domestic guards, and one by the man who had invested him with the purple; one had died in a fit of rage, and one with his retinue had perished in the flames of a burning house to which the Goths had set fire. Of the widows of these emperors, some had perished by poison, others had died of despair and broken hearts.

Against such miseries as these, how light and insignificant in the balance were all the wealth and power of the imperial office, and how unstable the condition of things in view of them! An apprehension, or foreboding of something dreadful impending, pervaded the more serious and thoughtful portion of society and tinged with solemnity their speech and writings. We discover it in the sermons of Chrysostom, and in the writings of Augustine and other Christian fathers. It was a condition of things, however, that stimulated the good and noble qualities of the great, as well as the corrupt and reckless frivolity of the degraded. The great and the good seem indeed to have reached an extraordinary stature, as if society were like a rank soil fattened by corruption, in which good plants and worthless weeds flourish alike with unusual vigor. This statement is borne out by a consideration of the remarkable men and women of that time. Contemporaneous with Chrysostom in the Church were Athanasius, Ambrose, Jerome, Augustine; in the State, Constantine the Great, Valentinian, Theodosius, and his son, Theodosius the Great; and among the distinguished women, besides Anthusa and Monica, were some of the most noble and saintly that the world has ever known. The Christian women indeed of that age surpassed the men in devotion to their religion. But for their strenuous opposition the Emperor Julian thought that his efforts to revive Paganism would have been successful.

Chrysostom having such a mother, who lavished upon him all her wealth of love, grew up, amid the twofold environment described, to manhood unstained by the vice for which Antioch was then notorious. As a child he was precocious; as a youth, diligent and ambitious of distinction. Under the instruction and training of Libanius, the rhetorician, he enriched his mind with classical learning, and with native powers of natural eloquence acquired the art of effective speech. Following the wish of his father's family, as is supposed, he studied the profession of law and entered upon its practice with the most brilliant prospects. He made some pleas in the law court which received much public applause and won the praise of his master, Libanius. Of all Libanius' pupils he was the favorite, and to his dying day the old teacher mourned that the Christians had stolen John from them. For John did not like the profession of the law. To his pure and upright soul it seemed tarnished by chicanery and rapacity, and the gain it held out to him he abhorred as "the wages of the devil."

PREPARES FOR THE MINISTRY

The influences that led him to abandon his profession of the law and at length enter upon that of the ministry were various. Chief among these was his friendship for a schoolmate, Basil, who afterwards became a bishop in the Catholic Church. "He accompanied me," says Chrysostom, "at all times; we engaged in the same studies and were instructed by the same teachers; as we went to our lectures or returned from them we were accustomed to take counsel together on the line of life it would be best to adopt."

The molding influence of school friendships! Who can measure it, or how powerfully it shapes the destiny of those whose hearts are knit together by it? The friendship between Chrysostom and Basil, ' there at the school of Libanius in Antioch, reminds us of that between Professor Charles Hodge and ,

Bishop John Johns in their early college days at Princeton. There was the same invincible attachment, the same mutual admiration and the same molding power of each over the other, resulting in the greatest benefit to both.

Basil decided upon a religious career and this decision separated him for a time from Chrysostom. But separation from his friend only increased Chrysostom's attachment to him and his discontent with his own profession. He began to withdraw from the worldly society about him and to give more of his time to the study of the Bible, which later in life, he said, was "the fountain for watering the soul." He sought the acquaintance of Meletius, the good and wise Bishop of Antioch, whose influence drew him in the same direction as Basil's friendship, and after a while induced him to receive baptism and accept the office of reader, then the initiatory step to the Christian ministry. Entirely in accord now in their thoughts and purposes, the two friends were reunited and pursued with ardor the religious life agreed upon. But for his mother's entreaty "not to leave her a second time a widow," Chrysostom would have gone with his friend into a monastery. Denied this wish, he resolved, as far as possible, to live the life of a religious recluse at home. He adopted an ascetic diet and monastic discipline, and devoted himself with his friend to a life of prayer, intense study of the Scriptures and meditation. Diodorus, a friend of the good bishop Meletius, and prior of one of the monasteries near Antioch, directed their studies. Chrysostom as a preacher owed as much, and possibly more, to the teaching of Diodorus than to that of Libanius. From Libanius he learned how to speak eloquently, from Diodorus he learned how to study the Bible whence he derived the substance of his speech. Diodorus in fact taught him the right method of exegesis, a method of literal common-sense interpretation of the Scriptures, like that of our English Bible scholars, in contrast to the allegorical and mystical interpretation characteristic of Origen and the Alexandrian School. He taught him also to view the truth of God's word in its relation to man's nature and needs, to see its practical applications, and to weave the stuff it afforded into garments suited to human wear in the various exegencies of life as they arise.

Their great piety and gifts soon attracted the attention of the Church to Chrysostom and his friend Basil, and, though so young, they were publicly spoken of as fit to be made bishops. According to the custom of that time they might any day be seized and compelled to accept the high office. So Augustine was dragged forcibly to the church, and ordained to the bishopric in spite of his protesting entreaties and tears. The two friends hearing what was in the air, were filled with apprehension and alarm, and agreed to act together, either to accept or evade together the unwelcome honor. Chrysostom, however, broke his promise. When the officers of the Church came to seize them, he contrived to have Basil captured and made bishop while he himself hid away and escaped. To the subsequent reproaches of his friend for having deceived him, he boldly answered that it was "an excusable fraud," which the good of the Church justified; and to soothe and reconcile him wrote a treatise on the "Priesthood," showing its preëminent dignity, and declaring the peculiar fitness of Basil to discharge the duties of bishop. This questionable act is the only blot on the early name of Chrysostom. It seems, however, to have been in accord with the lax morality of his age.

In a short time his mother died and he was free to indulge his wish to live in religious retirement from the world. Six years he thus spent in the seclusion of monastery and hermit's cell in the mountains to the south of Antioch. The day and the greater part of the night he spent in study, fastings and vigils. Bread and water formed his principal food. His zeal for the mortification of his fleshly appetite carried him to the extreme limit of asceticism. In fact, he injured his health and was obliged to return to the greater comfort of his former home in Antioch.

About this time he was ordained a deacon by his much revered bishop, Meletius, who soon after died, to be succeeded by Flavian, under whose direction Chrysostom performed his diaconal functions. In that day deacons "were essentially, as the name implies, ministers or aids to the bishop, and were often styled the bishops 'eyes,' or 'ears,' or 'right hand.'" Their duties consisted partly of service about the sanctuary in connection with the public worship, and services of relief among the sick and the poor in the parish. They were required to search out and bring to the notice of the bishop cases of distress, to distribute relief under his direction and to report to him moral and religious offenses. The office was a good training school for the ministry of the Gospel. During the five years that Chrysostom filled it, he labored with great zeal and activity, and stored his mind with a knowledge of human nature in its great diversity and variety, as displayed in the manners and practices of the people, that was of great value to him afterwards in his preaching.

His Personal Qualities

He possessed a keenly observant and discriminating mind with a genial, kindly spirit and a power of sympathetic imagination that enabled him vividly to imagine with exactness and sympathy the circumstances and scenes amid which men moved and lived. This is why he has ever been a favorite author with historians like Gibbon, and great preachers like Isaac Barrow and Cardinal Newman. They have found in his works the richest suggestions and most valuable matter suited to their purpose. He speaks and "writes," says Newman, "as one who was ever looking out with sharp but kindly eyes upon the world of men and their history, and hence he has always something to produce about them, new or old, to the purpose of his argument. I speak of his versatile recognition of men one by one, for the sake of that portion of good which has severally been lodged in them; his eager contemplation of the many things they do, effect, or produce; of all their great works, as nations or as states; of the graphic fidelity with which he notes them down upon the tablets of his mind, and of the promptitude and propriety with which he calls them up as arguments or illustrations in the course of his teaching as the occasion requires."

It was after such a long course of preparation, covering fifteen years of study in the schools of Libanius and Diodorus, and in the religious seclusion of the monastery and hermit's cell, and five years of practical training in the diaconate, in which he exercised his powers of observation to such good purpose, that he came at length upon the work of the ministry, being ordained presbyter by Bishop Flavian in 386, when he was in the fortieth year of his age. The course of preparation seems to have been long, but the work he was to do in the twenty years that remained of his life was great. Those twenty years were about evenly divided between the offices of preacher at Antioch and of Archbishop of Constantinople. Immediately after his ordination he was appointed by his bishop, Flavian, to preach in the principal church of the city where the bishop himself officiated. Chrysostom at once rose to the zenith of fame as a preacher, and for ten years his pulpit labors were incessant with no abatement of his popularity.

His Great Eloquence

"The people flocked to him," says Sozomen. "As often as he preached he carried them away one and all. They hung upon his words and could not have enough of them. He held them spellbound to the end." So close and all-absorbing was the attention he commanded and so great the crowd that thronged the church to hear him, that pickpockets plied their trade right there in the church with great success.

Let us try to get a true and clear conception of his personal appearance, manner, and qualities as a preacher. Like many men of commanding genius, Athanasius, John Wesley, Shleiermacher, Louis XIV, Bonaparte, he was little of stature, but of such dignity of bearing that he produced, as it were, an illusion of greatness. When he was speaking, especially, his witchery of speech made him often seem majestic, reminding one of what Boswell said of William Wilberforce: "I saw a mere shrimp of a man mount the platform, but as I listened he grew and grew until the shrimp became a whale." Chrysostom's diminutive stature was the less noticeable probably from the fact that he usually sat in a raised position when preaching, while the people stood, eagerly crowding as close as possible to him. He had a large bald head with a broad lofty forehead, deep-set piercing eyes, with a searching but benignant look, and an expressive mouth. That mouth from the epithet given him, "mouth of gold," was rich in tone and most opulent in expression.

He possessed extraordinary fluency. A contemporary compares it to the inexhaustible flow of the river Nile. And yet, as Cardinal Newman says:

"It was not by the fertility of his imagination, nor the splendor of his diction that he gained the surname of the 'Mouth of Gold.'" His oratorical power was but the instrument by which he readily, gracefully, adequately expressed, expressed without effort and with felicity, the keen feelings, the living ideas, the earnest practical lessons which he had to communicate to his hearers. He spoke because his heart, his head, were brimful of things to speak about. His unrivaled charm, as that of every really eloquent man, lay in his singleness of purpose, his fixed grasp of aim, his noble earnestness.

He combined in himself, as a study of his sermons shows, the excellencies of several preachers. He had the florid exuberance of Jeremy Taylor, the fire and vehemence of Savonarola, the declamatory splendor of Bossuet and the straightforward earnestness and practical good sense of John Wesley.

He often displayed in speaking an eager and impetuous spirit like that of a soldier rushing to battle. It was as if this son of a Roman soldier felt in himself the martial spirit of his father urging him on. You seem to hear in his sentences the notes of the bugle sounding the charge of the Roman legions. A discriminating student of his life, himself a distinguished orator and preacher, commenting on this characteristic of Chrysostom says: "There is something martial in all real oratory; the attack, the earnest seizing of the situation, the amassing of the powers, the gathering of manifold forces and hurling them all with resistless strength against the foe— this oftentimes constitutes the movement of the real orator, and in Chrysostom's life there was this martial power, not only in his tongue but also in his achievements."

CHRYSOSTOM

We here present to our readers one or two examples, asking them to remember while they are listening to or reading them, what a contemporary says of Summerfield's eloquence, that "every attempt thus to present the splendid effects of impassioned eloquence is like gathering up dew drops, which appear jewels and pearls on the grass, but run to water in the hand; the essence and the elements remain; but the grace, the sparkle, and the form are gone."

Chrysostom enjoins it as a duty upon every Christian to labor for the spiritual welfare of his fellowmen. He insists that "Neither poverty nor human station, nor business, nor family cares, nor bodily infirmity can exempt one from the obligation of this duty." "Say not," he says, "within thyself, I am a man of the world; I have a wife and children, these matters belong to the priests and the monks. The Samaritan in the parable did not say 'Where are the priests?' 'Where are the Pharisees?' 'Where are the Jewish authorities?' but seized the opportunity of doing a good deed, as if it were a great advantage. In like manner when you see anyone requiring bodily or spiritual care, say not within thyself, 'Why did not this, or that man attend to him?' But deliver him from his infirmity. If you find a piece of gold in your path you do not say, 'Why did not some other person pick it up?' but you eagerly anticipate others by seizing it yourself. Even so in the case of your fallen brethren, consider that you have found a treasure in them and give the attention necessary for their wants."

Those who noisily crowded forward to the Lord's Table he thus admonishes: "Approach with fear and trembling, with fasting and prayer; not making an uproar, hustling and jostling one another; consider, O man, what kind of sacrifice thou art about to handle; consider that thou, who art dust and ashes, dost receive the body and blood of Christ."

To those who would fain hurry away from the Eucharist before the service is done, he says: "What, when Christ is present, and the angels are standing by, and this awe-inspiring Table is spread before you, and your brethren are still partaking of the mysteries, will you hurry away?"

Though his style is exuberant, it is rarely redundant; every word is a telling word. At times it is strikingly epigrammatic. Examples: "The fire of sin is great, but it is quenched by a few tears." "Pain was given because of sin, yet through pain sin is dissolved." "Riches are called possessions, that we may possess them, not be possessed by them." "You are master of much wealth; do not be a slave to that whereof God has made you master." "Scripture relates the sins of saints, that we may fear; the conversion of sinners, that we may hope."

He held a rational Scriptural theology—an important condition of success for the preacher. He taught that "Man fell through his own indolent negligence; but his nature was not thereby essentially changed, it was only weakened." "Evil is not an integral part of man, it is not an inherent substantial force." "There is no constraint either to holiness or to sin; neither does God compel to the one, nor do the fleshly appetites compel to the other." "It is the moral purpose that is perverted when men sin. The whole burden of responsibility in sin must be thrown on the moral purpose." "If man's will was not unfettered, there would be no merit in goodness and no blame in evil." "We do not try to alter that which is by nature; sin, therefore, is not by nature, because by means of education, laws and punishments we do not seek to alter that. Though sin is not a part of man's nature, his nature is readily inclined to evil. But this tendency may be controlled by a healthy moral purpose."

While he thus insists upon the freedom of man's will and his actual responsibility for his conduct, Chrysostom also asserts human insufficiency to accomplish good without the divine assistance. He describes the power of sin over the heart in the strongest terms: "It is a heavy burden, more oppressive than lead; it is more terrible than a demon, it is a great demon; it is like fire. When once it has got hold on the thoughts of the heart, if it is not quenched, it spreads further and further, and becomes increasingly difficult to subdue." "Christ saw us perishing under the power of sin and He took compassion on us. His redemption plan embraces all, but it constrains no one. His purpose is limited by man's freedom of choice. God's election is not compulsory but persuasive. Only they who are drawn and taught by the Father can come to Christ; but away with the pretense that those who are not thus drawn and taught are emancipated from blame; for this very thing, the being led and taught, depends on their own moral choice." He maintains the equal divinity and distinct personality of the Holy Ghost. He maintains also both the humanity and the divinity of Christ. "Our nature could not have been elevated to the divine, if the Savior had not really partaken of it; neither could He have brought help to our race if He had appeared in the unveiled glory of His God-head; for man would have perished at the brightness of His presence."

In regard to the divinity of Christ and his continued presence and activity in the world, he holds the most orthodox opinions.

In his "Homilies against the Arians," he thus speaks of the obstacles overcome by Christianity and the proof which the wonderful successes of the Church afford as to the divinity of the founder of it: "In a short space of time Christianity had abolished ancestral customs, plucked up deeply-rooted habits, overturned altars and temples, caused unclean rites and ceremonials to vanish away. The customs abolished were not only venerated but pleasant; yet these were abandoned for a religion which substituted fasting for enjoyment, poverty for money getting, temperance for lasciviousness, meekness for wrath, benevolence for ill-will. Men, enervated by luxury and accustomed to the broad way, had been converted into the narrow, rugged path by multitudes under the whole heaven. These mighty results had been wrought by a few unlearned, obscure men, without rank, without money, without eloquence. And all this in the teeth of opposition of the most varied kind. Yet in spite of persecution and the disruption of social ties, the new faith flourished. How contrary to the common course of events, that He who was despised, weak and put to an ignominious death, should now be honored and adored in all regions of the earth! Emperors, who have made laws and altered the constitution of States, who have ruled nations by their nod, in whose hands was the power of life and death, pass away; their images are in time destroyed, their actions forgotten, their adherents despised, their very names buried in oblivion, present grandeur succeeded by nothingness. In the case of Jesus Christ all is reversed. During his lifetime all seemed failure and degredation, but a career of glory and triumph succeeded his death. How could such unprecedented marvels have come to pass but through the divine power and in obedience to that word of God which is creative of actual results? Just as when he said, 'Let the earth bring forth grass,' the wilderness became a garden, so when the expression of his purpose had gone forth, 'I will build my church,' straightway the process began, and though tyrants and people, sophists and orators, custom and religion had been arrayed against it, yet the word, going forth like fire, consumed the thorns, and scattered the good seed over the purified soil."

The most memorable occurrence that happened during the ten years of Chrysostom's pastorate in Antioch was the "Riot of the Statues," in 387 A. D. It arose in this way: In the following year of 388 A. D., the emperor, Theodosius the Great,

would celebrate the tenth anniversary of his own reign, and the fifth of that of Arcadius, his son, whom he had associated with himself in the empire. The army on such occasions claimed a donative of five gold pieces to each soldier. To raise the considerable amount thus required, Theodosius made a special levy upon the great cities. The edict which proclaimed the levy made upon Antioch, produced there a great outcry of discontent. The men openly uttered their complaints, and the women loudly lamented the hardship and ruin thus imposed on the city. A crowd gathered, which soon became a riotous mob and committed various acts of violence. The rioters rushed to the *pretorium* and forced their way to the governor's audience room demanding an abrogation or abatement of the levy. The governor was not there; but they were confronted by the statues of the imperial family set up there to give dignity to the place. A momentary awe checked and subdued them to silence, until a boy in the crowd hurled a stone at one of the statues by which it was shattered. The spell of reverence was thus broken, and the mob was emboldened to other acts of vandalism, until the different images of the Emperor and his father and the beloved Empress, who had recently died, were thrown down, dragged in the streets and mutilated. Soon their rage spent itself and then there came a revulsion of terror and dismay. Such acts of insult to the imperial family were treason of the worst kind. The Emperor, though a nominal Christian and man of noble qualities, possessed a quick and ungovernable temper. In his paroxysms of rage he showed no mercy. He might pardon the insult done to himself, but he was not likely to forgive that done to his noble father and his beloved wife, Flacilla, for whose recent loss his heart was still sore. A vision of direful retribution, of destruction and slaughter, such as was to befall Thessalonica three years later through the rage of Theodosius, arose before the mental sight of the terror-stricken city, and the people gave themselves up to feelings of anguish and despair. In this emergency the power of Christianity to soothe, control, comfort, and encourage was signally displayed. The aged bishop, Flavian, hastened in the depth of winter to Constantinople to intercede with the wrathful Emperor in behalf of the offending city, and Chrysostom, meanwhile, day after day, addressed the people who thronged to hear him speak upon the requirements of the situation. It was his opportunity to turn them to God, and he faithfully improved it. His eloquence sounded through the whole gamut of encouragement and persuasion. His words fell upon their anxious souls like the rays of the sun upon the darkness of night, by which the morning cometh. He urges them to a hearty repentance of their sin. He wrestles to win their souls; he convinces them of their past follies; he leads them to hope in God. Thus he saves them, whatever the Emperor might do. When Flavian returns at the end of some weeks with the imperial forgiveness, he finds the city chastened and purified, and three thousand converts ready for baptism. During his absence Chrysostom's preaching had infused in them a new spirit and life. It had proved itself a marvelous power to control and calm the seething vortex of passion. It had accomplished more to tranquilize and correct the city than many legions of soldiers would have done.

These sermons, relating to the "Riot of the Statues," have been preserved for us by the shorthand reporters of that time, probably revised by the preacher and published subsequently by his consent. We are privileged to read careful translations of them. They may be found in the ninth volume of "The Nicene and Post-Nicene Fathers."

In them the eloquence of Chrysostom probably reached the high-water mark. We are tempted to quote some passages from them, in spite of the peril of excess and the certain danger of utterly failing to give any true idea of the eloquence of the preacher in the absence of that unreportable personal charm so essential to the impression.

He thus describes the change produced in Antioch when the fear and dread of the Emperor's wrath had smitten it with silence and solitude: "Aforetime there was nothing happier than our city; now nothing is more melancholy than it has become. As bees buzzing around their hives, so before this, the inhabitants flitted daily about the forum, and all pronounced us happy in being so numerous. But behold, that hive hath now become solitary; for even as smoke drives away the bees, so hath fear dispersed our swarms. . . . They desert it as if it were a dungeon; they leap out of it as out of a fire. . . . Our calamity has become an enigma—a flight without enemies; an expulsion of inhabitants without a battle. . . . We have not seen the watch fires of barbarians nor beheld the face of enemies; yet we suffer what those do who have so been smitten. . . . There is a silence big with horror. Loneliness is everywhere. That dear hum of the multitude is stifled; and even as though we had gone under the earth, speechlessness hath taken possession of the town, while all men seem as stones. . . . For he who has been insulted hath not his equal in dignity upon earth. . . . On this account, then, let us take refuge in the King who is above. Him let us call to our aid."

Of what gives dignity to a city he says: "Learn ✔ what the dignity of a city is, and then thou wilt see clearly that if the inhabitants thereof do not betray it, no one else can take away its honor. Dost thou wish to learn the dignity of this city? I will tell it exactly, not that thou mayest know it merely, but that thou mayest emulate it also. This it is: 'It came to pass that the disciples were first called Christians at Antioch.' Dost thou wish to hear further of another dignity belonging to this city? A grievous famine was once approaching, and the inhabitants of Antioch determined, as each had the means, to send relief to the saints at Jerusalem. . . . They also sent Paul and Barnabas to Jerusalem, and cautioned the apostles to provide that pure doctrine should be distributed over the world. This is the dignity of this city. This makes it a metropolis, not in the earth only, but as related to the heavens. . . . I have heard many saying in the Forum: 'Alas for thee, Antioch! What hath befallen thee?' When I heard, I smiled at the puerile spirit, which gave vent to such words. When thou seest men dancing, drunken, singing, blaspheming, perjuring themselves, lying, then use such words as these: 'Alas for thee, O city! What hath befallen thee?' But if thou seest the Forum containing meek, modest, temperate persons, even though they be few, then pronounce the city blessed. When you wish to extol it; tell me not of the suburb of Daphne, nor of the height and multitude of its cypresses, nor of its flowing fountains of waters; nor of the great population which inhabits the town, nor of the safety of its markets and the abundance of its wares. But, if you can, speak of virtue, meekness, almsgiving, nightly visions, prayers, sobriety, true wisdom of soul, for these things commend the city."

He thus commends the example of Nineveh to Antioch, as worthy of its imitation. "Thus was that city agitated when it heard the prophet's voice, but instead of being injured, it was benefited by fear, for that fear became the cause of its safety. The threatening effected the deliverance from peril; the sentence of overthrow put a stop to the overthrow. . . . They did not flee from the city as we are doing, but remaining in it they caused it to stand. They fled not from their buildings, but from their sins. . . . They trusted for safety not to a change of habitations, but to a change of habits."

He puts into the mouth of their good bishop Flavian, interceding in their behalf, this appeal to the offended Emperor: "Were your statues thrown down? You have it in your power to set up others more splendid. If you remit the offenses of those who have done you this injury, and take not revenge on them, they will erect a statue to you, not in the forum, of brass or of gold, or inlaid with gems, but one arrayed in that robe, which is more precious then anything material, of clemency and tender mercy. Every man will thus exalt you within his own soul; and you will have as many statues as there are men who inhabit, or who hereafter shall inhabit, the entire world."

He thus exhorts them to find in the bee a good model for their imitation: "Whilst from the ant thou learnest industry, take from the bee a lesson at once of industry, and of mutual helpfulness. For it is not more for herself than for us that the bee labors and is every day weary; which is a thing especially proper for a Christian, not to seek his own things only, but the things of others. As, then, she traverses the meadows, that she may provide a banquet for another, so also do thou, O man. If thou hast accumulated wealth, expend it upon others. If thou hast the faculty of teaching, bury not the talent, but bring it forth publicly for those who need it. If thou hast any other special endowment, become useful by it to those who need the fruit of thy labor. Seest thou not that for this very reason the bee is more honored than other insects—not because she labors merely, but because she labors for others? For the spider also labors, and spreads his fine textures upon the walls, surpassing the utmost skill of women; but he is still without estimation, since his work is no way profitable to us. Such are they who labor and are weary, but only for themselves."

He thus touches upon the folly of the passion for riches: "A covetous man is one thing; a rich man is quite another. A covetous man is never rich. He is in want of many things, and while he needs so many things he cannot be rich. A covetous man is a keeper, not a master, of wealth; its slave, not its lord. He would sooner give one a portion of his flesh than of his hidden gold. As though he were ordered and constrained by some one to touch nothing of these concealed treasures, with all diligence he keeps them, abstaining from his own as if it were another's. Yet, indeed, they are not his own; for what he can neither determine to bestow upon others, nor yet to distribute to the needy, though in consequence he encounter punishment, how can he possibly count that his own? . . . Abraham was rich, but he was not covetous. . . . This man let us imitate, beloved. His lodging was rude, but it was more distinguished than kingly saloons. No king has entertained angels; but he, dwelling under an oak, and having only briefly pitched his tent there, was thought worthy of that honor; not receiving the honor on account of the meanness of his abode, but enjoying the benefit on account of the magnificence of it and the riches that were therein laid up. Let us adorn our souls before our houses. What doth thy house profit thee, O man? Wilt thou take it with thee when thou departest? But thy soul thou shalt surely carry with thee."

Speaking of the visible universe, he says: "Seest thou its greatness? Seest thou its beauty? Marvel at the power of Him who made it, at the wisdom which adorned it. This it was which the prophet signified when he said: 'The heavens declare the glory of God.' How, then, tell me, do they declare it? Voice they have none; month they possess not; no tongue is theirs; how then do they declare? By means of the spectacle itself. For when thou seest the beauty, the breadth, the height, the position, the form, the stability thereof during so long a period, being instructed by the spectacle, thou adorest him who created a body so fair and strange. The heavens may be silent, but the sight of them emits a voice that is louder than a trumpet's sound, instructing us not by the ear, but through the eyes. . . . Upon this volume the unlearned as well as the wise man shall be able to look, the poor man as well as the rich man, and wherever any one may chance to come, there looking upwards towards the heavens, he will receive a sufficient lesson from the view of them."

After various admonitions of this sort, he adds: "Say these things to others, and observe them yourselves. I know that in this place (i. e. the church) we become more reverent, and lay aside our evil habits (as profanity and slander). But what is to be desired is this, that we depart taking this reverence with us to where we especially need it. For those who carry water do not seek merely to have their vessels full when they are near the fountain, and then empty them when they reach home; but they set them down there with particular care, lest they be overturned, and their labor become useless. Let us imitate this process, and when we reach home let us strictly retain what has here been spoken; since, if ye have here gotten full, but return empty to your houses, having the vessels of your understanding there destitute of what here you have heard, there will be for you no advantage from your present replenishment. Show me religion, not at the season, but in the time of personal practice."

These quotations will suffice to show the remarkable qualities of the man and his deserved eminence. What powers of creative inagination and of original thought! What affluence of mind in beautiful and suggestive ideas pertinent to his theme and strengthening his argument! Not only was the flow of his words like that of the Nile, inexhaustible, but his mind like the Nile was charged with richness, which it dropped in its progress all along its course, for the fertilization of truth to the production of harvests of virtue.

A study of his sermons and of their effect gives the impression that Chrysostom was not only a great preacher for the age in which he lived, but one of the greatest of all the Christian centuries. In this opinion we are confirmed by the judgment of the late Dr. R. S. Storrs, who says that "among the great preachers of the world he held nearly, if not quite, the foremost place. I have read many sermons of Augustine and Gregory, not a few of the

great medieval preachers, from Bernard of Clairvaux to John Tanler; a goodly number from Bossuet, Massillon and other famous preachers of France,
with many of the English pulpit, from Taylor and
South to Robert Hall, Newman, Liddon and the
others, with our own Phillips Brooks, and I do not
know, for myself, where to find certainly the superior, in this special function, of this presbyter in
Antioch, fifteen hundred years ago."

A remarkable thing about the sermons of Chrysostom is their undecayed, enduring vitality. They are
not dry and lifeless like the specimens of an her-
barium, to which old sermons are often compared,
and justly, for their lack of interest to a present-day
reader. "His words," says Dr. Storrs, "were
living things; they are so still. There is a marvelous modernness in his sermons. No man can read
them after so many ages without feeling that he
who shot these shafts lived by the faith of the Son
of God."

The good such a ministry wrought in ten years
there in Antioch cannot be estimated. It was
simply immense, and stamped with God's manifest
approval. Chrysostom became more and more
the pride of the city as the fame of his eloquence
extended abroad. In 397 A. D. at the death of
Nectarius, the Archbishop of Constantinople, he
was appointed his successor. The Eunuch, Eutropius, the prime-minister of Arcadius, had heard him
in Antioch some years before, and believing that he
would add luster to the eastern capital and be found
subservient to his wishes, he persuaded the emperor

to place him in that high ecclesiastical position. The place was not of Chrysostom's seeking; indeed had it been openly offered him, he would have shrunk from the responsible charge, as in his young manhood he had shrunk from and evaded being made a bishop. But the option now was not given him, any more than it had been given in those early years to his friend Basil. Knowing that the people of Antioch would not willingly give up their favorite preacher, Eutropius got him away by stratagem. He sent word to Asterius, the imperial governor of Antioch, to invite Chrysostom to visit a martyr's shrine with him just outside the city. Well pleased to make the pious pilgrimage the preacher unwittingly accepted the invitation. At the holy shrine he was seized by imperial officers and in spite of his remonstrances hurried off by an escort of soldiers to Constantinople, and forcibly ordained to the Patriarchate of the Eastern Church.

The dignity to which he was thus summoned and in which he was installed by envious ecclesiastics was not a bed of roses. It was, in fact, a bed of thorns to him. He was too little of a courtier and too much of a saint to find it otherwise. The view of Eutropius and of the Emperor of the nature and obligations of the sacred office was much different from that of Chrysostom. They looked upon it as an ecclesiastical appendage to the court, and believed that the archbishop should be servile and pliant to the behests of the court. He, on the other hand, held that Christ alone was his Master; that he should aim chiefly to please him; that it was inumbent upon him as a faithful shepherd to watch ver the spiritual welfare of the flock committed to is care; to rebuke sin and vice wherever found; to e uncompromising in his assertion of the paramount claims and obligations of religion upon all like, the high and low, rich and poor, those who lwelt in palaces as well as those who lived in the meanest hovels.

So sharply differing, it was inevitable that ere ong he should come into collision with the court nd its pampered minions. At first, however, verything seemed fair and lovely. The eloquence hat had charmed his hearers in Antioch was greeted vith admiration and applause in Constantinople, nd for a short time he enjoyed the highest ministerial success and popularity. The Emperor and the empress performed with zeal the religious observances he recommended. At his suggestion a pilgrimage on foot was made by night to the shrine of a martyr located a considerable distance from the city. Those who engaged in it formed a vast torch-light procession, led by the archbishop and the Empress and her court. Chrysostom was in raptures at such docile and exemplary piety, and expressed his satisfaction in a laudatory discourse when they reached the shrine at dawn of day.

"Of what shall I most discourse?" he exclaimed. "The virtue of the martyrs, the alacrity of the city, the zeal of the Empress, the concourse of the nobles, the worsting of the devils? Women more delicate than wax, leaving their comfortable homes, emulated the stoutest men in the eagerness with which they made this long pilgrimage on foot. Nobles, leaving their chariots, their lictors, their attendants, mingled in the common crowd. And she, who wears the diadem and is arrayed in purple, has not consented along the whole route to be separated from the rest. The procession moved along like a stream of fire, or a continuous golden chain; the moon shone down upon the crowd of the faithful, and in the midst was the Empress, more brilliant than the moon itself, for what was the moon compared to a soul adorned with such faith?"

Only for a little while did this mutual admiration continue. As Chrysostom became accustomed to his new position and more familiar with the faults and sins of those to whom he ministered, and as he strove to correct them by rebukes and remonstrances, then coolness and estrangement, and at last bitter enmity arose. He found many of the clergy to be worldly, and indulging in practices that dishonored religion. Attempting to reform them, he incurred their hate and the hate of those who wanted religious guides that would not reprove them for sin.

Many Christians were passionately fond of the circus and the theatre, and indulged their liking for them to the neglect of religion, the loss of all spirituality and the leading astray of others. On Good Friday, near the end of the first year of Chrysostom's episcopate, they forsook the church and its solemn service for those places of amusement. On the next Sunday, having remarked upon the impiety of such conduct, he thus called to account each guilty offender: "What defence will you be able to make when you have to render an account of that day's work? For thee the sun rose, the moon lit up the night, choirs of stars spangled the sky; for thee the winds blew and rivers ran, seeds germinated, plants grew, and the whole course of nature kept in proper order; but thou, when creation is ministering to thy needs, thou fulfillest the pleasure of the devil. Say not that few have wandered from the fold. Though it be only one, yet it is a soul for which this visible world was created, for which laws and statutes and the diverse operations of God have been put in motion, yea, for whose sake God spared not His only Son. Therefore I loudly declare that if anyone after this admonition shall desert the fold for the pestilent vice of the theatre, I will not administer to him the holy mysteries or allow him to touch the holy table, but will expel him as shepherds drive out the diseased sheep from the fold, lest they should contaminate the rest."

Such severity toward sin and vice and worldly amusements aroused hate and opposition. He added to these the dislike of the court by his own austerity. His predecessor, Nectarius, used to frequent the court, and to give grand entertainments to the nobles and high officers, and indulged himself in luxurious habits of living. Chrysostom, always simple and abstemious in his habits, usually ate in solitude, and refused to set foot at court except upon business of the Church. He would not flatter the great by entertaining them, nor would he adorn their feasts. Thus he gradually fell out with the great court officers, with the Empress Eudoxia, and with the worldly clergy, though he warmly attached to himself the common people, and the saintly men and women of every class.

Eutropius, the prime minister, vexed at not finding him subservient to his wishes, showed his resentment by depriving St. Sophia of its ancient right of asylum. But by the irony of fate, he himself was the first to need that asylum, and Chrysostom generously asserted and obtained it for him, when disgraced and thrown from power because of the enmity of Eudoxia. Chrysostom, ruled by the instinct of a preacher, could not refrain from improving the occasion to impress an important lesson. On the day following the minister's downfall, which was Sunday, when the great church of St. Sophia was thronged with an eager, expectant congregation, suddenly the curtain that separated the nave from the chancel, was partly drawn aside and disclosed to the view of the multitude the cowering form of the wretched Eutropius clinging to one of the columns which supported the holy table. Then Chrysostom pointing to him as a visible example of fallen grandeur exclaimed: "Where now are the pomp and circumstance of yonder man's office? Where his torch-light festivities? Where the applause which once greeted him? Where the stir that attended his approach in the streets, the flattering compliments paid him in the amphitheatre? They are gone, all gone! One rude blast has shattered all the leaves, and shows us the tree stripped quite bare and shaken to its very roots.

These things were but as shadows which flitted away, as bubbles which burst, as cobwebs which rent. Therefore we chant this heavenly strain: 'Vanity of vanities, all is vanity.' For these are words which should be inscribed on our walls and on our garments, in the market place, by the wayside, on our doors, above all in the conscience and engraved upon the mind of everyone." As showing the protecting power of the Church and illustrating the wholesome truths of religion, the suppliant was an ornament to the altar. The spectacle of one lately at the pinnacle of power now crouching with fear like a hare or a frog, chained to yonder pillar not by fetters but by fright, would repress arrogance, and subdue pride, and teach them the truth of the Scripture: "All flesh is grass, and all the glory of man as the flower of grass."

The fall of Eutropius but increased the pride of Eudoxia. She ruled the weak-minded emperor, and through him the affairs of state. But she could not rule Chrysostom, nor make him connive at her sins. If she committed an offense against morals and religion, he censured her like any other offender. At this she grew first cool, and then furious at the preacher. She was to Chrysostom what Jezebel was to Elijah, or Herodias to John the Baptist, and both of these epithets he is said (but without good proof) to have bestowed upon her. Through her influence his path was more and more thorny. His enemies, having her countenance, plotted his destruction. Theophilus, Archbishop of Alexandria, took the lead, having associated with him a disrep-

ntable crowd of bishops and ecclesiastics whom
Chrysostom had mortally offended by his rebukes
and discipline for their corrupt practices. They
gathered in a synod, in a suburb of Chalcidon, at a
place called "The Oak," and there this "Synod of the
Oak" framed charges against Chrysostom and summoned him to appear before them and make answer
to the indictment. The charges were false, or absurd, but as there was no probability of his having
a fair trial before such a tribunal, Chrysostom
refused to appear before them and was condemned
for contumacy. The synod decreed that he should
be deposed from his office and called upon the Emperor to execute the decree. He, ruled by Eudoxia,
performed their bidding, and Chrysostom was secretly arrested and hurried away into exile.

When the people of the city learned of the ban-
ishment of their beloved preacher, great was their
indignation and loud their cry for his return. "Better that the sun cease to shine," they said, "than
that our Chrysostom's mouth should be stopped."
And they crowded the approaches to the imperial
palace as they pressed their demand. Heaven
itself seemed to second the demand. An earth-
quake occurred which shook the city, and violently
rocked the very bed on which the Empress slept.
Terrified at what she thought a manifestation of
the wrath of heaven she added her voice to that of
the people for Chrysostom's recall, and even wrote
a letter entreating his return. "I remember the
baptism of my children by thy hands," she said.
"God whom I serve is witness of my tears." Re-

called in haste, he returned to Constantinople in triumph amid the joyous acclamations of the people.

But the peace made with him by the Empress proved to be only a hollow truce. In her heart she hated him still, and was ready to break with him at the first opportunity. As there can be no concord betwixt Christ and Belial, it inevitably came very soon. The occasion was the erection of a statue of the Empress before the Church of St. Sophia, inaugurated with heathenish ceremony, which Chrysostom condemned. Fierce was her resentment when the report of his censure was brought to her, and from that time she relentlessly pursued him until his death. He was exiled again after a few months to Cucusus, a lonely mountain town on the borders of Cilicia. Hearing that he was cheered there by visits, letters, and gifts from his faithful friends, the implacable Empress had him removed thence by brutal soldiers to Pityus on the Caucasus, the most dreary spot in the empire. The journey with its hardships and privations was too much for his feeble body; he died on the way, September 14, 407, in his sixtieth year, his last words being: "Glory to God for all things," expressive of the sweetness of his spirit and the resignation with which he bore his sufferings.

Thirty years after his death, the relics of Chrysostom were brought back with great pomp to Constantinople at the command of the then reigning Emperor, Theodosius II, the son of Eudoxia. When they were deposited in the church appointed to receive them, the Emperor kneeling humbly and reverently above the reliquary, implored forgiveness for the injuries which his parents had done to the saint whose ashes it held. That kneeling Emperor typifies well the attitude of the Christian world toward the illustrious saint. He is numbered among the four great Fathers of the Christian Church by both the Greek and the Roman branches of it; he is extolled for the impartial purity and incorruptible integrity of his episcopal rule as well as for his surpassing eloquence, and spoken of generally with great respect by those held in highest honor. Great historians, like Gibbon and Milman, and great scholars and preachers, like Isaac Barrow, J. H. Newman and R. S. Storrs have been enthusiastic students of his works and admirers of his character.

There are few men in the history of the world whose names are more deservedly illustrious. To be forever a good example of faithfulness to duty and of noble Christian character, to continue through many centuries to be an instructor and inspirer of mankind by one's imperishable utterances, to have them the delight and nourishing food of successive generations of scholars and preachers—there are few achievements of men equal to this. In the firmament of the past on which the names of men of all degrees of greatness and glory are emblazoned, this man appears, therefore, as a star of the first magnitude, whose light neither the gathering mists of time nor the darkness of oblivion, which soon or late hides from human gaze most of those stars in the sky, can dim or quench. It remains a splendid beneficent beacon light for all time.

III

BERNARD OF CLAIRVAUX

III

BERNARD OF CLAIRVAUX

Among the great preachers whose names shed splendor upon the Christian faith, Bernard of Clairvaux holds a very high place. No name stood higher in the Christian world in the age in which he appeared, and since his death his fame has lingered down to the present time like a beautiful afterglow from his immense reputation and influence with his contemporaries. This long lingering splendor is a sure proof of his real greatness. Only the true giants among men, as well as the giants among mountains, retain so long the halo of glory that attracts the wondering gaze of the world. In influence he ranks next to Augustine in the history of Latin Christianity, whose scholars and ecclesiastics affectionately speak of him as "the last of the Fathers."

Born in 1091, in the last decade of the 11th century, his childhood was cradled and largely passed amid the intense excitement and religious enthusiasm created by the first crusade, in which his father, Tescelin, a noble knight and vassal of the great Duke of Burgundy, was engaged, and lost his life. His mother, Aletta or Alèthe, a woman of rare beauty of character and of deep piety, consecrated him on his birthday with passionate devotion to a religious life. This consecration held him fast in spite of the strong allurements of arms in that warlike age, or of study, to the charm of which he was deeply sensible.

From both parents Bernard inherited rare qualities. From his father, Tescelin, masculine courage, energy and a martial spirit, united with a sobriety of judgment and magnanimity of mind that fitted him for leadership; from his mother, Aletta,—besides elegance of person, beauty of features, a radiant countenance and gracious manners,—a love of nature that amounted to a passion, an affectionate, tender, spirit and ardent religious sensibilities. "To her he owed it, under God," says Dr. Storrs, "that while strong with the strongest, he was impassioned and fond as the most ardent woman, and it was her spirit in him which sighed and sorrowed, or rose to summits of Christian triumph." (R. S. Storrs, D.D., "Bernard of Clairvaux.")

He was as happy in his place of birth in the neighborhood of Dijon, the capital city of Burgundy, as in his parentage. "The skies of Burgundy," says the historian, "judging from the illustrious people it has produced, have for centuries ripened wits as well as wines." Besides Bernard and the illustrious warriors and churchmen of his own and earlier times that shed their luster upon it, there is a splendid galaxy of names belonging to more recent epochs. Bossuet was born there, and Buffon, and Madam de Sévigné and Lamartine; and there originated the order of the Golden Fleece, instituted three centuries after Bernard for the glory of Knighthood and of the Church, representing in name at least, the wealth and the warmth of the prosperous province.

In his father's Castle of Fontaines, the third son in a family of six sons and a daughter, Bernard grew up amid the choicest influences and the highest social advantages that the times could give. While he was yet a child his father was taken from him, and the care and responsibility of his training devolved on his mother. She deeply impressed the stamp of her own spiritual character upon him. "If ever a mother's wish and prayer and Christian counsel determined the character and career of a son," says Dr. Storrs, "those of the mother of Bernard determined his. After her death, which occurred while he was still a youth, her image remained vividly with him. He remembered her words and meditated affectionately on her plans for himself." For a little time, as he was just entering manhood, he seemed to turn away from those plans and to be drawn by the example of two older brothers to a martial career, upon which they had entered. The martial spirit, which he had inherited from his father, and the spirit of the times impelled him that way. But his mother's memory brought him back to the religious life to which she had dedicated him. The story of his conversion is interesting: "He was riding toward the camp of the Duke of Burgundy, to join his brothers who were already there, when the image of his mother, disappointed and reproving, took possession of his mind. He retired to a church by the roadside to pray, and from that hour his course was determined and his purpose unchangeable to lead a religious life."

In that age, a religious life meant retirement from the world to the seclusion and ascetic practices, the fastings, the vigils and strict regulations of a monastery. To this Bernard resolved to give himself. He purposed, however, not to go alone, and with sublime courage he resolved to win to the same religious life he had embraced those two elder brothers whose example had for a while turned his heart away from it toward a military career. This was not an easy thing to do. His oldest brother, Guido, was already married and the father of children; his next brother, Gerard, was a daring soldier, with a martial spirit and soaring ambitions, and already in high repute for wisdom and bravery in action. But Bernard was one whom great difficulties only stimulated to greater effort, and the heavenly fire which had subdued his heart to penitence and high resolve had touched his lips likewise with overpowering eloquence. His brothers, his uncle, and more than twenty others besides, were induced by his eloquence to join him in his purpose to forsake the world. It is said that "Mothers hid their sons, wives their husbands, maidens their lovers, and companions their friends, lest they should be drawn away by him."

Leading such a company of men, most of them from influential families, Bernard and his companions would have found a welcome at almost any monastery in the land. He might have gone to the greatest of Burgundian abbeys, the rich and

famous abbey of Clugni, where life was easy and
the religious rule then far from strict. But he chose
to go to Citeaux, the smallest, poorest and strictest
of them all, at that time presided over by an Eng-
lishman, Stephen Harding, whose sanctity all men
respected, but whose austere rule and discipline
most shrank from, so that his monastery, recently
founded, was very small and in a languishing condition. The strict discipline and poverty, which
had repelled others, was an attraction to Bernard
and his companions, whom he had inspired with
his own enthusiasm and devotion. He rejoiced
to endure the hardest things for the love of Christ.
The greatest self-mortification delighted him. He
endeavored by means of it completely to subdue
all bodily appetites and passions, so that, delivered
from their clamor or control, he might easily dwell
in an atmosphere of religious meditation and spiritual rapture. He took food, not to nourish life or
derive from it strength, but to postpone death and
keep himself from fainting. It was usually only
a bit of bread moistened with warm water with
no delicacy to please the palate. He regarded sleep
as almost an utter loss of time, during which one
was but as a dead man. As the delicacy and weakness of his body forbade his undertaking heavy
tasks and hard labor, he compensated for that by
assuming the most menial offices, like that of wash-
ing dishes and greasing the shoes of the brethren.

The coming of Bernard and his company to
Citeaux resulted in such an increase of its prosperity
and numbers, that it could not accommodate the

crowd that flocked to it. It was obliged to do what a beehive does with its swarming inhabitants—send out colonies to form other hives. In less than three years it sent out three colonies; Bernard was chosen the leader of the third. A band of twelve, representing the twelve apostles, with their young abbot, then twenty-four years old, representing Christ, bearing a cross and leading in a solemn chant, they marched forth to establish for themselves another home in the valley of Clairvaux, one hundred miles distant. It was at the time a wild and desolate place which formerly had borne the name of "The Valley of Wormwood." The name was typical of the experiences they encountered. They suffered the bitterness of hunger, of cold, of extreme privation, ere they became established. More than once they became discouraged, and would have given up their enterprise but for the unfaltering faith and indomitable perseverance of Bernard. He was their example and their inspiration.

Salt at one time failing them, he sent one of the brethren to a neighboring village for a fresh supply, but without money to pay for it. The monk demurring, in the belief that if he went empty handed he would return in like manner, Bernard said: "Be not afraid; He who has the treasure will be with thee and will supply the things for which I send." When the monk returned with more than he had gone for, the abbot said to him: "I tell thee, my son, that nothing is so necessary to a Christian man as faith. Have faith, and it will be well with thee all the days of thy life." At another time when they were brought almost to the verge of despair on account of their destitution and began to talk of returning to Citeaux, "where at least the means of maintaining life could be commanded, Bernard kneeled and prayed till he felt that a voice from heaven had answered him." To their question, what he had prayed for, he simply answered: "Remain as you are, and you will know"; and shortly relief came to them from three different sources. After a period of hard struggle, filled with such incidents, whose effect was to inspire them with more complete confidence and reverence for their leader as one peculiarly favored of heaven, they overcame all obstacles and achieved a marvelous success.

That wild and desolate valley became through their labors a paradise of beauty, fertility and plenty, well deserving its name of Clairvaux, or "bright valley." Formed by two lines of converging hills opening toward the east and coming together at the west, where the monastery stood, the valley was bright with sunshine in the morning and with the glory of the sunset reflected from its hills long after the monastery lay in the shadows that fell upon it in the late afternoon. It was bright in spring with blossoming orchards and smiling gardens; and in autumn with the golden fruit and the ripening harvest that the industry of the brotherhood had created out of the wilderness of forest and marsh land which they found there at their coming. In time, the original twelve multiplied by accessions as the parent institute of Citeaux had done, so that it was obliged in turn to send out colonies. A hundred and sixty of these went from it in Bernard's own lifetime, one of which founded the celebrated "Fountains' Abbey," in England, whose beautiful ruins as seen today form one of the notable objects of interest to American travelers in the mother country. But wherever they went and however beautiful the new homes they established, these colonists reluctantly left the valley of Clairvaux and the monastery where the presence and rule of Bernard were a constant benediction, and they incessantly longed to return thither. In time it was greatly enlarged to accommodate those who entreated to stay, so that it contained within it at the time of his death seven hundred monks. Here at Clairvaux, Bernard spent the most of his life, nearly forty years, with those occasional absences which the service of the Church or of the State required.

THE MONASTIC SYSTEM

It is proper that, at this point, we should dwell awhile upon that remarkable institution of monasticism, with which Bernard stands associated. We should make a great mistake, if, misled by our prejudices and Protestant training, we should pass a sweeping condemnation upon it as though based solely upon religious infatuation, and fraught only with mischief to mankind. Dr. Storrs says truly, that "No institution exists for centuries and continues to attract the reverent regard of many of the best and most cultured of the time, which has not a foundation in wide and wholesome human tendencies or which does not minister, more or less successfully, to recognized moral needs of mankind." This is true, we think, of that monastic life so passionately embraced by Bernard, and which as exemplified in him must be confessed to have had an attractive charm, and produced a wholesome effect. Its essential idea and purpose was a life of retirement and seclusion from the world for the sake of religious meditation, self-collection and the formation and recovery of those ideals of character and conduct that are most worthy and fit to regulate the soul. So defined, it may be said that the germs of monasticism are clearly discernible in the Bible. We find them in the lives of the ancient prophets, Moses and Elijah, in John the Baptist, even in Christ and his Apostles.

It was under the impulse of the monastic spirit, so to speak, that they occasionally withdrew from the noise and bustle and excitement of this crowded, bewildering worldly life, which we all know so well, and of which we often become weary. The solitude of the desert, of mountain, or of sea, was under such circumstances as grateful and as restful to them as is the stillness of night under the quiet stars to one oppressed with "the cares that infest the day"; or as is the repose of sleep, when exhansted with the day's toil. In this view of the matter we may affirm that monasticism is a product of man's spiritual wants and necessities, that it sprang up to satisfy cravings and impulses of which all people of any degree of spirituality are at times conscious. When the pressure of life becomes heavy and burdensome, and one feels his weakness and the smallness of his own unaided resources; when one is confronted by great and perplexing problems, for the solution of which he has no light, then it is natural for him to look for relief and light in retirement from the world and converse with God. The words of Christ to his disciples: "Come ye apart into a desert place and rest awhile" seem suited to his need, and the saying of the prophet: "My people shall dwell in a peaceable habitation and in sure dwellings and in quiet resting places," equivalent to a divine direction, obeying which he may, and thus only may, perhaps, attain that righteousness "whose work," according to his prophet, "shall be peace and whose effect, quietness and assurance forever." Thus the troubled and harrassed soul is prompted to seek and often finds what the poet extols as a "gift sublime"

> ". . . that blessed mood,
> In which the burden of the mystery,
> In which the heavy and the weary weight
> Of all this unintelligible world
> Is lightened."

The needs of nature and of religion demand occasional indulgence of this craving for retirement and seclusion from the world.

It is a necessity for all deeper and most fruitful souls. "Man must retire at intervals within himself in reflection and silence, to do the best things," says one of the greatest of our American preachers. The examples of Christ and of the Apostle Paul intimate that such seclusion is especially needful both as a preparation for successful work in the ministry and as a means of spiritual invigoration amid its exhausting labors. All the great preachers of the past have by means of it replenished their stores of thought and been girded with strength for the deliverance of their messages. Chrysostom, Augustine, Savonarola, Baxter, Howe and Edwards thus prepared their pinions for higher flight. And "in chambers of scholars," says Dr. Storrs, "in how many schools of sacred learning, where outward things for the time at least have been excluded, and no echo has been heard of the furious and mercenary rush of society, have men come to the loftiest efforts and successes of intellectual and spiritual life? There philanthropies and missions have been born; there sublime intuitions of truth have given new import to the Scriptures; and there immortality has become to the soul asserting kinship with God, a proximate presence."

The religious system of monasticism was contrived so as to promote by its regulations and discipline the spiritual life of those submissive to it. Life among them was occupied with worship, study, and work, and for the pursuit of these objects they solemnly vowed to observe in practice the virtues of obedience, chastity and poverty or self-denial. The Cistercian monasteries, of which Clairvaux was one, represented, as we have intimated, a reform in the ancient Benedictine discipline, which, as in the case of the famous abbey of Clugni, had become lax and corrupt through their acquisition of riches and spiritual declension. The monastery of Citeaux, which Bernard had originally joined and to which his coming had given great prosperity, compelling it to colonize, was the mother of this new order, and Clairveaux was her third daughter.

At Clairveaux, therefore, monasticism was presented in its best form. Let us try to imagine, if possible, the sort of life they lived there during the days of Bernard. The daily services of religion were seven in number, in accordance with the example of the psalmist, Ps. 119; 164, "Seven times a day do I praise thee." These were known as "The Canonical Hours," and were as follows: 1. *Nocturnes*, two o'clock in the morning, when it was believed that Christ rose from the dead; 2. *Prime*, or *Matins*, six o'clock in the morning, when it was believed Christ's resurrection was announced to the women; 3. *Tierce*, nine o'clock, when Christ was condemned and scourged by Pilate; 4. *Sext*, twelve (noon), when Christ was crucified and darkness was over all the earth; 5. *Nones*, three o'clock in the afternoon, the hour of public prayer in the temple, and when Christ gave up the ghost; 6. *Vespers*, six o'clock, the hour of evening sacrifice in the temple, and when Christ was taken down from the cross; 7. *Compline*, or "Even-Song," solemnly sung about seven o'clock, when Christ's agony began in the garden.

Thomas Fuller after giving these divisions, or

"hours," of their religious day, adds the following comments. In regard to the first: "It was no fault, for the greater haste, to come without shoes, or with unwashen hands (provided sprinkled with holy water) to this night's service. And I find no expression to the contrary but that they might go to bed again; but a flat prohibition after matins, when to return to bed was accounted a petty apostasy."

In regard to the last, called also the "Completory," it completed the duties of the day. This service was concluded with that versicle of the psalmist: "Set a watch, O Lord, before my mouth and keep the door of my lips," Ps. 141; 3. With this was connected the injunction strictly observed: "Let none speak a word after 'completory,' but hasten to their beds." The rule was, in regard to these "hours": "Let all at the signal given (the tolling of a bell in England, hence called the "Ringing Island") leave off their work, and repair presently to prayers." "This canon was so strict," says Fuller, that "writers having begun to frame and flourish a text letter were not to finish it, but break off in the middle thereof."

Of another rule, that "those who are absent in public employment, be reputed present in prayers": "There was a particular commemoration made of them, and they by name were recommended to divine protection." Those also were to observe the same hours. "Be it by sea or land, on ship, in house or field, they were to fall down on their knees, and though at distance, and very briefly, yet in some sort to keep time and tune with the convent in their devotions." (See Fuller's "Church History of Britain," Book 6, Sec. 2.)

From the standard work of Dr. R. S. Storrs, "Bernard of Clairvaux," we take the following brief summary of the life pursued at Clairvaux in Bernard's day: "The rule of Benedict was strictly observed in it during the lifetime of Bernard, and as long as his influence remained dominant there. According to this, the abbot, though elected by the monks, afterwards represented among them the Divine Master, and to him was to be rendered respect, veneration, and immediate obedience. Among things insisted on, these were prominent: no sensuality, no idle or jesting words, humility, patience under injuries, contentment with meanest goods or employments, constancy in religious service, regularity in labor. For offences, chastisement; for the incorrigible, expulsion. Of course, no personal property was permitted. Each of the monks served in his turn in the kitchen, or at the table. Meals were to be eaten, but accompanied with the reading of Scripture. ('This,' says Fuller, 'was St Austin's rule. *Ne solae fances sumant cibum, sed et aures percipiant Dei verbum.*') A spiritual lecture was to be given each night before 'compline'; after 'compline' silence resigned. In summer, work was required from 'prime' till ten o'clock; from ten to twelve, readings, reflection, and perhaps rest; after 'nones,' labor again till even-song. In the winter, the hours differed somewhat, and the outdoor work was limited or suspended; but the succession of work, reading, and prayer continued." (Lec. IV.)

It must be confessed that the system and life thus described was adapted, one would think, to promote a vital piety and good conduct in those who consecrated themselves to it. And they did this among the Cistercians in the time of Bernard and for generations after. The statement of the writer in "The Catholic Encyclopedia" concerning them is undeniable: "Their abbeys during their golden age (1134–1342) were so many sanctuaries of the most fervent prayer, of the severest discipline as well as of untiring and constant labor."

The piety thus developed and nurtured in their inmates was not their only fruit. They yielded other benefits to mankind of inestimable value, of which none can question the reality and importance, though they may deny and scout at their religious and social influence. As teachers of what, for · those times, was scientific agriculture; as drainers of fens and swamps; as clearers of forests; as makers of roads; as tillers of reclaimed soil; as architects of durable and even stately buildings; as exhibiting a type of orderly government in a rude and chaotic age; as mitigating the ferocity and cruelties of war and the savage spirit it engenders; as showing the superiority to warlike pursuits of peaceful employments, and the refining influence of literature, art and Christian charity; as students and transcribers of both sacred and classical literature in their *Scriptoria;* as the collectors of precious libraries connected with their monasteries; as the teachers and founders

of schools, they have won the everlasting gratitude of mankind.

Their manifest good work attracted to them men
of the highest class and noblest character. "Princes
and kings," says Dr. Storrs, "were gladly numbered among the lay brothers. Some of them fully
entered the convents, and men of the highest rank
and repute were found serving faithfully in kitchen,
or mill, cutting faggots, gathering crops, or de-
lighting to drive the pigs to the field."

What then was the error of monasticism?

*The error of monasticism was in supposing that an
occasional want of the soul justified a permanent separation and seclusion of the best and most devout people
from the world and its society for the sake of religion.*
They thus converted what should be an occasional
spiritual discipline and refreshment into a constant
self-indulgence, which so used became at length
unhealthful and the source of serious ills.

Let us not, in reprobating the mischief that arose
and brought this institution into widespread disrepute, be blind to the thing perverted.

Occasional retirement from the world for prayer,
reflection and quiet, undisturbed study of God's
truth, that one may enjoy a "Sabbath of the Soul,"
and have a clear vision of this truth, is essential to
our highest spiritual welfare. It is indispensable
to the successful minister. In the still "retreat"
and solitude thus obtained one gains admission to
the "audience chamber of God," and acquires the
moral elevation, the deep convictions and consequent moral earnestness that make him eloquent

and impressive as a preacher. "The eloquent man," says Emerson, "is not merely a beautiful speaker, but one who is inwardly drunk with a certain belief. This terrible earnestness makes good the ancient superstition of the hunter that the bullet will hit its mark which is first dipped in the marksman's blood."

The eloquence for which Bernard became famous was the eloquence of a message that had first been dipped in his own blood. It was a matter of heart experience, and not merely a doctrine of his creed; and it was perhaps largely due to his monastic life and its large opportunity for quiet meditation and uplifting of his heart in prayer to God in that age of storm and distraction, that he attained at length this experience. He seems to have experienced all the benefits, and to have been preserved from all the dangers connected with such a life. "From these dangers, even the subtlest," says Dr. Storrs, "Bernard was preserved not only by the grace of God in his sincere and ardent soul, but by his assiduous study of the Scriptures, and by the multitudinous activities, within the convent and beyond it, which constantly engaged him. When at home he preached every day, besides taking his faithful part in the customary labors. He wrote treatises, rich in the products of careful reflection, and with passages of remarkable beauty and power as well as of high spiritual thought. His letter writing was constant, of vast extent and variety, often concerning the gravest matters. His letters were addressed to men of all classes and conditions and on all sorts of subjects, from the highest themes of truth, duty, and Christian experience, to the humblest particulars of familiar affairs."

He was the counselor and influential advisor of kings and popes. "His utmost energy was called for and was exerted in the successive crises which confronted him in the Church and in the State, and nothing seems to have occurred in France or in other related countries during the last thirty years of his life, concerning directly or indirectly the honor and interest of religion, which was not brought to his personal notice, on which his governing, practical genius was not intensely busy." Thus, though living apart from the world, he was sufficiently concerned with its great interests to keep his heart in healthy sympathy with mankind.

The chief interest, however, which he has for us is not that of a representative of the monastic system, or that of an ecclesiastical statesman, but that of a great preacher, whose eminence was due, to some extent perhaps, to his peculiar religious life and environment, but due far more to the personal characteristics which distinguished him. What these characteristics were, and wherein his power as a preacher chiefly lay we will now attempt to show.

As to his personal appearance and physical qualifications: These were such that "he persuaded the eye before the ear heard him." He was of about the middle height, but the veneration and respect he inspired made him seem taller. His figure was slight and his movements were graceful. His features, possessing a refined and saintly beauty, an inheritance from his mother, were yet marked with lines of strength that made his face commanding. It was lighted up with expressive eyes which ordinarily looked only gentleness, tenderness and benevolence, but "which glowed at times as if with divinest fires." Delicate health and physical infirmity made him seem, at first, like one near to death, and gave great solemnity to his words. There was, however, no impression of feebleness in his speaking. His ardent spirit so energized his fragile frame and physical powers that he displayed great vivacity and astonishing vigor as he advanced in his discourse.

He had a remarkable voice, "which quivered like a harp string or rang like a trumpet in its changing emotion." (Storrs.) There was a power of entrancement in its clear, far-reaching tone which repeatedly enthralled great multitudes, and such a manifestation of spirit as made the impression that he was a heaven-sent messenger.

His mental qualities were still more extraordinary; among them, *a rich and fertile imagination.* "One would hardly know," says Dr. Storrs, "where to find a brighter example of the power which is imparted to the preacher by this noble, if sometimes dangerous, faculty. Whatever his subject, however familiar, or apparently trivial, there is *always a transfiguring light thrown upon it* by his imagination, which is like the light upon Italian hills. *His suggestive faculty* was quick, active and fruitful of thought. Sometimes he indulged it too much, so much that a hearer would find it hard to discover the relation between his text and the sermon which followed; for 'the text is often hardly more than the nest, from which like the eagle he lifts himself on eager wing to touch, if he may, the stars.'"

He possessed *an extraordinary power of mental abstraction*. When meditating upon his sermons in his convent cell, or in the rustic arbor with an enchanting view of the lovely valley, to which he often retired, he became lost in thought and insensible to everything without. Though his love of nature amounted to a passion and he was alive to her every suggestion and influence, and though he found in her an interpreter of revelation, so that he says, "whatever he had learned of the Scriptures and of their spiritual meaning had chiefly come to him while he was meditating and praying in the woods and fields," yet when occasion required he could exclude everything from his mind and become engrossed in whatever subject claimed his attention. This is an invaluable power. To it Isaac Newton attributed whatever preëminence over other men he had won in science. The preacher needs it, to be able to elaborate his thought amid the distractions of the world.

But the *most important qualifications of Bernard*, as of every great preacher, *were moral* and *spiritual*. These had their roots in and were nourished by his religious faith. This faith was that in which he was instructed in his youth, when the teaching of the Catholic Church was, as compared with that of later times, much closer to original primitive Christianity and more in harmony with the sacred Scriptures. Luther extols him, as "the most God-fearing and pious of monks"; and Calvin, as "a pious and holy writer, above his time, pungent and discriminating in rebuke of its errors." "He accepted, without reserve, the system of Christianity as it had come to him from the past, as it seemed to him set forth in the Scriptures, as it was associated with the deepest and subtlest longings and attainments of his spiritual nature. He believed it because he felt it. He could truly say of it: 'All my springs are in Thee.' The sphere of truth had to him an atmosphere about it full of tints and sunny splendors, in contemplating which his soul delighted, and by which the truth seemed freshly verified. He was a contemplative yet a most practical mystic." (Storrs.)

The criterion of its truth, or reality, was its power and tendency to bring man's spirit nearer to God. That evidence of its divine authority Bernard himself had received to a remarkable degree. Neander and other close students of his life and character dwell much and often upon his deep and large religious experience. He was not content with a traditional faith; he was not satisfied with anything less than a personal verification of it obtained through his own moral perceptions and spiritual intuitions as these came to him in prayer, earnest study and deep meditation upon the Scripture teachings.

Having thus verified it, he was, in his preaching, a *witness* to its truth. He spoke as one who had himself received and heard it from God. "No doubt fettered his powers. Celestial impulses were felt to vibrate on his uplifting words." The conviction and certainty which belong to such a preacher, resounding in his tones and looking forth from his eyes, gave to his utterances a thrilling effect.

This ability to bear credible witness to the truth is the supreme qualification of the preacher. It stood first in the qualifications of the apostles. It is first always. It is the source of other qualifications. Besides certainty and conviction, it gives to the preacher earnestness, spirituality, a tender Christlike love of souls, intrepid boldness, the authority which invests a messenger from God. These qualities were characteristic of Bernard. Historians and contemporaries say of him, that "the doctrine which he taught came to men illumined, and spiritually emphasized by their clear perception of his profound experience of it"; that "he spoke as one who had communion with heaven"; that "he seemed to reverence every man and to fear no man"; that his influence was so immense that "he was at once the leading and governing head of Christendom, more the pope than was the pontiff himself," and that "his persuasive power was so great that he led men captive and constrained them almost against their wills to do his bidding"; that "the Germans who could not understand a word he said, were carried away by his preaching equally with his own more excitable countrymen."

· The following remarkable example of the subduing power of his eloquence is reported by historians. It was connected with a famous dispute as to the right of succession to the papacy, which occurred in Bernard's time. Of the two claimants, Anacletus 2d and Innocent 2d, Innocent at last prevailed, chiefly through the influence of Bernard. Opposed to him was the powerful Count of Aquitaine, who in his fierce opposition deposed those bishops in his dominions who favored Innocent, and filled their vacant places with creatures of his own choosing. "He was a man of vast stature and of gigantic strength with a peculiarly violent, sensual and intractable temper." He feared not God nor regarded man.

When Innocent had become established in the papal chair, Bernard in company with the papal legate waited upon this fierce prince to induce him to give in his allegiance to the generally recognized pope, and to reinstate the deposed bishops. The pope he was willing to recognize, but the bishops he refused to restore. "They had offended him past forgivness and he had sworn never to be reconciled to them. Argument was vain; as well argue with a wild beast." Bernard broke off the useless discussion, and proceeded with his companions to the church to celebrate mass. The count remained at the door, an unrepentant rebel to the Church. When the host had been consecrated, Bernard with lifted arms and flashing face advanced with it toward him and said: "We have besought you and you have spurned us. These servants of God have entreated you and you have despised them. Behold, here comes to you the Virgin's Son, the Head and Lord of the Church which you persecute. Your judge is here, 'at whose name every knee shall bow, of things in heaven and things on earth, and things under the earth.' Your Judge is here, into whose hands your soul is to pass. Will you spurn Him also? Will you despise Him as you have despised His Servants?"

"An awful silence," we are told, "fell on the assembly and a dread expectation. The furious and implacable count, pierced in spirit, fell to the ground, and lay there speechless. Lifted by his knights, he could not stand, and fell again foaming at the mouth. Bernard bade him rise and listen to the judgment of God. He presented the Bishop of Poictiers, whom he had violently expelled from his see, and commanded the count to give him, then and there, the kiss of peace, and restore him to his seat. He meekly obeyed and with a kiss led the bishop to his place. He who had an army at his back, and who himself could, by reason of his brute strength, have smitten Bernard into instant death with one blow of fist or mace, yielded to the onset of his overwhelming will. Nor only for the time; he gave himself, from that time on, to repentance for sin and the service of religion."

This incident shows a man of masterful force, resolute spirit, and indomitable will, as well as of intrepid courage. One might think it indicated also a haughty, presumptuous spirit; but that would be a mistake. Though at the impulse of duty he did not hesitate, as God's minister, to rebuke or expostulate with kings and popes and great nobles, he was, and, notwithstanding the honors and applause he received, he continued to be, one of the most humble and self-depreciating of men. "The humility of his heart," we are told, "surpassed the majesty of his fame, so that when receiving the profuse honors and adulation of princes or of peoples, he did not seem to himself to be Bernard, but some one else substituted for him; he only recognizing himself in his proper personality when he resumed familiar talk with the humbler of his brethren."

Perhaps it may be truly said, that when in his high moods of spiritual exaltation and of eloquence, he was another person. Those moods were due to the descent of the Spirit of God upon him, or to his becoming suddenly possessed by truths and ideas which under the operation of the spirit lifted him above his usual self. There are instances in the Bible where the spirit of God came upon men with transporting power. (Examples: Samson, Elijah, Elisha, Isaiah, etc.) Most of us can remember seasons in our experience, when we have been lifted to such exaltation of mind and high achievements by inspiring ideas and spiritual influences, that, as we look back upon them from the lower plain to which alas! we soon descended and on which we usually move, it seems as if it was some one else that felt and spoke and did thus. Our study of the life of Bernard has made the impression upon us that his amazing eloquence is to be explained in this way. The "Spirit of God came upon him" at those times, and with this unction from on High his speech possessed an irresistible and marvelous power.

We give two more instances, as Dr. R. S. Storrs has described them in his fascinating volume: "He preached once in Paris, in the schools of philosophy, where men were too busy with engrossing disputations to give any practical heed to his words, and the discourse apparently produced no effect. He went home to pray, with sobs and groans, with deep searchings of heart and a passion of tears. He was in anguish of spirit, lest God had forsaken him. The next day he preached again, with the unction and energy derived from this divine communion, and large numbers were converted and gave themselves to God at the hand of his servant."

The other instance is his discourse at Spires before the Emperor Conrad, whom he sought to enlist in the second crusade, which Bernard, unhappily for his fame, was chiefly instrumental in causing: "At Frankfort, Bernard had had audience with the emperor, but had failed to impress him with the duty or the privilege of taking part in the crusade. Subsequently, at Spires, he saw him again, but without effect. The only answer he obtained from him was, that he would consider the matter, consult his advisers, and give his reply on the following day. On that day, Bernard officiated at mass, the Emperor being present. Suddenly, without invitation, moved as he felt by the divine spirit, he began to preach. At the end of the discourse, turning to Conrad in the crowded cathedral, and feeling himself as much alone with him as if the earth had swung out of sight and only they two remained to remember it, he addressed him, not as an emperor, but as a man. His whole soul flung itself forth from his impassioned lips, and he was for the time as one inspired. He pictured the coming tribunal of judgment with the man then before him standing there in the presence of the Christ who says to him, 'O man, what ought I to have done for thee, which I have not done?' He set forth the height and splendor of royalty, the riches of the emperor, the wise counsels he could command, his virile strength of mind and body, for all which things he must give account. The whole scene of the coming judgment seemed palpably present to the mind of the preacher, while it flamed as a vision through his prophetic admonitory words. We may conceive that the cathedral itself appeared to darken in the shadows and to tremble with the echoes of ethereal thunders, as 'He who cometh with clouds' was foreshown. At last the Emperor, bursting into tears in the midst of the discourse, exclaimed: 'I acknowledge the gifts of the Divine favor; nor will I prove ungrateful for them. He assisting me I am ready to serve Him, seeing that on His part I am so admonished.' 'The Emperor took the holy banner from the hand of Bernard, a multitude of nobles followed eagerly his example and the second crusade was launched upon its turbulent way."

Besides this remarkable unction, he possessed *the equally important qualification of a saintly character.* "Remember to give to your words the voice of a noble virtue," he once said to a young abbot, whom he was instructing in the art of preaching. He himself was an eminent example of his own teaching. His eloquence well exemplified Emerson's definition of being "the best speech of the best soul." His evident piety and the striking fruits of it in his life caused him to be regarded as a genuine saint by all classes. He was canonized only twenty years after his death. Men coveted his blessing as certain to bring celestial good; they imputed to him heavenly wisdom; he spoke with the authority of one enjoying the special favor and the direction of heavenly powers. "His very character seemed an evangel."

One more qualification and our characterization of him is finished. *He was a "gospel" preacher* in the truest sense of the word. The truth with which he charged his sermons and the motives to which he appealed were almost wholly evangelical. Man's lost condition through sin and God's redeeming love and grace as expressed in the person and work of Christ viewed as man, savior, priest, and king, these doctrines were the warp and woof of his sermons. These doctrines form a great magazine of spiritual power. The motives that are touched by them are the strongest and most potent known to man. Appealed to, or stimulated and strengthened by them, men rise to greater things than otherwise would be reached by them. In Bernard's case, these doctrines were both the source of an irresistible eloquence and the spring of a seraphic piety.

How lofty and irresistible, at times, was his eloquence, the examples given sufficiently indicate; how ardent his piety is shown by his hymns. Examples of these hymns may be found in most of our hymnals. Originally put into Latin verse, good English translations of them have been made. The following are the first lines of four that are now generally familiar:

> "O sacred Head, once wounded."
> "O Jesus, King most wonderful."
> "Jesus, thou Joy of loving hearts!"
> "Jesus, the very thought of Thee."
> (In the *Manual of Praise*, Oberlin.)

Where in the whole field of hymnology can one find expressed more ardent love for Christ, or more complete trust and devotion than in these hymns? They match those of Charles Wesley. They are the breathings of a soul ravished with the love of him whom they extol.

The most of his sermons that have come down to us, in the fragmentary reports of them made by some of the brethren at Clairvaux, are characterized by the same sweetness of spirit and warmth of evangelical sentiment as these hymns. "They are," to quote an admiring Catholic eulogist, "at once so sweet and so ardent that it is as though his mouth were a fountain of honey and his heart a furnace of love."

Being such a man, with such extraordinary gifts and qualifications for preaching, and achieving by it such marvelous results, what shall we say of his eloquence? Considering its triumphs and effects, it seems to have realized, in the largest measure, that witchery of speech, mysterious, inexplicable, which is so wonderful in the highest eloquence. As a poet of the highest genius is born, not made, so with such a preacher. His eloquence is a gift of God. No art or industry could fabricate it.

And yet Bernard's example is full of instruction for all preachers and students preparing for the ministry. It emphasizes in particular the following things:

(1) *The value to the preacher of occasional seasons of seclusion from the world, for close study of God's word, for meditation and the replenishment of his spiritual force by prayer and communion with God.* Without this the mind is in danger of becoming unspiritual, professional, destitute of any fresh, clear vision, or inspiring thought. Religious seclusion for the purposes named is as needful for the health of the soul, as rest and sleep for the health of the body. By means of it the exhausted fountains of life are refilled, as the fountain of an intermittent spring is replenished by a period of seeming inactivity. "The spirit needs meditation as the day needs the night" is a maxim of experience. Without the night we should never see the stars; without meditation, we should lose sight of spiritual verities that give an ineffable grandeur to our being. It is the preacher's office to explore the depths of those heavens in which these verities lie hidden, and direct the attention of men to them. Without meditation and prayer he cannot successfully do either one or the other.

(2) *The life of Bernard emphasizes also the importance to the ministry of combining with such sea-*

sons of seclusion 'from the world a constant living contact with the world and an active interest in its affairs. It was this living contact with the world and active interest in its affairs that preserved Bernard from the common evils associated with monasticism. It is with men as with water. Water is purified and clarified by being occasionally withdrawn from the turbid stream in which it flows. Pausing in its onward rush in the still placid pools that occur here and there in its course, it precipitates the sediment which has defiled its purity, and it better reflects the heavens in its tranquil surface. But entirely withdrawn from the stream and separated long from it, so that it does not feel its quickening pulse, the water of the pool becomes stagnant, and the place is converted into a malarial swamp. So it is, I say, with men. Therefore the minister must, with his seasons of seclusion for prayer and study and meditation, join such an interest in the world and such an active part with mankind as will preserve his heart from corruption. He can do this by diligently exercising his pastoral function, by performing those ministries to the sick, the poor, the tempted, and by discharging the duties to society and the state, incumbent on him as a citizen, and which the ministry is so well qualified to perform.

(3) *The life of Bernard emphasizes the importance of a genuine experience by the minister of the truth he preaches.* "Instructed by the Mistress Experience," says Bernard, "I will sing of mercy and judgment." His profound religious experience made

him an impressive and convincing witness to the great doctrines of the Bible. So is it with any successful minister. The true prophet will not be content, unless he has such à testimony to give. Others may be satisfied with a tradition; he must hear the voice of the spirit for himself and verify or reject the doctrine which tradition affirms.

In what has been said of Bernard we have confined ourselves to his remarkable personal qualities, his saintly virtues, his eminent abilities and admirable achievements. Scarcely a word has been given to faults of character or conduct. On this account we may be accused of excessive eulogy to the discredit of the truthfulness of our study of the man. No doubt he had faults of character and conduct. He carried his abstinence and asceticism to an absurd extreme, to the great injury of his health and the perpetuation of a false standard of conduct. His resolute encouragement of the second crusade was most unwise and disastrous. He was chiefly responsible for its mischief. It was a chimerical enterprise, doomed from the start to melancholy failure, and involving the sacrifice of many precious, heroic lives after incredible hardships and sufferings. But probably the worst thing that can be alleged against him is his theological persecution of and intolerant treatment of Abelard at the famous Synod of Sens, A. D. 1140.

Abelard was one of the most celebrated men of his time; like Bernard he was of noble family, of the province of Brittany. Possessing an eager inquiring mind and displaying extraordinary abilities as a youth, he was provided by his father with larger educational advantages than usual for those times. Study was an enthusiasm with him, and he gratified his passion by attendance upon the most famous schools of the kingdom. At the age of twenty, he went to Paris, and studied at its schools of philosophy and letters. Handsome, brilliant in thought and speech, accomplished and engaging in manners and address, he attracted attention and admiration wherever he went. While yet a very young man he himself became a teacher, and opened schools at Melun, at Corbeil, and on the height of Saint Genevieve, to which many pupils were attracted, upon whom he made such an impression of mental power, sagacity and extensive knowledge that the saying became current among them, that Abelard "knew whatever was knowable." At the age of thirty four he became the head of that great school of Paris, which developed later into its famous University.

From studies in philosophy and science, his eager mind turned its attention to theology, and he aspired to become equally a master in that. His effort as a theologian, says Dr. Storrs, was "to present a rational philosophy of the Christian religion, and, without denying its transcendent truths, to so commend them to the intelligence of men as to win for them just mental assent, and to reconcile with them the more searching and inquisitive thought of the time." The effort seems to us to have been commendable and deserving of the approbation of the ruling authorities of the Church instead of their condemnation. It is not improbable that they would have given their approval had Abelard exhibited along with his effort a persuasive and conciliatory spirit. But he was derisive and imperious towards his critics, impatient of dissent, and of the hesitation of cautious and timid minds, answering their objections with scorn and a haughty disdain. Men are not prone to give to new ideas and novel statements a ready acceptance, if those who propose them exhibit an unamiable temper. These novelties may be supported by good reasons, but their reasonableness will not be perceived under the circumstances. Those opposed will refuse to be convinced, if the advocate uses the lash of caustic speech to overcome their resistance. Instead of converts he makes them determined adversaries.

Cousin calls Abelard "the father of modern rationalism." The effect of his teaching was to unsettle the faith of his disciples in the traditional teachings of the Church. "The bold young man," says the historian Michelet, "simplified, explained, humanized, everything. He suffered scarcely anything of the hidden and the divine to remain in the most commanding mysteries. It seemed as if the Church till that time had been stammering, while Abelard spoke out." But in the opinion of the leaders of the Church it was fit that she should stammer in speaking of the mysteries of her faith. In her view they were incomprehensible, and she looked upon his effort to explain them as irreverent and profane. Bernard thought so, and placed himself decisively among Abelard's adversaries, after a careful examination of his published writings, deeming him "a rash adventurer on a dangerous path, if not a concealed enemy of the truth." He abhorred him both as a teacher of damnable error subversive of the faith of the Church, and as a wicked, immoral man, who had seduced for the gratification of his lust the beautiful and accomplished Heloise, of whom his biographer says, "her century put her at the head of all women," and the annals of the convent of which she afterwards became abbess, "as most illustrious in learning and religion."

"The men," says Dr. Storrs, "represented colliding tendencies. Two systems, two ages, came into shattering conflict in their persons. It was heart against head; a fervent sanctity against the critical and rationalizing temper; an adoring faith in mysterious truths, believed to have been announced by God, against the dissolving and destructive analysis which would force those truths into subjection to the human understanding. It was the whole series of the Church Fathers, fitly and signally represented by Bernard, against recent thinkers who questioned everything, who refused to be bound by any authority."

It was many years, however, after their antagonism was felt and known, before these two men met to join issue in open discussion before the Council of Sens. Abelard, skilled in dialectics and a practised debater, who had been victorous in many wordy conflicts with opposers, was eager for it and requested it as a privilege; Bernard went to it reluctantly and consented only when urged to it by the earnest entreaty of friends and the authoritative summons of the archbishop of Rheims, to call this bold innovator to account for his heresies and defend the faith of the Church from their mischief.

The Council was an imposing assembly, at which were present the king of France and many nobles and prelates of high rank. A considerable part of it consisted of the friends and followers of Abelard, who expected that he would successfully defend himself from the accusations with which he was charged. Bernard, put forward as the champion of Orthodoxy and the defender of the Church, entered upon his task simply and naturally. "He had collected passages from the writings of Abelard, seventeen in number, which he judged heretical and contrary to the faith of the Church, and he called for the reading of these, that Abelard might declare whether he recognized them as his own and then might either retract or defend them. A hush of attention and expectancy pervaded the assembly. But the clerk had hardly begun to read when Abelard rose and interrupted him, to the astonishment of all, by saying that he would not then discuss the points in question, that he appealed to the pope for judgment; then abruptly left the hall. Bernard, amazed at his action, tried to stop him. He earnestly assured Abelard that nothing of harm was intended to his person, that he might answer freely and in perfect security, that he would be heard with patience, and would not be checked or smitten by a premature sentence. In vain; he would not be detained, and "Abelard went from the council to the street on that June day a beaten and broken man." Why he did so, what the cause of his sudden panic and flight from this council to which he had come so confident of vindication, is one of the puzzles of ecclesiastical history.

After he had gone, Bernard insisted, notwithstanding, that the trial proceed by the examination of the passages taken from his writings, and a judgment upon them be given by the council. Fourteen of them in regard to the Trinity and the divine nature of Christ, his redemptive work, and the nature of sin as rooted in the present intention were condemned. At the request of the bishops, the action of the council was reported by Bernard to the pope, and, in turning over the case to him for decision he energetically urged the prompt condemnation of the defendant; and Abelard, largely through Bernard's influence, was condemned by the pope with his writings, which were consigned to the flames. He was furthermore enjoined to keep silent thereafter, and sentenced to be imprisoned in a convent, the condemnation being determined upon and the sentence proclaimed before Abelard, who was on his way to Rome, reached the holy city. Such treatment, of course, was unjust, but it was according to the habit of those times, and excused with the plea that Abelard's heresies were very dangerous and fast spreading, and that prompt action was imperative to arrest them. But injustice and wrong are not excused for such reasons;

they remind us of the clamor to Pilate against Jesus and his teaching as dangerous to the Jewish hierarchy.

Abelard found a friend and protector in Peter the Venerable, the abbot of the rich monastery of Clugni, one of the noblest churchmen of his time, as strictly orthodox as Bernard himself, sweet-spirited and benignant, whose Christian character is shown by a reported saying of his: "The rule of Benedict is always subordinate to the law of charity." With him at Clugni, Abelard spent the remaining two years of his sad and eventful life, the pathetic story of which he tells in his "History of Calamities." "It is one of the saddest books ever written," says Dr. Storrs; and Rémusat, Abelard's biographer, says: "No better instruction can anywhere be given of the misery which may come with the most beautiful things of the world, genius, learning, glory, love."

We are glad to say of him, that through the mediation of the good Abbot of Clugni he became reconciled before he died with Bernard, who even became his friend and was so spoken of by him; that he was pardoned his offenses by the pope, and "permitted again to use and enjoy the sacred offices from which for a time he had been debarred." We are furthermore told that, in those last years, "his manner was humble, he was diligently observant of the sacraments and of prayer, that he was truly penitent for his past sins, and that the good Abbot said in view of his good influence upon them, that "a divine arrangement had sent this honored philosopher and servant of Christ, enriching the monastery with a gift more precious than of gold and topaz." In view of all which, we may acquiesce in the words of his biographer: "We need not mourn too much for his sad life; he lived in keen suffering and he died in humiliation, but he had his glory, and he was beloved."

Bernard and Abelard were regarded as rivals in their time, and the followers of Abelard accused the former of jealousy because the eminence of their master was eclipsing his fame. But a study of Bernard's life and character does not allow us to believe this. Anything like jealousy or envy was foreign to his breast. He was lifted by his genuine goodness and sanctity above such infirmities, even if his great influence had not made him superior to them.

The fact that Bernard was able by his influence to defeat and crush Abelard was no evidence either that Abelard's work in life was a failure. There was much that was good in his ideas and philosophical opinions, and this good remains a permanent blessing to mankind. He was the originator of what is known as "the moral theory of the atonement," that "it was needed and intended to enkindle in us such love toward God as should effectually incline us to do His will, and make us ready for suffering and service in His cause." Dr. Storrs sums up correctly, we think, the truth in regard to him: "As we think of him in his relations to the Abbot of Clairvaux we may confidently believe that while they never might have been able to see eye to eye in their contemplation of the problems of theology, as presented in their time, they did attain a perfect harmony when passing beyond the mortal limitations. . . . And certainly we know that the special impulses represented by either, perhaps represented extravagantly by either, have been combined ever since and will be to the end, in the historic development of the Church."

IV
RICHARD BAXTER

IV

RICHARD BAXTER

1615–1691

Richard Baxter is the most interesting and picturesque figure among the old English divines. "If he had lived in primitive times," says an eminent English bishop, "he would have been one of the Fathers of the Church." Born November 12, 1615, of pious parents of the middle class, he received a careful religious training. His first decisive religious impressions were experienced in his fifteenth year. To dispel remorse for a petty theft of fruit from a neighbor's orchard, he took up and began to read an old, torn volume which he found at home, "Bunny's Resolution," by a Jesuit author. It excited in his troubled soul the desire for a religious life, which resulted in his conversion. His decision to enter the ministry, formed in his nineteenth year, was due to the serious impressions made by his mother's death and his narrow escape from death which occurred about the same time. He was journeying on horseback in winter. At a certain place, where the frozen road ran between high, steep banks, he met a heavily loaded wagon. To avoid it, he urged his horse up the steep side of the road. His saddle-girth broke and he was thrown before the wheel of the wagon. In a moment he would have been crushed, had not the horses suddenly stopped, as by some supernatural intervention, and he was dragged away from destruction.

His early education was defective. Though one of the most learned men of this time, he had no University training. "My faults," he says, "are no disgrace to a University, for I was of none. I have little but what I had out of books and the inconsiderable help of country divines." His appetite for reading was keen and in the indulgence of it he was omnivorous. There is in his autobiography an oft-quoted passage, where he speaks of the wide range of his reading, of which the following extract is only a portion: "I have looked over . . . Erasmus, Scaliger, Salmasius, Casaubon and many other critical grammarians. I have read almost all the physics and metaphysics I could hear of . . . whole loads of historians, chronologers and antiquaries. I despise none of their learning. All truth is useful; mathematics, which I have least of, I find a pretty manlike sport. But if I had no other kind of knowledge than these, what were my understanding worth?—I have higher thoughts of the schoolmen than Erasmus had; I much value the method and sobriety of Aquinas, the subtilty of Scotus and Occam, the plainness of Durandus, the solidity of Ariminensis, the profundity of Bradwardine, the excellent acuteness of many of their followers [giving the names of more than twenty] and many others. But how loath should I be to take such sauce for my food and such recreations for my business! The jingling of too much and too false philosophy among them oft drowns the noise of Aaron's bells." He had, however, his favorite authors, to whom he gave a more particular study, among them, Richard Hooker; and a careful examination of Baxter's works shows that he had studied deeply and learned much from the "Ecclesiastical Polity."

Baxter was ordained for the ministry in his twenty-third year in Worcester Cathedral. After preaching here and there for two years or more without any stated charge, he entered upon his pastorate at Kidderminster in 1640, when he was twenty-five years old. "There are some three or four parishes in England," says Dean Stanley, "which have been raised by their pastors to a worldwide fame. Of these the most conspicuous is Kidderminster. Kidderminster without Baxter would have nothing but its carpets."

A Remarkable Preacher

His preaching was characterized from the start by great evangelic earnestness. He so felt the importance of the soul's salvation and the adequacy of the gospel for it, that he thought that "if men only heard this as they ought, they could not but repent. And I was so foolish as to think that I had so much to say of such convincing force for the truth that men could scarcely be able to withstand it."

Baxter's qualifications as a preacher were extraordinary. He had all the fervor and intensity of

Whitefield united with great reasoning power. Besides this, he had what he calls "a familiar moving voice," which he knew how to manage so that every thought was uttered with its proper intonation and in which was heard "the accent of conviction." He took great pains with the preparation and delivery of his sermons. It is evident from some passages in his writings, that he made a careful study of the art of preaching and that he gave much attention to both the matter and the manner of his public addresses. "In the study of our sermons," he says, "we are too negligent. We must study how to convince and *get within men*, and how to bring each truth to the quick, and not leave all this to our extemporary promptitude. . . . How few ministers preach with all their might! There is nothing more unsuitable to such a business than to be slight and dull. What! speak coldly for God and for men's salvation! Let the people see that you are in earnest;—Men will not cast away their dearest pleasures upon a drowsy request. A great matter lies in the very pronunciation and tone of speech. The best matter will scarcely move men if it be not movingly delivered. See that there be no affectation, but let us speak as familiarly to our people as we would do if we were talking to any of them personally. We must lay siege to the souls of sinners. In preaching there is intended a communion of souls and a communication from ours unto theirs. I have observed that God seldom blesseth any man's work so much as his whose heart is set upon success." From "The Reformed Pastor.")

His personal appearance in the pulpit matched well with his entrancing voice, unmistakable sincerity and earnestness of spirit. His countenance in speaking was animated, and lighted up by large, serious eyes, which looked the entreaty that his tongue uttered. Delicate health, from which he suffered nearly all his life and by which he was often brought near to death, lent additional force to his speech. His words were those of "a man that was betwixt living and dead," so that, in his own phrase, he "preached as a dying man to dying men." But there was no suggestion of feebleness in his speaking. Such was the strength of his reasoning and the grip of his thought, and his ardent spirit so energized his fragile frame and physical powers that he made the impression of remarkable tireless vigor as he advanced in his discourse. His style was that of genuine oral address, a real *talking* style, though he usually read his sermons. We have the evidence of this in his published works, like the "Call to the Unconverted," which contain the substance of sermons actually preached. Many of their passages are but transcripts or extracts from those sermons, preserving for us the style and forms of thought which marked his preaching. Evidently this was marked, as Archdeacon Trench says, by "a robust and masculine eloquence." He had a strong imagination, and used it with rare effect when proper; but he possessed also the judgment and self-restraint not to use it when there was danger from its use of diverting the hearer from serious attention to the truth presented.

Nothing can be wiser from a rhetorical point of view than some of his remarks upon the sort of style required for successful preaching:

"The plainest words are the most profitable oratory in the weightiest matters. Fineness is for ornament and delicacy for delight, but they answer not necessity. Yea, it is hard for the hearer to observe the matter of ornament and delicacy, and not be carried from the matter of necessity; for it usually hindereth the due operation of the matter, keeps it from the heart, stops it in the fancy and makes it seem light as the style. . . . All our teaching must be as plain and evident as we can make it. If you would not teach men, what do you do in the pulpit? If you would, why do you not speak so as to be understood?" (From "The Reformed Pastor.")

He preached with a conviction amounting to certainty of the truth of the Scriptures, due to a remarkable personal religious experience which he had in sickness. Having this conviction, he endeavored to impart it to his hearers. To this end it was his practice "so to study the Scripture as to find passages of it capable of simple explanation and appeal, which would fasten readily upon the hearer's mind and would occupy his daily thoughts until he was entirely possessed by the fact of the immediate necessity and wisdom of guiding himself by it." So believing the Bible, and so trying to have others believe it, he proved the saying true, that "nothing can withstand the force of the man who upon the most awful of all subjects is absolutely sure of what he says, and is resolved that others shall be so, too."

He possessed, furthermore, as a crowning excellence a real *passion* for saving souls. "It was Baxter's meat and drink," says Dr. Bates, his eulogist, "the life and joy of his life, to do good to souls." Not Whitefield, nor Wesley, nor the most ardent for evangelistic conquests in the ministry of later times, surpasses Baxter in this quality. This was his chief distinction as a preacher and gave efficacy to all his gifts, his persuasive voice, his countenance, his powers of reasoning, his rare felicity of language, his rich religious experience, his spirituality.

Possessing these remarkable qualifications for preaching, no doubt he preached at times with great eloquence. The proof of it is still perceivable in his published works and sermons. They abound in passages which no one can read unmoved. If printed discourses, two hundred and fifty years after they were uttered, contain such subtle fire, able to kindle a cold reader to spiritual fervor, what must have been the flame that burned upon his tongue? It was an eloquence that attracted and impressed all classes, educated men and substantial citizens, likewise the humblest and poorest. "My public preaching," he says, "met with an attentive, diligent auditory. The congregation was usually full, so that we were fain to build five galleries after my coming, the church being the most commodious that ever I was in." It produced an immediate good effect upon the life of the community. "On the

Lord's days there was no disorder to be seen in the streets, but you might hear a hundred families singing psalms and repeating sermons as you passed them."

INTERRUPTION OF WORK BY THE CIVIL WAR

The breaking out of the Civil War, in a year or two after his advent to the town, interrupted the good work so well begun in Kidderminster. Through the powerful influence of certain royalist families the town took the side of the king; but Baxter, though a zealous churchman and loyal to the royal family, was suspected of sympathizing with the Puritan party in the conflict because of the more obvious harmony of his religious opinions and practice with theirs, and he was publicly denounced as a traitor, and threatened with violence by the vicious and turbulent spirits of the town whose sins he reproved. At the entreaty of his friends he accordingly left the place and took refuge in the walled town of Coventry, where for two years he labored diligently, preaching twice weekly to the people and the soldiers,—"taking nothing from either but his diet" for his service. "Like men in a dry house who hear the storms abroad," he and his friends there heard the dreadful rumors and sounds of the raging conflict. One day while he was preaching he heard the cannonading of the battle of Naseby. At length he was induced to become the chaplain of Whalley's regiment in the Parliamentary army and followed it fearlessly into many a hard battle and desperate siege, marching

Bible in hand with Cromwell himself to the storming of Basing House.

Baxter figured during the war in other scenes not quite so heroic though showing an equal stoutness of heart. The Parliamentary army abounded in enthusiasts and sectaries of every stripe, who were as ready for a theological tilt with opposers as for a battle with cavaliers. Baxter feeling it incumbent on him to defend the faith and to expose error—he could not sit still and keep silent when what he deemed dangerous heresy was being promulgated —never failed to improve any opportunity offered to encounter these men in argument. So whenever, for the sake of making converts to their opinions, they appointed a public meeting in any place, he would go to it and talk them down. One instance is described by him. "A cornet and troopers of Pitchford's regiment appointed a meeting in a certain church. I thought it my duty to be there also. I found a crowded congregation of poor, well-meaning people who came in the simplicity of their hearts to be deceived. I took the reading desk, and the troopers took the gallery, and I alone disputed against them from morning until almost night. If I had but gone out first, they would have prated what boastful words they listed, and made the people believe that they had got the best of it. Therefore I stayed it out until they first rose and went away. The crazy babblers were so discouraged that they never met there again. But, oh, the abundance of nonsense they uttered that day!" He did not suppose, however, that he had confuted them. "There is no confuting a man that saith nothing," he dryly remarks. "Nonsense is unanswerable, if thou hast enough of it."

OPPOSITION TO CROMWELL

It is said of Baxter that "he feared no man's displeasure and hoped for no man's preferment." His attitude toward Cromwell proves this. It was an attitude of mingled respect and disapproval. He respected him for his prowess and military genius which were attended with such constant success, and for his Christian character and devotion to the interests of religion, by reason of which he says: "Godliness had countenance and reputation, also, as well as liberty; whereas before it was the way of common shame and ruin." It was this personal regard for Cromwell's character and work that had drawn Baxter to the Puritan camp and its service as chaplain. But he remained all the time unalterably opposed to Cromwell's ambition to rule, and fearlessly criticized his usurpation of political power and authority. He went so far in his opposition as to think seriously, at one time, of trying to get up a counter movement to Cromwell's ambitious policy. Fortunately for him, he was stopped in his endeavor by illness. Cromwell would certainly have arrested him with an iron hand, and Pitchford's troopers would have been found only too willing to silence with their muskets the irrepressible man that had baffled their tongues. Having been given the opportunity, later, to preach before Cromwell, when

Protector, Baxter preached on 1 Cor. 1:10, against the divisions and distractions of the Church, and, intending to rebuke him for what he believed his sin, showed "how mischievous a thing it was for politicians to maintain such divisions for their own ends, that they might fish in troubled waters." "My plainness," says Baxter, "I heard was displeasing to him and his courtiers, but they put up with it." Soon after that sermon Cromwell sent for Baxter, once and again, for interviews with him, with the aim to vindicate himself from his charges and disarm his hostility, but without apparent effect. "He began a long and tedious speech to me," says Baxter, "of God's providence in the change of the government and how God had owned it. . . . But I told him that we took our ancient monarchy to be a blessing and not an evil to the land; and humbly craved his patience that I might ask him how England had ever forfeited that blessing, and unto whom that forfeiture was made."

"A few days after he sent for me again to hear my judgment about liberty of conscience (which he pretended to be most zealous for) before almost all his privy council; where, after another slow tedious speech of his, I told him a little of my judgment. . . . I saw that what he learned must be from himself, being more disposed to speak many hours than to hear one, and little heeding what another said when he had spoken himself." This is a shrewd criticism of Cromwell's character. Baxter's contemporaries would have said, probably, that it was equally true of Baxter himself.

He was hardly just at this time in his estimate of the Protector and his policy. Cromwell understood then the doctrine of religious liberty better than Baxter did, and he was not actuated wholly by selfish ambition as his critics affirmed, but largely by a sincere regard for England's welfare. His patience with Baxter showed great magnanimity. "Had Baxter," says Orme, "used the same freedom with the royal successors of Cromwell which he used with him he would most probably have lost his head." In what he said and did he displayed indeed a fearless courage and he acted from conscientious motives, which was admirable; but we cannot give him credit for wisdom and prudence. He himself confessed as much afterwards. In his "Penitent Confessions," Baxter says: "I am in great doubt how far I did well or ill in my opposition to Cromwell; whether I should not have been more passive and silent than I was."

His Return to His Work in Kidderminster

A sickness, by which he was brought nigh to death, and his dissatisfaction with the course of things, led to his severance of his connection with the Puritan army and his return to Kidderminster, at the almost unanimous entreaty of his flock, after an absence of four years. Those four years, with the exciting experiences that filled them, are to be looked upon simply as an interesting episode in Baxter's ministry there. The sad things he had witnessed, the waste and ruin and tragic incidents of the war, served to intensify his earnestness and spur him on to greater diligence and activity in his work. His preaching reflected the deeper earnestness of his spirit and rose to a higher pitch of eloquence. For the space of fourteen years, from 1646 to 1660, he now labors there in Kidderminster as a preacher of the gospel with unsurpassed zeal. "Of all the admirable preachers," says Davies, his biographer, "who have influenced the religious life of the English people, Baxter unquestionably has the preëminence. No one has so convincingly reasoned in the pulpit as he, so powerfully urged, so effectively taught and moved the conscience to right decision."

His Successful Method in the Cure of Souls

Baxter's ministry in Kidderminster was also remarkable for the success with which he united in it the pastoral work of family visitation and private religious conversation with his public preaching. His passion for souls did not stop with the labors of the pulpit, nor did his conception of the duties of the minister limit his efforts for their spiritual welfare to such preaching. Both his love of souls and his conception of what is due from the minister to his flock, constrained him to labors outside the pulpit for their benefit. He says: "We should know every person that belongs to our charge; for how can we 'take heed to the flock of God,' if we do not know them? Does not a careful shepherd look after every individual sheep, and a good physician attend every particular patient? Why then should not the shepherds and the physicians of the church take heed to every member of their charge? Apostolic example and precept urge this. Paul taught the people publicly and from house to house, 'warned every man and taught every man that he might present every man perfect in Christ Jesus'; and he charges ministers of the gospel to 'watch for souls as those that must give an account.' " The superior effectiveness of "this private way of preaching" especially recommends it, he asserts. "One word of seasonable advice has done that good which many sermons have failed of doing. . . . Yea, I have found that an ignorant sot, who for a long time had been an unprofitable hearer, has got more knowledge and remorse of conscience in half an hour's close conversation than he did by ten years' public preaching."

The reasons why this private, personal method of dealing with individual souls was so effective, are by him thus stated:

"We have the best opportunity to imprint religious truth upon the heart when we can speak to each one's particular necessity, i.e., his particular case, and address him in regard to it with familiar importunity.

"By this means you will hear their objections, and discover what it is that resists the truth, and so may be the more able effectually to convince them. We can here answer their objections, drive them to a stand, urge them to discover their purposes for the future, and to promise to use the means of reformation.

"In private we may speak in a much plainer manner than we can in public. In public we cannot use such homely expressions nor so many repetitions as their dullness requires, but in private we may.

"In public our speeches are long, we quite overrun their understandings and their memories, so that we lose their attention, and they know not what we have been saying; but in private we may take our hearers with us as we go, we have them as interlocutors in what is said, and easily hold their attention."

It was not until after some years that he undertook this private work. "My apprehensions of it were too small and of the difficulties too great. I thought that the people would scorn it and that only a few would submit to it. The work seemed strange to me and I thought my strength would never go through it." Having ventured, however, upon the experiment, the success of it more than met his expectations. "I find the difficulties," he says, "to be nothing to what I imagined, and I experience the benefits and comforts of the work to be such that I would not wish to have neglected it for all the riches in the world. I cannot say that one family hath refused or that many persons have shifted it off. I wonder at myself that I kept from so clear and excellent a duty so long. We never took the rightest course to demolish the Kingdom of Darkness till now." His rule was to "take each person alone and discourse with him privately. I find by experience that in general people will bear plain and close dealing about their sin and their duty when you have them alone better than when others are present."

His passion for saving souls prompted him to take another forward step with a view to pressing the truth home upon every individual in his parish; he invited the more devout and intelligent Christians of the Church to coöperate in the effort with him, saying: "The good work is likely to go on but poorly if none but ministers are employed in it." In this he anticipated by one hundred years the ideas and opinions of John Wesley in regard to the importance and value of lay activity in the Church. He anticipated Wesley also in adopting the conference and prayer meeting as an evangelizing agency and a means of the development of Christians through the exercise of their gifts. He testifies that "many of them were able to pray very laudably with others, while the temper of their minds and the innocency of their lives was more loud than their parts." Such meetings, usually held weekly, Baxter caused to be started and maintained in different parts of his parish; they formed a part of the net which he spread for souls in Kidderminster, whereby he sought to catch as many for Christ as possible.

We have dwelt at this length upon the manner in which Baxter fulfilled his pastoral function, because it forms an essential part of his ministerial work in Kidderminster. Without it he could not have accomplished the remarkable work he wrought there, a work so great that it transformed the moral and religious character of the town and gave it, as Stanley says, "a world-wide fame." "When I first came there," he says, "there was about one family in a street that worshipped God; when I came away there were some streets where there was not one family that did not so, and that did not by professing serious godliness give in hopes of their sincerity. In those families which were the worst—those of inns and alehouses—usually some persons in each house did seem to be religious. If not the elders, their children; and then the elders were made more kindly disposed because of the children. Many children did God work upon at fourteen or fifteen or sixteen years of age. This did marvelously reconcile the minds of the parents to godliness, and they that before talked against godliness would not hear it spoken against when it was their children's case."

The Reformed Pastor

Another result of his pastoral work of visitation for religious conversation with individuals should be mentioned. It led to the writing by him of "The Reformed Pastor," in which he describes the work undertaken for the spiritual benefit of his flock, its method and success, that other ministers might be stimulated and encouraged to undertake a similar work for their people. From that book we have derived our account of what he did in this particular line in the "Cure of Souls." "It prevailed with many ministers," he says, "to set upon that work which I there exhort them to. Churches either rise or fall as the ministry doth rise or fall."

This book, by reason of its "thoughts that breathe and words that burn," and its great influence upon subsequent generations of ministers, is one of the most notable in the religious literature of the world. Dr. Philip Doddridge speaks of it as "a most extraordinary performance," and asserts that "nothing would have a greater tendency to awaken the spirit of a minister to that zeal in his work, for want of which many good men are but shadows of what by the blessing of God they might be if the maxims and measures laid down in this incomparable treatise were strenuously pursued." It is a book of undecaying vitality and, consequently, of perennial value. In this belief, the founder of Wellesley College, Mr. Henry C. Durant, in his awakened zeal for the spread of religion, bought up a large number of them for distribution among the ministers of Massachusetts, to the great spiritual profit, no doubt, of those ministers and their congregations.

BAXTER'S PUBLISHED WORKS

Boswell once asked Dr. Johnson which of Baxter's works he recommended him to read. "Read any of them," he replied, "they are all good." This, however, was a careless answer. Baxter's works are not all good, nor is any one of them equally good throughout. If there were no other reason, he wrote too much for uniform excellence. His published works numbered more than 170 volumes. Besides this, many of them, being controversial and upon questions no longer living, would now be to any one but a church historian dull and unprofitable stuff to read. He often began a controversy in his young manhood without sufficient consideration, and was forced later to shift his ground, and so fell into self-contradictions and glaring inconsistencies, which his opponents pointed out to his discomfiture. One of them compiled a volume composed of the irreconcilable utterances discoverable in Baxter's works, and entitled it "A Dialogue between Richard and Baxter." Bishop Burnet truly says, he "meddled in too many things," and "was most unhappily subtle and metaphysical in everything." But whatever may be the contradictions and unprofitable stuff found in any work, such were the genius and piety of the man that, as Dean Stanley says "there run through it golden threads and solid strands which redeem 'it from ignominy, and at times are woven into patches and fringes of glorious splendor."

In his old age he confessed as a fault the controversial propensity and errors displayed by him in earlier years and thus explains how it happened: "To tell the truth, while I busily read what other men said in these controversies, my mind was so prepossessed with their notions that I could not possibly see the truth in its own native and naked evidence; and when I entered into public disputations concerning it, though I was truly willing to know the truth, my mind was so forestalled with borrowed notions that I chiefly studied how to make good the opinions I had received, and ran farther from the truth. Yea, when I read the truth in Dr. Preston's and other men's writings I did not consider and understand it, and when I heard it from them whom I opposed in wrangling disputations, or read it in books of controversy, I discerned it least of all; till at last being in my sickness cast far from home, where I had no book but my Bible, I set to study the truth from thence and so by the blessing of God discovered more in one week than I had done before in seventeen years' reading, hearing and wrangling."

HIS PRACTICAL WORKS

Baxter's great merit as an author rests chiefly upon his practical works. The most notable of these, besides the "Reformed Pastor" are: "The Saint's Rest," "A Call to the Unconverted," "Reasons for the Christian Religion," "The Right Method for a Settled Peace of Conscience," "The Crucifixion of the World by the Cross of Christ," "Dying Thoughts," and "Reliquae Baxterianae" —"Baxter's Narrative of his Life and Times." The "Saint's Rest" was his first as well as most widely known book. It was written in his thirty fourth year, when "sentenced to death" by his physicians. Its design was to be "a directory for getting and keeping the heart in heaven by heavenly meditation," and he put into it such directions as he had found good for himself when expecting soon to die. Books of this kind, in which are distilled the heart's real experiences and which, as John Milton says, "preserve as in a vial the purest efficacy and extraction of the living intellect that bred them," touch men most deeply and live long. The "Saint's Rest" is, therefore, still a live book. So likewise are his other practical writings that have been mentioned. Their thoughts are good for all time, and expressed in a remarkable style. "There reigns in it," as Archbishop Trench says, "a robust and masculine eloquence, nor does it want from time to time rare and unsought felicity of language, which once heard can scarcely be forgotten." These words of Trench concerning Baxter's style, "rare and unsought felicity of language," express the literal truth about it. It was "rare," but not, like the style of Cardinal Newman and Stevenson, the result of painstaking toil and long effort. Its "felicity" was "unsought"; it was natural to him, the unstudied manner in which his thought expressed itself. "Probably," says one of his admirers, "he never consumed forty minutes in as many years in the mere selection and adjustment of words." And Baxter himself says of his published writings: "I scarce ever wrote one sheet twice over, nor stayed to make any blots or interlineations, but would fain let it go as it was first conceived." His earnest mind in its expression of the good thoughts within him chose instinctively the right language, such language as most aptly and happily clothed what he wanted to say.

It must be confessed, however, that all his practical writings have one obvious fault, that of *redundancy of thought*, not of language. Though Isaac Barrow affirms that "they were never mended," the affirmation is not strictly true. They have been really improved and made more readable by considerable abridgment. It is the fault of an affluent mind that from its fulness overflows to excess. But in every book he wrote there are passages that are remarkable for their conciseness, force and beauty. There are gems of thought on almost every page, which enrich the unprofitable stuff, as the diamonds the blue ground in the South African mines, in which they lie embedded. Take the following examples: *"When half is unknown, the other half is not half known." "Truth is so dear a friend, and he that sent it is so much more dear, that whatever I suffer I dare not stifle or conceal it." "The melody of music is better known by hearing it than by reports of it. So there is a latent sense in us of the effects of the gospel in our hearts, which will ever cause us to love it and to hold it fast."*

BAXTER'S WORK AFTER THE RESTORATION OF THE MONARCHY

At the Restoration, Baxter, because of his prominence in England as a clergyman and religious writer, and his great influence among the Dissenters and Moderate Churchmen, was invited to take a leading part in the consideration and discussion of some of the questions which then engaged the attention of the nation, the king and his court. Holding a foremost place among these questions was, whether concessions should be made and pains taken to gain the Dissenters or not, especially the Presbyterians, to representatives of whom the king at Breda, before his return to England, had promised that if restored to the throne of his father he would grant "liberty and consideration for tender consciences," and that "no man should be molested for differences of opinion in matters of religion." Lord Chancellor Hyde, the Earl of Clarendon, was apparently for concession, and, Bishop Burnet says, "got the king to publish a declaration, soon after his restoration, concerning ecclesiastical affairs, to which if he had stood, very probably the greatest part of them might have been gained. But the bishops did not approve of this, . . . and instead of using methods to bring in these sectaries, they resolved rather to seek the most effectual ones for casting them out."

The bishops managed, by rekindling the animosities produced by the Civil War, and by infusing into the mind of the king distrust of the loyalty of the Dissenters, to bring over the king to their side. Burnet says that under his compliance, however, the king concealed the design of favorable legislation for popery. "Nothing could make toleration for popery pass (he thought) but the having great bodies of men put out of the Church and put under severe laws, which should force them to move for a toleration and should make it reasonable to grant it to them. And it was resolved that whatever should be granted of that sort should go in so large a manner that Papists should be comprehended in it." The King's "Declaration" was no doubt shaped by this secret purpose and was less moderate and conciliatory than had been anticipated. "When we received this copy of the Declaration," says Baxter, "we saw that it would not serve to heal our differences. We therefore told the Lord Chancellor that our endeavors as to concord would all be frustrated if much were not altered in the Declaration." Baxter was chosen to put their objections to it in a petition, which he wrote with his usual warmth and frankness. When this was laid before his associates, "they were troubled," says Baxter, "at the plainness of it. It

was not my unskillfulness in a more pleasing
language, but my reason and conscience upon foresight of the issue which were the cause." He refused
to alter it, until "they told me it would not so much
as be received and that I must go with it myself, for
nobody else would." The petition, as altered, was
still "ungrateful" and rejected by the Lord Chancellor.

Finally, after considerable more parleying, the
following course, according to Baxter's account
(abridged), was decided upon: "A day was appointed
for his majesty to peruse (in their presence) the
Declaration, as it was drawn up by the Lord Chancellor, and to allow what he liked, and alter the rest
upon the hearing of what both sides had to say."

The following account of the interview of the
Nonconformists with the king is given by Baxter:
"The business of the day was not to dispute, but as
the Lord Chancellor read over the 'Declaration,' each
party was to speak to what it disliked, and the king
to determine how it should be, as he liked himself.
. . . The great matter which we stopped at was
the word 'consent'(where the bishop is to confirm
by the 'consent' of the pastor of the church). . . .
The King would by no means pass the word 'consent'
either then, or in the point of ordination, or censures;
because it gave the ministers a negative voice [thus
limiting the bishop's power and authority]. I insisted
that, though 'consent' be but a little word, it was
necessary to a very desirable end, *union*, which would
not be attained if no consent were allowed ministers
in any part of the government of their flocks.

"The most of the time being spent thus in speaking to particulars of the Declaration, as it was read, when we came to the end, the Lord Chancellor drew out another paper and told us that the king had been petitioned also by the Independents and Anabaptists, and though he knew not what to think of it himself and did not very well like it, yet something he had drawn up which he would read to us, and desire us also to give our advice about it." Thereupon he read, as an addition to the declaration, "that others also be permitted to meet for religious worship, so be it they do it not to the disturbance of the peace, and that no justice of peace or officer disturb them!"

Had this "addition" been promptly accepted by both parties and incorporated in the declaration, and the whole at once enacted into the law of the realm, the "union" sought would have been achieved. But after the reading of it, "all were silent," says Baxter. "The Presbyterians perceived, as soon as they heard it, that it would secure the liberty of the Papists; and Dr. Wallis whispered this in my ear, but entreated me to 'say nothing,' and to let the bishops speak to it. But the bishops would not speak a word, nor any one of the Presbyterians. . . . I knew, if we consented to it, it would be charged on us that we spoke for a toleration of Papists and Sectaries; and if we spoke against it, all sects and parties would be set against us as the causers of their sufferings. At last, seeing the silence continue, I thought our very silence would be charged on us as consent, if it went on, and therefore, I said only this: "This reverend brother (pointing to Dr. Gunning, a leader of the Episcopal party) even now speaking against the sects, named the Papists and the Socinians; for our parts we desired not favor to ourselves alone, and rigorous severity we desired against none; but we distinguished the *tolerable parties from the intolerable*. For the latter, such as the two sorts named by that reverend brother, for our parts, we could not make their toleration our request."

It was one of the faults of Baxter that he was not always self-consistent in what he said and did. We have here a notable instance. Previously, in the days of Cromwell's protectorate, he was on the committee to settle the fundamentals of religion as a basis of toleration and religious liberty, and what he then proposed as fundamental was objected to as something "which might be subscribed by a Papist or Socinian." "*So much the better*," was Baxter's reply, "*and so much the fitter it is to be the matter of concord*." At the time of the conference with the king and Clarendon he was probably of the same opinion still, though what he now said in objection to "the addition" seemed opposed to the former opinion. The explanation of it is, that he *volunteered at this time to speak for the Presbyterian members of the conference, rather than for himself*. As we look back upon it, the objection thus prompted was ill-timed and most unfortunate, defeating the cause of toleration and religious liberty most dear to his heart. If Baxter, always too forward to speak, had restrained his tongue on this occasion with the rest, the religious toleration, not only of the Papists, which the king

desired, but of all the Nonconformist bodies, Presbyterians, Independents, Anabaptists, Quakers and
Socinians (tolerance of which the Episcopalians
opposed), would have been then and there secured.

Why did he not say "Yes"? Because he did not
now openly avow his former opinion undisturbed by
the disapproval which he read on the faces of those
about him. "I should as willingly be a martyr for
charity as for faith," is one of his famous sentences.
It is a pity that this sentiment did not fortify his
resolution at that moment. But the intolerant
atmosphere he breathed may have clouded at the
time his spirit,—or he may not have reached the
positive conviction of his later years. Why did not
the Presbyterians say "Yes"? Because John Knox's
hatred of popery was still felt by them. Why did
not the bishops say "Yes," and avoid the infamy they
incurred by the "Act of Uniformity," the "Test
Acts," and the cruel persecutions they relentlessly
waged against the Nonconformists the next twenty
five years? Because they remembered the persecutions of the Romish Church under Mary Tudor a
hundred years before, and shared the horror of the
majority of the English people for the papacy on
account of them; a horror kept alive among the
English people by Fox's "Book of Martyrs," which
with his Bible John Bunyan carried with him to his
prison, and the reading of which made him and other
sufferers from Episcopal intolerance prefer to endure
these sufferings rather than purchase religious liberty
by extending it to Papists. The dread of having
their land come again under the dominion of the

Romish Church haunted, and still haunts, the majority of the people of Great Britain like a persistent nightmare.

"When I went out from the meeting I went out dejected," says Baxter, "satisfied that the form of government outlined in that 'Declaration' would not be satisfactory, because the pastors had no government of the flocks."

Before it was published, however, it was so modified through the influence of two great nobles, that the chief objection found in the conference over it was removed. "The word *consent* in regard to confirmation and the sacrament was put in, though not as to jurisdiction." Because of this concession Baxter agreed to "do his best" to induce all to conform according to the terms of the Declaration.

To strengthen the bond which held him but slightly to the State Church, the Lord Chancellor offered him the bishopric of Hereford, which he declined.

THE SAVOY CONFERENCE

In his "Declaration" the king had intimated that the liturgy of the Church should be revised and certain alterations adopted to meet the wishes of the Nonconformists. In fulfillment of this promise a commission was issued under the great seal empowering chosen representatives of both sides to meet for the purpose. The Archbishop of York and twelve bishops represented the Episcopal side, and eleven Nonconformist ministers, of whom Baxter was one, the other side. The place of meeting for the consideration and discussion of the alterations desired was the Savoy palace, the official residence of the bishop of London. In this conference, which was limited to three months and recognized in English history as singular and notable, Baxter was the protagonist of the Nonconformist party. At its opening meeting the Bishop of London, speaking for his side, said, as Baxter reports: "it was not they but we (the Nonconformists) that had been the seekers of this Conference, and who had desired alterations in the liturgy; and therefore they had nothing to say or do till we had brought in all we had to say against it in writing, and all the additional forms and alterations which we desired." "I was wholly of his mind," says Baxter, "and prevailed with my brethren to consent. We accepted of the task which they imposed upon us, yet so as to bring all our exceptions at one time, and all our additions at another time."

In the division of this task, the companions of Baxter distributed among themselves the selection of exceptions to the Common Prayer Book, and he took the additions or new forms to be proposed. With characteristic energy and dispatch he performed his work in a fortnight, and finding his brethren still toiling over theirs, took hold and helped them with a paper of such exceptions as occurred to him.

When they submitted their work to the bishops, they found them indisposed to accept any of the changes proposed, and ready stoutly to defend liturgy and prayer book, as if it were a profanation to alter them in any particular, though after the

conference, when the heat of their joint discussion was over, they agreed among themselves to considerable additions and alterations.

Bishop Burnet gives an interesting contemporary view of the conference. He says: "The two men that had the chief management of the debate were the most unfit to heal matters, and the fittest to widen them that could have been found. Baxter was the opponent, and Gunning (afterwards made bishop of Ely) was respondent. He was noted for a special subtlety of arguing. All the arts of sophistry were made use of by him on all occasions in as confident a manner as if they had been sound reasoning. Baxter and he spent some days in much logical arguing to the diversion of the town, who thought here were a couple of fencers engaged in disputes that could never be brought to an end, or have any good effect."

No "good effect," or gain to religion, or to the cause of truth ever resulted from such a discussion. Baxter himself learned this, later, to his complete satisfaction, and describes the result in most expressive language: "*I have perceived,*" he says, "*that nothing so much hindereth the reception of the truth as urging it on men with too harsh importunity, and falling too heavily on their errors; for hereby you engage their honor in the business, and they defend their errors as themselves and stir up all their wit and ability to oppose you. In a learning way men are ready to receive the truth, but in a disputing way, they come armed against it with prejudice and animosity.*"

And so the efforts which Baxter and his Nonconforming associates made for the religious peace and concord of their torn and distracted land, and from which they had hoped so much, ended in utter, disastrous failure. The "Convocation" soon adopted additions to the prayer book that made it still more repugnant to them, and Parliament passed an Act of Uniformity with new forms of subscription that were far harder to bear than the old ones were. The baleful mischief wrought by the Act to the civil and religious welfare of England is thus candidly stated by that eminent churchman, the late Professor Benjamin Jowett, Master of Balliol, Cambridge; "On August 22, the Nonconformist ministers (2000 of them) were finally expelled by the Act of Uniformity. That was the greatest misfortune that has ever befallen this country, a misfortune that has never been retrieved. For it has made two nations of us instead of one, in politics, in religion, almost in our notion of right and wrong; it arrayed one class of society permanently against another, and many of the political difficulties of our own time have their origin in the enmities caused by the rout of August 22, 1662, called 'Black Bartholomew's Day,' which Baxter vainly strove to avert."*

Baxter, though a minister of the Established Church and greatly beloved by most of the people of his parish which he had so greatly blessed by his ministry and exalted to a place of lasting honor among the parishes of the Christian world, was deprived by the ecclesiastical authorities of his charge in Kidderminster. His offense was the

---

* Sermons, Biographical and Miscellaneous, by Benjamin Jowett—E. P. Dutton & Co., Pub.

unpardonable one in the eyes of the restored monarchy and the ruling churchmen, of being eminent for piety and of holding the religious opinions of the discredited Puritan party, that had ceased from power with the death of Cromwell, and of earnestly reaffirming the doctrines of their own great divines, Jeremy Taylor and Chillingworth, in regard to religious toleration and liberty of conscience, and of having endeavored in conference with them to get their consent to have these doctrines incorporated in the law of the land for the sake of its peace and the religious quiet of all. On this account his reasonable request to be formally invested by the new government with the vicarship of the town was refused and he was practically deposed, after two years, from the ministry. Though the most powerful preacher in England, he was forbidden to preach, or minister to any other flock, and thus doomed to silence for nearly the remainder of his days, a period of about thirty years.

For this exclusion of Baxter from his minsterial work, Morley, his diocesan bishop, was chiefly responsible. He had acquired for Baxter an implacable dislike, most unchristian and indefensible, from which he never relented.

And because of Baxter's prominence in the religious world he was ever an object of bitter persecution. "When I sit in a corner," he says, "and meddle with nobody and hope the world will forget that I am alive, court, city and country are still filled with clamors against me." No unprejudiced, fair-minded man can read of the unjust treatment he received from court and prelates, especially from Bishop Morley, without hot indignation.

But God gave to him the comfort of good friends, among whom was Sir Matthew Hale, and a romantic consolation in the shape of a lovely wife, Margaret Charleton, a young woman of beauty, refinement, and of high social position, who, touched by his wrongs and reverencing his saintly character, delicately offered herself to him in marriage, to be the sharer of his obloquy and the comforter of his heart in his affliction. Her friends and acquaintances endeavored in vain to turn her from her purpose. They disparaged him as a man of ignoble birth, of "a family so obscure that no one could tell whence he came." "True," she replied, "but *I know where he is going and I want to go with him.*" "It was rung about everywhere," says Baxter, "partly as a wonder, partly as a crime, and the king's marriage was scarcely more talked of than mine." The marriage proved a happy one; and with the blessing of his wife's society and love he found it easy to endure the trials of ejectment from the ministry with its enforced silence and continued persecution in addition to the misery of poor health.

Though his tongue was silenced by the ban put upon his preaching, his pen continued to be busy in spite of his poor health. Some of his best works, like "Dying Thoughts" and the "Narrative of His Life," were produced in this period. "The Dying Thoughts," like "The Saint's Rest," was written by him primarily for his own use. He was for a long time "unresolved whether anyone else should ever see it." He finally gave it to a publisher in the hope that "the same thoughts may be useful to others that are so for me. If those men's lives were spent in serious thoughts of death who are now studying to destroy each other and tear in pieces a distressed land, they would prevent much dolorous repentance." The "Dying Thoughts" contains just such thoughts, expressed in Baxter's best style, as are appropriate and helpful to one nearing death, or supposes he is, because of failing health. They exhibit the calm serenity of one who through the power of the gospel is able to contemplate death not only with composure but with a holy joy. The book has given comfort to many people in the prospect of death. It gave consolation, in particular, to the celebrated Lord William Russell before his execution, a judicial murder in the reign of Charles II.

Some of the works of Baxter, written at this time with the most excellent intention of promoting religious harmony, failed sadly of their purpose. Instead, like his endeavors at the Savoy conference, they drew upon him a more bitter and determined hostility and much savage criticism and abuse. The cause, apparently, was his unfortunate, offensive manner of approaching and attacking the position of opponents. Orme, his biographer, says—in comparing his character and mode of discussion with those of the celebrated Dr. Owen—"Baxter was sharp and cutting, and disposed to push matters further than the circumstances of the times admitted. The deportment of Owen was bland and conciliating compared with that of Baxter. Hence Owen frequently made friends of enemies, while Baxter often made enemies of friends."

A notable illustration of this is found in his famous controversy with Edward Bagshaw, a former friend and champion of his cause against Bishop Morley, who took offense at a book published by Baxter, entitled "A Cure for Church Divisions," which Bagshaw thought reflected too severely and unjustly upon some Dissenters, and wrote a reply to it. This reply called out from Baxter a rejoinder, which Bagshaw answered with "A Defense." This, Baxter hotly declared to be "full of untruths which the furious and temerarious man did utter out of the rashness of his mind." This drew from Baxter "A Second Admonition" to Mr. Bagshaw, "written to call him to repentance for many false doctrines and especially fourscore palpable untruths in matters of fact." Again Bagshaw replied with "A Review: All of Mr. Baxter's Calumnies Refuted," to which Baxter finally rejoined with "The Church told of Mr. Edward Bagshaw's Scandal." Of this last rejoinder, Baxter says: "About the day that it came out, Mr. Bagshaw died a prisoner, which made it grevious to me to think that I must seem to write against the dead"; and then, as if condemning his own part in the controversy as utterly futile and foolish, he adds: "While we wrangle here in the dark we are dying and passing to the world that will decide all our controversies; and the safest passage thither is by peaceable holiness."

Doubtless his feeling of the shocking impropriety of this bitter controversy, in view of its sad conclusion

was heightened by the thought that Mr. Bagshaw
had once been his friend and former defender.

> "Each spoke words of high disdain
> And insult to his heart's best brother:
> They parted, ne'er to meet again!"

*　　*　　*　　*　　*

"I cannot forgive myself," he says, later on in life,
"for rash words or deeds by which I have seemed less
tender and kind than I should have been to my near
and dear relations.　When such are dead, every sour
or cross provoking word which I gave them maketh
me almost unreconcilable with myself, and tells me
how repentance brought some of old in the hurry of
their passion to pray to the dead whom they had
wronged to forgive them."

The affair with Mr. Bagshaw had no transient
effect on Baxter's mind.　It appears to have wrought,
besides the compunction of heart shown by the
words that have been quoted, a deep and permanent
change in him.　Whereas he had been, as Dean
Stanley says, "provokingly contentious, at times
captious beyond endurance," sharp and cutting in his
reproofs, and disposed (in his eagerness to refute
opponents in controversy), as Orme says, "to push
matters further than the circumstances of the times
admitted," he became at last tolerant and gentle
toward those who differed from him in their religious
and theological opinions, until he arrived at the
point of saying: "Almost all the contentions of
divines,—the sects, the factions, the unreconciled

feuds, the differences in religion, which have been the taunt of the devil and of his emissaries in the world, have come from pretended knowledge and of taking uncertain for certain truths. Richard Baxter, by God's blessing, on long and hard studies hath learned to know that he knoweth but little, and to suspend his judgment of uncertainties and to take great, necessary and certain things for the food of his faith and comfort, and the measure of his church communion."

He made the motto of those last years of his life the now familiar maxim of all tolerant Christians: "*In necessary things unity, in unnecessary things liberty, in all things charity,*" which he had discovered in a Latin treatise of Rupertus Meldenius, an obscure German writer and conciliatory theologian of the seventeenth century, and "which," says Dean Stanley, "has gradually entered into universal literature and been deemed worthy of the great Augustine, who, I fear, with all his power and piety never, or hardly ever, wrote anything so good or so wise as this."

The great change wrought in Baxter bore precious fruit in his last uncompleted literary work, the "Narrative of His Own Life," published after his death. We refer especially to the last twenty pages or thereabouts of the First Part, where he reviews the changes that had occurred in his own mind, and in his opinions and conclusions "since the unriper times of his youth." "It stands," says Dean Stanley, "in the very foremost rank of autobiographical reflections; and I make bold to say that in permanent practical instruction it as much exceeds anything even in the 'Confessions' of Augustine, as in ordinary fame it falls below them." Stanley's attention was directed to it as a remarkable piece of literature by Sir James Stevens. "Lose not a day in reading it," Stevens said. "You will never repent of it." "That very night I followed his advice," says Stanley, "and I have ever since, publicly and privately, advised every theological student to do the same." As Stanley pronounces it "the very flower of Baxter's writings" I shall be justified in dwelling upon and quoting from it at some length.

Contrasting what he was and thought as a young man with what he had become through his enlightening experiences and the mental growth and studies of years, he says: "I was then like a man of quick understanding that was to travel a way which he never went before, or to cast up an account which he never labored in before. . . . I am now like one of a somewhat slower understanding, who is traveling a way which he hath often gone, and is casting up an account which he hath ready at hand, so that I can very confidently say, my judgment is much sounder and firmer than it was then."

In his review he touches upon a considerable number of subjects, all interesting, but our limited space forbids our reference to but few. The quality, however, of "his riper thoughts," as contrasted with those of "the unriper times of his youth," in which, as recalled, he says: "I find the footsteps of my unfurnished mind and of my emptiness and insufficiency," may be guessed by quoting what he says on these few topics selected:

The Profit of Meditation on Heavenly Blessedness

"I perceive that it is the object which altereth and elevateth the mind, which will resemble that which it most frequently feedeth on. It is not only useful to our comfort to be much in heaven in believing thoughts; it must animate all our other duties and fortify us against every temptation and sin. The love of the end is the poise or spring which setteth every wheel a-going."

Increasing Consciousness of Personal Ignorance in Spite of Growing Knowledge

"Formerly I knew much less than now, and yet was not half so much acquainted with my ignorance. I had a great delight in the daily new discoveries which I made, and of the light which shined in upon me, like a man that cometh into a country where he never was before, but I little knew either how imperfectly I understood those very points whose discovery so much delighted me or how many things I yet was a stranger to. I now find far greater darkness in all things, and perceive how very little we know in comparison of that of which we are ignorant. I have, therefore, far meaner thoughts of my own understanding though I know that it is better furnished than it was then."

Good and Bad Men

"I now see that good men are not so good as I once thought they were, . . . that nearer approach and fuller trial do make the best appear more weak and faulty than their admirers at a distance think; and I find that few are so bad as either malicious enemies or censorious professors do imagine. In some, indeed, I find that human nature is corrupted into a greater likeness to devils than I once thought; but even in the wicked, usually, there is more for grace to take advantage of than I once believed."

Church Communion

"I am not so narrow in my principles of Church communion as once I was. I am not for narrowing the Church more than Christ himself alloweth us nor for robbing him of any of his flock. I can now distinguish between sincerity and profession, and that the profession is credible that is not disproved. . . . I am more sensible of the sin and mischief of using men cruelly in matters of religion, and of pretending men's good and the order of the Church for acts of inhumanity and uncharitableness. Such know not their own infirmity, nor yet the nature of pastoral government, which ought to be paternal and by love; nor do they know the way to win a soul, or to maintain the Church's peace. I do not lay so much stress upon the external forms of worship. Judgment and Charity are the cause of it. I cannot be so narrow in my principles of Church communion as many are, that are so much for a liturgy, or so much against it; so much for ceremonies, or so much against them, that they can hold communion with no church that is not of their mind and way. . . . I cannot be of their opinion, that think God will not accept him that prayeth by the Common Prayer Book; and that such forms are a self-invented worship, which God rejecteth; nor yet can I be of their mind that say the like of extempore prayers."

Differences and Church Divisions of Christians

"I am more afflicted by the disagreements of Christians than I was; except the case of the infidel world, nothing is so bad and grievous to my thoughts as the case of divided churches; and, therefore, I am more deeply sensible of the sinfulness of those prelates and pastors of churches who are the principal cause of these divisions. How is the conversion of infidels hindered by them and Christ dishonored! I think most divines do study differences a hundred hours for one hour that ever they study the healing of differences, and that is a shameful disproportion. Do not bend all your wits to find what more may be said against others, and to make the differences as wide as you can, but study as hard to find out men's agreements and to reduce the differences to as narrow a compass as possible. Be as industrious for the peace of the Church among others as if you smarted for it yourself; seek it, and beg it, and follow it, and take no nay. Be sure that you see the true controversy, and distinguish all that is merely verbal from that which is material; and that which is about methods and modes and circumstances from that which is about substantial truths; and that which is about the inferior truths, though weighty, from that which is about the essentials of Christianity. Lay the unity of the Church upon nothing but what is essential to the Church. Seek after as much truth and purity and perfection as you can but as not necessary to the essence of the church or any member of it. Tolerate no error nor sin so far as not to seek the healing of it; but tolerate all error and sin, consistent with Christian faith and charity, so far as not to unchristian and unchurch men for them. . . . Acquaint yourselves with healing truths and labor to be as skillful in the work of pacifying and agreeing men as most are in the work of dividing and disagreeing. The least contested points are commonly the most weighty."

His Zeal for Truth Limited to Fundamentals

"I have lost much of the zeal which I had to propagate any truths save the mere fundamentals. When I perceive people to think they know what indeed they do not—which is too common—and to dispute those things which they never thoroughly studied, or to expect that I should debate the case with them, as if an hour's talk would serve instead of an acute understanding and seven years' study, I have no zeal to make them of my opinion . . . and am apt to be silent and leave them to themselves."

The Blindness to Its Evidence of Opponents to Truth

"We mistake men's diseases when we think there needeth nothing to cure their errors but only to bring them the evidence of the truth. Alas! there are many distempers of the mind to be removed before men are apt to receive that evidence. In controversies, fierce opposition is the bellows to kindle a resisting zeal, when if they be let alone and their opinions lie awhile despised they usually cool and come again to themselves."

The Sin of Pride

"I am much more apprehensive than long ago of the odiousness and danger of the sin of pride, especially in matters spiritual. I think so far as any man is proud, he is king to the devil and utterly a stranger to God and himself. It is a wonder that it should be a possible sin to men that still carry about with them in soul and body such humbling matter as we all do."

Mutability of Mind

"I find a great mutability as to the apprehensions and degrees of grace, and consequently find that so mutable a thing as the mind of man would never keep itself if God were not its keeper. When I have been seriously musing upon the reasons of Christianity, with the concurrent evidences methodically placed in their just advantages before my eyes, I am so clear in my belief of the Christian verities that Satan hath little room for a temptation; but sometimes when the foresaid evidences have been out of the way, or less upon my thoughts, he hath by surprises amazed me and weakened my faith in the present act."

Suffering the Lot of the Church

"I am more apprehensive that suffering must be the Church's ordinary lot, and true Christians must be self-denying cross-bearers even where there are none but nominal Christians to be the cross-makers; for ordinarily, God would have vicissitudes of summer and winter, day and night, that the church may grow externally in the summer of prosperity, and internally and radically in the winter of adversity; yet, usually, their night is longer than their day, and that day itself hath its storms and tempests."

His Chief Solicitude

"I am more solicitous about my duty to God, and less solicitous about his dealings with me, being assured that he will do all things well and that there is no rest but in the will and goodness of God."

CONCLUSION

"This much of the alterations of my soul since my younger years. . . . What I have recorded hath been especially to perform my vows. I have done it also to prevent the defective performance of this task by overvaluing brethren who were unfitter to do it than myself; and that young Christians may be warned by the mistakes and failings of my unriper times, to learn in patience, live in watchfulness, and not be fierce and proudly confident in their first conceptions; to reverence ripe, experienced age and to beware of taking such for their chief guides as have nothing but immature and inexperienced judgments with fervent affections and free and confident expressions."

Our quotations from Baxter's last work show that his mind was continually progressive, growing in spiritual insight, and freedom of thought and charity of opinion to the very end.

"These counsels of moderation," as Dean Stanley calls them, men are slow to hear in times of heated controversy and bitter resentment like those in England during the Civil War and the reigns of the two last of her Stuart kings, but when the sky clears and a serener atmosphere comes, then they are heeded as sane and Christian. They so slowly make their way, because strong prejudices and theological and political rancors are slow to cool, like the lava of a volcano which is warm to the touch and glows with inward fire long after the eruption; but, nevertheless, they prevail at last by their intrinsic reasonableness and persistent power.

We have an impressive proof of this in the case of Baxter, showing the increasing acceptance of his liberal ideas among all classes of English people. In a public place in Kidderminster, a striking statue was erected and dedicated to the memory of Baxter with appropriate and impressive ceremonies, July 28, 1875. On the pedestal of the statue is the following inscription:

"Between the years 1641 and 1660
this town was the scene of the labors of
Richard Baxter
renowned equally for his Christian learning
and his pastoral fidelity.
In a stormy and divided age
he advocated unity and comprehension
pointing the way to the Everlasting Rest.
Churchmen and Non-conformists
united to raise this Memorial. A. D. 1875."

Dean Stanley made on the occasion a notable address, in which Baxter's character and work were highly eulogized; of which "unity and comprehension," the things which Baxter had labored so hard to promote among English Christians but apparently in vain, were the key notes. This event, occurring more than two hundred years after the Savoy conference, shows that the character and work of a good man, however much misunderstood and misrepresented during his lifetime, will certainly at length be recognized. Much still remains, to be sure, to be accomplished before his aim will be fully realized. But sooner or later it will be done. The growing spirit of mutual toleration and respect among all Christians presages it; the prayer of Christ for his disciples, "that they all may be one that the world may believe," assures us of it.

Baxter's writings and words, often and widely quoted, have powerfully wrought for this end. As gems of thought they have enriched our modern literature, and are symbolized by one of nature's wonders. Far to the north, beyond our Great Lakes and the Canada line, there is a ledge of jasper conglomerate, fragments of which torn off by the forces of the Ice Age and carried southward by glacial action are found, scattered all over Ohio, Indiana, Illinois and even beyond the Ohio River, in Kentucky, and the Mississippi, in Iowa. They have been gathered up to adorn public parks and buildings, and to enrich the geological specimens of college museums, have been wrought into tombstones for cemeteries, and into doorsteps to private dwellings, all of them reminding the intelligent observer of the distant ledge whence they originally came. This ledge, with its fragments so widely scattered, is typical of the writings of Baxter and his influences.

IN THE COURT OF JUDGE JEFFRIES

In 1685, when seventy years of age, and enfeebled by the ill health and ailments which greatly reduced his strength, "so that I did but live," he says, Baxter was brought to trial before the infamous Lord Chief Justice Jeffries for his "Paraphrase on the New Testament," recently published, which was described in the indictment as "a scandalous and seditious book against the government." The chief charge was, that in certain passages indicated, he had reflected on the prelates of the Church of England and so was guilty of sedition. But as no bishops or clergy of the Church of England were named, and the author in this very book had spoken honorably of the bishops of this Church, his counsel truly said that they who had drawn up the information were the libelers in applying to the English prelates the severe things that the book contained against unworthy bishops of the Church of Rome, spoken of in Church history, who "were the plagues of the Church and of the world."

To this Jeffries said that Baxter was "an enemy to the name and thing, the office and persons of bishops"; and when the prisoner ventured to speak in defense of himself, the Chief Justice interrupted and silenced him with unbridled ferocity and such reviling abuse as this: "Richard, Richard, dost thou think we'll hear thee poison the court? Richard, thou art an old fellow, an old knave; thou hast written books enough to load a cart, every one as full of sedition, I might say treason, as an egg is full of meat," and much more of the same sort. When he ended, he told the jury "that if they believed the accused meant the bishops and clergy of the Church of England in the passages which the information referred to—*and he could mean nothing else*—they must find him guilty." When the judge had finished his charge, Baxter said to him: "Does your lordship think any jury will pretend to pass a verdict against me upon such a trial?" "I'll warrant you, Mr. Baxter," he replied. The jury fulfilled his expectation: Baxter was sentenced to a heavy fine and imprisonment until this was paid.

He went to prison and remained in it for two years—when the fine was remitted by the king. While in prison he was cheered by visits from friends; among whom were some of the most respectable clergy of the Established Church, who deplored the injustice he received. After his release, he continued to live in London, preaching occasionally for his friend Sylvester while his strength permitted. These closing years of his life were full of suffering, but he continued his writing nearly to the end, the productions of his pen showing that the ardor and clearness of his mind were unimpaired. A friend speaking of the good many had received from his writings, he replied: "I was but a pen in God's hands; what praise is due to a pen?" Cotton

Mather, of New England, visited him the day before he died, and speaking some comforting words to him, he replied: "I have pain, there is no arguing against sense, but I have peace, I have peace."

He died, December 8, 1691, in London, in the reign of William and Mary, surrounded by attached friends and reverenced by the better portion of the religious world. When life was almost gone, he was asked by one of these friends how he did. "Almost well," was his significant reply, in anticipation of the fulfillment of his hope, that "after the rough tempestuous day we shall at last have the quiet silent night—light and rest together—the quietness of the night without its darkness."

V

BOSSUET

V

BOSSUET

1627–1705

Adorning the four sides of the imposing fountain in the public square before the Church of St. Sulpice, Paris, are four sitting statues of heroic size. They represent four great French preachers, Bossuet, Fléchier, Fénelon, and Massillon, the fame of whose eloquence, as it was most signally displayed in Paris, the city now cherishes as an important part of her civic glory. Of these interesting figures with their noble faces, that of Bossuet is fittingly reckoned the most striking, as he was the most distinguished of the four in life for his pulpit eloquence. He was the greatest, indeed, of all the illustrious preachers that adorned the reign of Louis XIV. and made it the Golden Age of the French pulpit. A study of his life is interesting and instructive as revealing the method by which a great preacher may be said to have made himself. We have found a delightful guide to such study in M. Eug. Gandar, the author of an elaborate French work entitled "Bossuet Orateur; Études Critiques sur les Sermons,"* a work crowned with honor by the French Academy.

As shown by this interesting work, Bossuet became the great preacher he was, not by any easy

* Paris, Errin et Cie, 1888.

development of his powers, but by a course of strenuous toil, and studious, intelligent self-discipline. Endowed by nature with a remarkable genius, *born* an orator if any man ever was, he combined with his native genius and its rare capabilities an industry quite as remarkable, so that he illustrated in his person the saying, "Great genius is an infinite capacity for hard work." He early revealed his extraordinary gifts. In the Jesuit school of Dijon, his native city, he showed especial aptitude for the ancient classics, the translation of which into modern speech has always proved an .excellent discipline for the development of the power of ready, precise and copious expression of thought. He was dedicated by his parents to the ministry. St. Bernard of Clairvaux was born in the same province, in the neighborhood of Dijon, and was constantly held up to him, in the conversations about the home fireside, as a model of piety and eloquence. To complete his preparatory course for the ministry, Bossuet was sent to Paris, at the age of fifteen, to the famous College of Navarre. Its headmaster at that time was Nicolas Cornet, whose virtues and skill as a teacher were thus gratefuly acknowledged by Bossuet in the funeral oration he pronounced in his honor: "I, who found in this man, with many other rare qualities, an inexhaustible treasure of sage counsel, faithfulness, sincerity, and constant, unfailing friendship, cannot refuse to him here some tribute of a mind which in its early youth he cultivated with a fatherly kindness." Under the stimulating influence of this wise teacher he achieved distinction in every line of study except mathematies, for which he thought he had no faculty.

His brilliant achievements in the College soon became noised through the city, especially his eloquent religious addresses in the College Chapel, and he was invited to give proof of his eloquence for the edification of the select company that assembled in the *salon bleu* of the Marquise de Rambouillet. He was brought into their presence and given a subject, having only a few minutes for its consideration, but no book. Thus tested, this youth of sixteen extemporized an eloquent sermon, which was prolonged until after midnight; at which one of the wits present said, he "never heard one preach *so early and so late.*"

For a wonder these attentions and flatteries did not turn his head. He remained unspoiled. M. Gandar says, "The progress of years and sober reflection put Bossuet on his guard against the illusions of youth, even when these seemed justified by the flattering *éclat* of the plaudits given him." The admiration he received assured him that he possessed the natural gifts of an orator; they did not delude him into thinking that he was already a consummate orator. So he labored to make himself such with unwearied assiduity.

Of what M. Gandar calls "*les illusions de la jeunesse,*" by which he meant the *conceits* common to bright young men, and from which Bossuet was preserved by his sober judgment, or which he soon outgrew with the progress of years, two may well be mentioned. They are, first, that mere fluency, or readiness of speech, such as Bossuet had exhibited at the Hotel de Rambouillet, is enough to make one a successful and effective preacher; and, second, that the resources of an active, inventive mind, independent of any help derivable from intelligent and fruitful studies, are adequate to make one a successful preacher. In the progress of years, both of these *conceits* are likely to be taken out of a man: they must be, indeed, if he achieves any success. In the case of some, however, the correction comes late— too late to retrieve the mischief of their early foolishness.

Of the first of these mistakes—the overvaluation of fluency—it is so common and disastrous that fluency has come to be regarded by intelligent people as a "fatal gift." It is "fatal," because apt to incline its possessor to trust unduly to it, to the neglect of the careful thought and thorough study indispensable to successful public speaking. It is fatal to the lawyer and legislator as well as the preacher. Lord Chief Justice Russell, of England, in a recent address to a society of law-students in London, is reported to have spoken of this faculty of ready speech somewhat as follows: "It was his opinion that facility of speech is liable to degenerate into glibness of speech, and, judging from his own experience, the man who speaks glibly does not, as a rule, speak impressively or instructively. In the flood of his eloquence there is usually a dearth of ideas. What is wanted is not words, words, but thoughts, thoughts, thoughts." Bossuet had the good sense early to perceive this danger and to labor diligently to improve his preaching in the essentials of thoughtfulness and adaptation to the spiritual needs of men. Four things were paramount in his conception of what is demanded of the good preacher, which things were more and more marked in his preaching. They were right thoughts, right words, right feelings—feelings in entire sympathy with the truth uttered—and untrammeled freedom in the delivery of this truth. The thoughts which he deemed most "right" or appropriate for the preacher's sermons, were the great, *necessary* truths of religion. "Speak to me of necessary truths," he said on his deathbed. These truths he loved with increasing ardor, and labored to make attractive. "He is under the charm of the truth he declares," says M. Gandar, "and he thinks it so beautiful that none can tire of hearing it, as he could not tire of speaking of it." This feeling sometimes, in the early years of his preaching, betrayed him into prolixity.

With these ideas and sentiments, more or less clearly defined, Bossuet entered upon his work. At Metz he began, spending six years in that provincial city—years of hard study and the diligent performance of the various duties of his sacred calling. He spoke of them afterward as the years of his apprenticeship, in which he laid the foundations of his ministerial success. There he found that "season of truce" between the educating discipline of school and the exacting business of the world, in which the power of thought freely develops and ripens.

It is by a curious incident in French history that the knowledge of those studies and ideas, by which he fashioned himself, is furnished us by Bossuet. When at the height of his fame, the Abbé d'Albret, the nephew of Marshal Turenne, the great French general, was created Cardinal de Bouillon at the age of twenty-six. The event provoked considerable criticism, about the French court and in the church, so that the young Cardinal felt it important, if possible, to show the world that the victories of his great uncle and his public profession of the Catholic faith were not the nephew's only titles to his promotion. The pulpit offered him an obvious but perilous means of vindication. Diffident, however, of his ability to shine in the pulpit, he sought instruction from Bossuet as to "the studies indispensable" for making a great preacher. Bossuet, a devoted friend of the young Cardinal's family, wrote out the instruction desired. It covers but a few pages, "written without a pause of his pen," and "with no time to revise them"; but these pages are justly esteemed "precious" by M. Gandar. Their interest is chiefly autobiographic. The directions they contain are *recollections* of the method Bossuet himself had used. The essential things, he says in substance, are "ample knowledge, such as comes from the thoroughgoing habit of exploring subjects to the bottom, that one may have plenty to say; and piety." "Fullness of mind gives fertility of mind, and fertility of mind insures a pleasing variety."

First in importance for the replenishment of the

mind is the knowledge of the Scriptures. In studying these, he should not spend much time over obscure passages and difficult texts, nor in turning
the pages of commentaries to find out their explanation. He must not expect to know everything in the
Bible, for this is a book of which one could never
know everything. He should ascertain what is clear
and most certain, and *fill his mind* with the substance
of the sacred books, *with the primary purpose of
nourishing his own piety.*

For the further replenishment of his mind the
Cardinal should study the Church Fathers. Not
content with giving a general direction, Bossuet
speaks of the Fathers individually, and of the particular benefits to be gained from each. St. Cyprian
would teach him the art of handling the Scriptures
so as to clothe himself with their divine authority.
Tertullian, in whom he himself had found a congenial spirit, "would give him many striking sentences," Augustine would explain the doctrine of
Christianity: *"Sa theologie est admirable; il élève
l'esprit aux grandes et subtiles considerations."* Chrysostom would afford him "excellent models of simple eloquence adapted to the common people and
well fitted to instruct and move them." Lest the
amount of reading thus marked out for the indolent
young Cardinal should appall him, Bossuet tells him
it is not so long and difficult a task as might appear.
"It is incredible," he said, "how much may be accomplished, *provided one is willing to give some time
to the effort, and to follow it up a little."*

In this brief outline of study *"pour former un*

orateur," Bossuet gave a transcript from his own experience during those years of his early manhood at Metz. He was a constant, diligent student of the Bible, so that Lamartine says, "in Bossuet the Bible was transfused into a man." Thence he derived that "*accent* of authority" which characterized his preaching. "We must not seek the explanation of this," says M. Gandar, "in the imperious bent of his mind." If he sometimes has an oracular tone, it is because he presents to his hearers, as he says and believes, "*une doctrine toute Chrétienne, toute prise des Livres Saints et des Écritures apostolique,*" "*simple et naïve exposition des maximes de l'Évangile.*" It is not himself whom he calls upon them to believe. "Listen," he says, "it is the Saviour who speaks; it is a question of heeding His word."

In regard to his diligent study of the Fathers of the Church, evidence of it is found in his sermons and funeral orations as well as in his explicit declaration, that at Metz he read the most of the Fathers. The fabric of his discourses is *shot through*, as with threads of silver and gold, with the thoughts and sayings of the Fathers. He relies upon their support, he breathes their spirit, he uses their expressions: he imitates them, cites them, paraphrases them.

The Bible and the Church Fathers thus formed, so to speak, his solid diet. He had also for a lighter diet the writings of Corneille, whom he admired "for his force and vehemence"; the Letters of Jean Balzac, who had "enriched" the French tongue with "beautiful sayings and noble phrases," and from whom he "obtained some idea of a fine and delicately turned style"; and the works of Tacitus in the French version of d'Ablancourt, which he liked because he found there "examples of the sublime and the grand," which "ought to be," he thought, "the style of the pulpit." To this style, it may be said, his natural bent inclined him as well as his studies and the fashion of the time. Indeed, his early pulpit style exhibits the faults of occasional grandiloquence and pompous amplitude. He had not learned, as he came to learn later, the value of self-restraint, the force of condensed expression, the merit of not saying too much; in short, that, *in writing and speaking, half oftentimes is more than the whole.*

But with these faults there were associated extraordinary gifts and abilities. He had a pleasing and sonorous voice that easily filled the largest cathedral. He had a heart responsive to the truth he uttered, and *vitalizing* it with genuine emotion. He thus had the ability of investing the trite themes of religion with fresh interest, "infusing," as Dean Church says, "a sense of serious reality into the commonplaces of the pulpit." Lastly, he had the power of unfettered freedom in the pulpit. Though he wrote out his sermons at the first and continued to do this for nearly twenty years, until he reached the meridian of his fame as a preacher, he did not attempt to commit to memory what he had written, and require of himself verbal exactness in its delivery. Such bondage would have hampered him, he said, and quenched the fire and force and freedom of his utterance. He wrote beforehand for the same reasons that Alexander Hamilton and Daniel Webster wrote their famous pleas, to sift and clarify his thoughts, to determine their arrangement for the best effect, and to shape their expression with sufficient definiteness to save him from uncertainty and hesitation in speaking. Having done this, he trusted himself to his powers of utterance under the impulse of his heart, as inspired and quickened at the moment by the truth. He thus secured in preaching choiceness and strength of thought, felicity of language, and the power of easy, sustained flight which caused him later to be called "the Eagle."

With such qualifications, natural and acquired, Bossuet soon gained at Metz a great reputation. The people of the city thronged to hear him; strangers passing through were told about him, and attended upon his preaching as the chief attraction of the town.

One of the remarkable things about the sermons of those early years is that they contained striking thoughts and passages like those found in the best sermons of his later days. The same fact has been noted in the lives of other great preachers. Dr. Brown, in his recently published Yale Lectures upon "Puritan Preaching in England," says of Dr. Alexander Maclaren, of Manchester, that "the survivors of his Southampton congregation [to which he ministered in his young manhood], while willing to admit that he is more forceful and more cultured in the 'nineties than in the 'fifties, still contend that he has never reached higher levels than he frequently did in the days when he was their minister." A similar declaration is made by M. Gandar concerning Bossuet's early preaching at Metz. "Bossuet," he says, "will be, some day, more self-contained, more even and chastened in his style, but he will never speak in a more elevated and impressive fashion. There is in the best parts of the Panegyric of St. Bernard [one of his discourses at Metz], the same indescribable charm which we shall find later in the sermons preached at the Louvre and in the 'Funeral Orations.'"

Such examples suggest that a young preacher of promise is somewhat like a young song-bird—a wood thrush, for instance—which, though its song has not the full strength, sustaining power, and superb quality of the song of the mature bird, sings nevertheless the same song essentially, though in a feebler key, and affords a similar delight to those that hear it.

Perhaps all preachers of promise manifest these tokens of excellence in the early years of their ministry. In the first five or six years of their preaching, generally, you will find clear intimations of their best thought and pulpit power. But many lack what Dr. Bushnell calls "the talent of growth"; or, having it, they do not stimulate it. They do not grow in pulpit power; they do not possess an insatiable desire to do so, or put forth unwearied efforts to realize this desire; they quickly reach their limit of improvement, and after a short period of moderate success exhibit a gradual declension of preaching power.

Bossuet had "the talent of growth" to a remarkable degree. He was also both ambitions of excellence and willing to pay the full price for it. His was a good example of what an eminent public man of today calls "the strenuous life." He left little to chance; he was resolute of purpose to improve himself to the utmost; he sets before us the example of "a man who could easily win admiration by the mere exercise of his natural gifts, but who for forty years never ceased toiling to satisfy his high ideal of excellence and make himself more perfect."

Two means of self-improvement employed by him at this stage, and which had a marked influence upon him, here demand our attention. They were: (1) the study of the best living models of pulpit eloquence, and (2) the writings of Pascal.

After four or five years of uninterrupted labor in Metz, he made a visit to Paris, and remained there about a year and a half, excepting the time required for a short visit to Dijon, his native city, and two or three flying visits to Metz, demanded by the duties of his position there. His purpose in going to Paris was to hear and to be heard: to hear the renowned preachers of the metropolis, that "his eyes might be opened to his own defects"; that he might learn to speak both "to the level of his audience, and to the height of his subject," and that he might clear his pulpit style of dryness, tautology, and all antiquated phrases and provincialisms: and to be heard by "audiences accustomed to hear the best preachers," that he might encounter the criticism of their standard of judgment.

Among the distinguished preachers whom he heard, four are specially mentioned by M. Gandar: Senault, Superior of the Oratory in the Faubourg St. Jacques; Leboux, who had the honor of being selected by the Queen Mother to preach two successive series of sermons at the palace of the Louvre before the young king and the court; Godean, whose preaching is described as marked by "seriousness," "unction," and "an indescribable charm," which reminded his hearers of the graces of St. Francis de Sales, or gave them a foretaste of the "sweetness of Fénelon"; and Claude de Lingendes, the Jesuit, "an almost perfect orator, condensed, earnest, sometimes pathetic and even terrible, whose hearers were seen to rise from their seats with a pale face and downcast eyes, and depart from the church without speaking a word, greatly moved and thoughtful."

The hearing of these preachers produced a salutary change in Bossuet's preaching. His style became more studied and even, his periods more symmetrical and marked by sustained dignity of language. His models were not less anxious to speak properly than to think truly, and they did not separate from a scrupulous attachment to the truth the fear of wounding the tongue, the ear—the proprieties. In imitating these models, however, he encountered the same danger that his studies of Corneille and Balzac and Tacitus had before exposed him to—the danger of being stilted, of losing his simplicity and naturalness, of becoming unreal, of filling with clouds and emptiness those heights where he affected to move.

From this danger he was saved by the influence of Pascal, whose "Provincial Letters" opportunely appeared, and became the talk of the town at the very time of Bossuet's visit to Paris. This famous work, which marks an epoch in French literature, gave a new and better model of prose to the French language, as well as a new and purer standard of morals to the Catholic Church. Pascal corrected the false taste of the time by commending to general acceptance the following sound principles of rhetoric: that the repetition of a word or phrase, if necessary to the clear meaning or force of a sentence, is not to be condemned; that useless antitheses for the sake of symmetry are, like "false windows," absurd; that euphuisms, "to mask nature," or "to make great what is little or little what is great," are to be avoided; that a *conventional* eloquence is not true eloquence; that a *continuous eloquence* soon becomes wearisome; that he who expresses himself naturally is likely to be listened to with less effort and more pleasure; that one *should do honor to the word: but only that the word may do honor to the thought.*"

Bossuet, then thirty years of age, readily came under the influence of this "peerless writer," as Mme. Sevigné calls him. This influence is shown, not in any sudden and entire alteration of his natural tendency to majesty (*majesté romaine*, as M. Gandar calls it), but in the fact that he afterwards exhibited a more chastened taste, and had "*the grand art of not saying too much,*" combined with the power of coining felicitous words and phrases that stuck in the memory. The influence of Pascal is visible in the manuscripts of Bossuet, as seen in the way he worked over and reshaped the thoughts and passages found in the sermons of his early years which he thought worthy of being used again in his later sermons. While he preserves the ideas and much of the old language, he prunes it without mercy, "bringing," Dean Church says,* "what was a diffuse and florid piece of amplification into the compass of a few, nervous, compact sentences, where every word tells."

Were these ceaseless efforts to perfect his pulpit-style commendable? We think so. A good style is like the feather that wings the archer's shaft. The better the style that conveys the truth, the more surely it is carried home to the mark. The aim of the preacher is to arrest attention, to impress the mind, to lodge the truth in the memory and heart, so that it may, by its natural operation, purify the heart and change the life. A good pulpit style, including action as well as words, assists this aim. To the degree that it sends the truth home, so that it possesses the mind with haunting and inspiring power through the action and words that drive it in, will be the preacher's power. The whole past history of the pulpit proves this. The examples of the great preachers illustrate the fact. This consummate power imparted by a rare style to the preacher's eloquence, and derived by Bossuet from his study of Pascal, was revealed after his return from Paris.

His return was hastened by the arrival in Metz, a fortnight before, of the Queen Mother, Anne of

* See Occasional Papers, 2 vol.; vol. 1:14. London, MacMillan & Co., 1897.

Austria, with the young king and court. The Queen Mother, who is represented in the annals of the time as occupied with acts of charity and devotion, and as eager to hear all preachers of renown, desired to hear the young preacher whose eloquence was the pride of the city, and had recently won applause even in the capital where he had preached. At any rate, a few days after his return, he preached (at her request), before herself and the royal court, a panegyric of St. Theresa. It marks an epoch in his pulpit career because of its surpassing merits, and indicates the "beginning of his maturity." "There were sagacious people in the brilliant assembly that heard it, who confidently predicted that such eloquence would some day produce a great noise in the church."

The fame, thus foretold, came two years later, when Bossuet was called to Paris to preach the Lenten sermons at the Louvre. For the following ten years, from 1660 to 1670, he was in constant request in Paris for Lenten sermons, Advent sermons and French orations. The audiences that gathered to hear him were composed of all classes and conditions of men. "Court and city flocked to listen; the queens went from the palace, and the nuns of Port Royal from their seclusion; Condé, Turenne, Madame de Sevigné, and other famous contemporaries." Scholars, nobles, sages—the *élite* of society —mingled with the crowd. Never was the fascination which eloquence has for all classes of mankind more signally displayed; never was the indescribable witchery of eloquent speech more truly exercised by human lips. For the hour, while sitting before him, those hearers sat entranced; they were almost literally spellbound.

Those were the years of his meridian splendor as a preacher; the years when his sermons were richest in thought, in wealth of knowledge and sentiment, in suggestive and picturesque language. At the close of the *Carême* (Lenten sermons) given at the Louvre in 1662, the King himself expressed his enthusiasm by sending a personal message to Bossuet's father, to felicitate him for having such a son.

But in the funeral orations over Henrietta Maria, Queen of England, her daughter, the Duchess of Orleans, and the great Condé, Bossuet displayed the most remarkable powers—powers of thought and spiritual discernment, and powers of a varied, exquisite style: the power of swift, condensed narrative, which places before us the substance of a long chapter or volume in a few sentences, as in the description of Condé's victorious leadership at the battle of Rocroi; and the power of epigrammatic as well as pathetic expression, which enabled him, by the use of a few simple words, to thrill and lift his hearers to sublimest heights of feeling, or to move them to irrepressible tears, as they hung upon his lips.

Take, for example, his account of the birth, childhood, and development to a beautiful womanhood, and of the sudden death of Henrietta, the Duchess of Orleans, daughter of Charles I., King of England.

"This princess, born near a throne, had a mind and heart superior to her birth. The misfortunes of her family could not crush her in her early youth, and from that time on she exhibited a grandeur which owed nothing to fortune. We say with joy that heaven plucked her from the hands of the enemies of her royal father, to give her to France. Precious, inestimable gift— if only it had been made more lasting! . . . Alas! we cannot dwell a moment upon the glory of this princess without having death come straightway to darken everything with his shadow! O death, withdraw from our thought, and suffer us to be beguiled, for a little while, of our grief by the remembrance of our joy! Recall now, sirs, the admiration this English princess inspired in all the court. Your memory will portray her better, with all her traits and incomparable loveliness, than my words could ever do. She grew up amid the benedictions of all classes, and the years ceased not to bring to her new graces. . . .

"Nevertheless, neither the esteem she inspired nor all her great advantages affected her modesty. . . . Men spoke with rapture of the goodness of this princess who, in spite of the cliques and parties common to courts, won all hearts. She exhibited incredible tact in treating the most delicate matters, in removing hidden suspicions, in terminating all difficulties in such a manner as to conciliate the most opposite interests."

"Irremediable sorrow! that the subject of such just admiration should become the subject of boundless regret! . . . O woeful night, in which, on a sudden, resounded, like a clap of thunder, that astonishing news, 'Madame is dying! Madame is dead!' . . . And there, in spite of that great heart, is this princess, so admired and so beloved,—there as death has made her for us!"

It is only a faint conception of the beauty and pathos of the original that our poor translation can give. Of the original only is the remark of Guizot true, "Bossuet alone could speak like that." If we have conveyed, however, a hint of the style of this matchless orator, or, by what we have said of it, may lead some of our readers to seek out the original, and peruse it for themselves, it will be enough.

This masterpiece of commemorative eloquence, given in August, 1670, marks the culminating point in Bossuet's career as a preacher. For more than thirty years subsequently he continued to exercise his great gifts and attainments in the pulpit. He was the leader of the Church of France in his time— more potent in its affairs than the Pope himself. To the end of his life he continued to be a student and a learner, taking up the study of Hebrew in his later years, and achieving a laudable scholarship in it, that he might be a better interpreter of the Bible. His vigor and vitality seemed to be unfailing; so that when, at length, he died, men were astonished, it is said, at "this mortal's mortality."

Our purpose has been, not to give a *panégyrique* upon Bossuet, but an *étude*—a study of him as a pulpit orator, and of the methods by which he made himself such. His character was by no means faultless, nor his life blameless. His treatment of Mme. Guyon was harsh; of Fénelon, ungenerous. In his discussions with Protestants he was not quite fair, and so his polemic triumphs were delusive. The truth cannot be determined by fallacious arguments nor settled by the plaudits of admirers. Nothing is settled until it is settled aright. The questions in controversy will recur until the demands of truth and justice are met. Bossuet also rests under the stigma of having approved the Revocation of the Edict of Nantes, and for that cruel act, by which Louis XIV. dispeopled his kingdom of his choicest subjects, and drove fifteen hundred thousands of them into exile, despair, or falsehood, Bossuet lauded him for "piety," and placed Louis "among the peers of Constantine and Theodosius." These are great blemishes upon Bossuet's good name; but they are faults to which good men are liable in an intolerant age. Luther, whom Bossuet resembled in several respects, was dishonored by them. Guizot, a staunch Protestant, characterizes Bossuet, however, as, for his time, "moderate and prudent in conduct as well as opinions," though his moderation "did not keep out injustice." On the whole our study of Bossuet has led us to accept as just the estimate of M. Gandar. He says: "In trying to account for the admiration of his genius, I have learned to honor Bossuet's character. While not daring to say that Fénelon thought of him, when he defined an orator as one '*qui ne se sert de la parole que pour la pensée et de la pensée que pour la vérité et la vertu,*' assuredly Bossuet fulfilled this idea in his best preaching, as in his *Carême* du Louvre."

In conclusion: An interesting question of supreme importance is here pressed upon our attention as worthy of consideration. How did it happen that the "Golden Age of the French Pulpit," in which Bossuet, Fénelon, Bourdaloue, and Massillon preached with such remarkable eloquence, remained, in spite of their preaching, notoriously wicked, dissolute and godless? Why were there no spiritual or moral results worthy of such pulpit fame? Those great preachers ought to have wrought, one naturally thinks, a great reformation in morals, and a great improvement in the religious tone and character of French society. But this natural expectation was not realized. Compared with the preaching of Baxter and other Puritan divines, or with the preaching of Whitefield and the Wesleys, the preaching of Bossuet and his illustrious contemporaries of the French pulpit was barren and fruitless. Its unfruitfulness does not seem to us entirely due, or mainly due, to the difference in doctrine, or because the doctrine of the French preachers was Catholic and that of the English preachers, Protestant, though this probably would be taken into account by some. We believe that in spite of the errors, from a Protestant standpoint, of the French Roman Catholicism of that day, it contained Christian truth enough if heeded, to convert men from their sin and develop in them genuine piety and beautiful Christian characters. The holy lives and the Christian characters of Fénelon, De Saci, Arnauld, "Mother" Angelica, and other famous Post Royalists prove this.

The reason why the preaching of those great pulpit orators was so barren of good fruit was due, we think, to the artificial and frivolous character of their age joined to the corrupting influence of the French king and his court. Affectation and vain display, insincerity and religious hypocrisy were found everywhere, in the court, in the army, in the salons, and even in the assemblies of public worship. Life was like a theatrical performance. It lacked the ring of sincerity and reality; it was not taken seriously. Genuineness of action or speech was rare. This characteristic of the times made the French people, in Paris especially, and in the social atmosphere of the court at Versailles and elsewhere, not ashamed to amuse themselves with sacred things, ready to entertain themselves with the preaching of a precocious youth in the salons of the fashionable quarter, and with the eloquent sermons of the great preachers in the chapels of the palaces, and in the churches and cathedrals of the city. The preachers could not but feel the demoralizing influence of this wide-spread atmosphere of insincerity. Aware of the seductive influence of flattery, and of the admiration and applause of the great, they really tried to resist it, but in spite of all they could do, it dulled the edge and diminished the power of their preaching. Their earnest and sincere endeavors were thus frustrated.

The preaching of the pulpit surely reflects the character and sentiments of the auditory. If the hearers habitually regard it as a fictitious performance, they make it so and it degenerates into rhetorical cant. There is a great difference between speaking *to* an audience, like a prophet with a divine message, and speaking *before* an audience like an actor for their entertainment. In the one case, the speaking is a genuine message that commands attention, convicts and persuades, and results in appropriate action; in the other, a make-believe utterance that produces no deep or permanent moral effect.

The king, Louis XIV, was chiefly to blame for all this. Vain, imperious, worldly-minded, selfish monarch that he was, fond of adulation and bent upon the gratification of his lust of power and of sensual pleasure, there was no sincere desire in his heart to

186

hear God's truth or to obey it. His seeming piety was a sham, his apparent interest in the preaching of the gospel by the great preachers of his age only the interest of a playgoer in consummate acting. As with the king, so with his courtiers and the fashionable people who thronged the royal chapels and the churches. They too regarded the sermons of the preachers as something like a theatrical performance, only a pleasant entertainment. Their eloquent appeals and exhortations might generally be admired for their rhetorical splendor, but few took them seriously to heart. The preachers knew that this would be the case, and they were disheartened in their endeavors to have it otherwise. They could not, they finally did not, expect the spiritual results that would have been looked for under different psychological conditions. Their preaching lacked the notes of earnestness and sincerity that marked the preaching of Bernard of Clairvaux, Luther, and Baxter. It was artificial to a degree that is traceable in their published sermons, but of which quality there is no trace in these preachers. "I would as soon doubt the gospel's verity," says Coleridge, "as the sincerity of Baxter." *Sincerity*, the downright sincerity of an earnest soul that speaks from a heart throbbing with emotion its message of salvation, which has been tested in its own experience and been found blessedly true, this must characterize the preacher whose ministry of the Gospel is attended with great reformations of religion and morals. It marked the ministries of those great preachers whose characters and careers we have previously sketched; it might have marked that of Bossuet could he have resolutely risen by the assured help and grace of God above the general insincerity of his nation at that time.   Failing to do this, succumbing weakly to its demoralizing influence, he failed of the highest result, though inferior to none of those preachers in natural gifts and rare accomplishments, and the purity of his original aims.

VI

JOHN BUNYAN

VI

JOHN BUNYAN

1628–1688

Among the old English divines of the Anglican Church, there were men of great genius, eloquence, and learning. Such were Richard Hooker, Joseph Hall, Thomas Fuller, and Jeremy Taylor; but Dr. Thomas Arnold says: "I hold John Bunyan to have been a man of incomparably greater genius than any of them, and to have given a far truer and more edifying picture of Christianity."

This man of extraordinary genius, however, was born in the humblest class of society and had but few educational advantages. "I never went to school," he says, "to Aristotle and Plato, but was brought up in my father's house in a very mean condition among a company of poor countrymen." Born November 30, 1628, at Elstow, Bedfordshire, into the family of a tinker, "of that rank that is meanest and most despised of all the families in the land," as he says, and brought up by his father to the same calling, the whole extent of his acquisitions from the poor instruction and brief school days given him, was "to read and write according to the rate of other poor men's children." But God plants a great mind where he will, and gives the highest powers of intellectual and moral achievement to people dwelling in the most unequal and diverse conditions. Rome had two illustrious moralists, of about equal eminence, who stood high above all others; one was the slave Epictetus, and the other the Emperor Marcus Aurelius. God made the slave the teacher and peer of the emperor in genius and virtue, to show men that in the bestowal of his highest and best gifts he is no respecter of persons. Bunyan's genius was developed and trained in the school of Providence. It came slowly to maturity, and to the glorious fruitage it finally yielded only by the hard and various discipline of sin and remorse, of a wonderful experience of God's grace, and the vicissitudes of family affliction, a soldier's life, poverty, religious persecution and long imprison-' ment for conscience sake, where celestial visions brightened his dreary captivity as with the glory of heaven, and qualified him to write his immortal allegory, "The Pilgrim's Progress," which Thomas Arnold extols for its "edifying picture of Christianity," "with none of the rubbish of the theologians mixed up with it."

Among his lesser writings is an autobiography, which he entitled "Grace Abounding," that is similar in character and the nature of its interest to Augustine's "Confessions." This small book, which one could read in three or four hours, might be called, "The history of a benighted soul in its struggles to find the light." The struggles it describes are mainly those of the spirit with sin and doubts and fears. All else that happened in the course of his life he seems to have reckoned of little account. It was the age of Cromwell and the great civil war. He scarcely refers, however, to the stirring events of his age, of which he was a spectator, or in which he was an actor, or a listener to the talk about him. He gives no dates, he mentions only a few localities, he alludes to but few of the exciting things then occurring in the world. He confines his narrative almost entirely to things that had some close relation to his spiritual development. "Time and place, outward circumstances and passing incidents, were nothing to him, about whom fell alternately the shadows of hell and the splendors of heaven." The estimate of Bunyan, in this personal review of his life, as to what was most important and valuable in his experience, has come to be accepted by the world as its own. The supreme interest of his life is found in the vehement spiritual struggles he has here graphically depicted, and it is particularly instructive as revealing the manner in which the Christian faith lifted him, and may lift any miserable sinful man, out of a wretched condition, and exalt him to a place of honor and happiness.

Taking up some of the most notable things in this sketch of his past life, it is pleasing to observe that while confessing his humble birth, he speaks respectfully of his parents and of their willingness to do for his welfare all they could. He is not ashamed of them, or of the social condition he inherited from them. "Though I have naught to boast," he says, "of noble blood, or of a high-born state, according to the flesh, all things considered, I magnify the heavenly Majesty that by this door he brought me into this world."

According to his own account of himself as a boy, youth, and young man, he was a rough, reckless, and most unpromising young fellow:—

"I had but few equals for cursing, swearing, lying, and blaspheming the holy name of God."

"So settled and rooted was I in these things, that they became as a second nature to me. . . ."

". . . so that until I came to the state of marriage, I was the very ringleader of all the youth that kept me company, in all manner of vice and ungodliness."

Naturally his influence upon his companions was very pernicious. "I was one of the great sin-breeders," he says, "the neighbors counted me so, my own practice proved me so." He tells how one day as he

"was standing at a neighbor's shop-window, and there cursing and swearing and playing the madman, after my wonted manner, there sat within the woman of the house and heard me; who, though she was a very loose and ungodly wretch, yet protested that I cursed and swore at that most fearful rate that she was made to tremble to hear me; and told me further, that I was the ungodliest fellow for swearing that she ever heard in all her life, and that I by thus doing was able to spoil all the youth in the whole town, if they came but in my company."

From these passages and others found in his writings in regard to the sins of his youth and early manhood, it might be supposed that he was guilty of nearly all the sins forbidden in the decalogue. But this would be a mistake. When those who wished to discredit him as a preacher and religious writer accused him of unchastity, he replied:—

"My foes have missed their mark in this; I am not the man. . . . If all the fornicators and adulterers in England were hanged by the neck till they were dead, John Bunyan, the object of their envy, would be still alive and well."

Macaulay, Froude and some other writers have expressed the opinion that the sins for which Bunyan so severely condemned himself, were, excepting his shocking profanity, but trivial offenses, like playing ball or "cat" on Sunday, and ringing the church bell on festive occasions, which his morbid conscience magnified into great proofs of wickedness; but faults graver than these seem implied in the words: "Had not a miracle of precious grace prevented, I had not only perished by the stroke of Eternal Justice, but had also laid myself open even to the stroke of those laws which bring some to disgrace and open shame before the face of the world." If sorrow could have sobered and subdued him, its discipline was not lacking. In his sixteenth year, his mother died, and a favorite sister, a month later. Shortly after, he joined the Parliamentary Army, "a finishing school to the hardened sinner," he says. He was at the siege of Leicester and probably in the desperately fought battle of Naseby.

"When I was a soldier [he says], I, with others, was drawn to go to such a place to besiege it; but when I was just ready to go, one of the company desired to go in my room; to which, when I consented, he took my place; and coming to the siege, as he stood sentinel, he was shot in the head with a musket ball, and died.

"Here were judgments and mercy; but neither of them did awaken my soul to righteousness."

Going home from the war, he married. The young couple were so poor that they did "not have so much household stuff as a dish or spoon between us both." But his wife brought him, notwithstanding, a precious dowry—the memory of a godly father and pious home, and two religious books, "The Plain Man's Pathway to Heaven" and "The Practice of Piety," which had a wide circulation in those days. These books he read with his wife, and they made a deep impression on his mind. Their influence, joined to that of his wife, produced in him a notable outward reformation, and a show of piety and religious zeal that led him

"to go to church twice a day, . . . and there very devoutly both say and sing, as others did. . . . I adored . . . all things belonging to the church, the high place, priest, clerk, vestment, service and what else."

". . . . Then I thought I pleased God as well as any man in England. My neighbors were amazed at this my great conversion, from prodigious profanity, to something like a moral life; and, truly, so they well might be, for this, my conversion, was as great as for Tom of Bedlam to become a sober man."

Nevertheless he says,—

". . . as yet I was nothing but a painted hypocrite. . . . I did all I did, either to be seen of, or to be well spoken of by men. . . ."

". . . I was all this while ignorant of Jesus Christ; and going about to establish my own righteousness; and had perished therein, had not God in mercy showed me more of my state by nature."

Finding in the Scriptures that the Israelites were accounted God's chosen people, he thought: "If I were one of this race, my soul must needs be happy"; and he tried to make out that he was of Hebrew descent, but his father, who had no desire to be thought a Jew, gave such an emphatic negative to his aspirations and inquiries in this direction that he was forced to give them up.

"But God [he says], the great, the rich, the infinitely merciful God did not take advantage of my soul to cast me away, but followed me still, and won my heart by giving me some understanding, not only of my miserable state, which I was very sensible of, but also that there might be hopes of mercy; taking away my love to lust and placing in the room thereof a holy love of religion. Thus the Lord won my heart to some desire to hear the word, to grow a stranger to my old companions, and to accompany the people of God, giving me many sweet encouragements from several promises in the Scriptures."

Of Bunyan it may be truly said that he was, to a rare degree, a Providential man, "a chosen vessel," like the apostle Paul, shaped by God for a great work. It is not possible to understand his remarkable character and career, or his vast influence for good as a preacher and writer, except we have this conception of him. This alone can explain the various agencies used by Providence to bring him "out of darkness into his marvelous light," to train and fit him for his appointed mission of teacher of practical Christianity to the world, especially to common people.

Three of these agencies may be particularized as most prominent and worthy of mention. They were a group of poor women of Bedford, the Bible, and the religious persecution of the Anglican Church in that day, by which he was shut up in prison.

NINE GREAT PREACHERS

Of his introduction to those poor women and the good he received from them, Bunyan himself thus tells us:—

"Upon a day, the good providence of God called me to Bedford, to work on my calling; and in one of the streets of that town, I came where there were three or four poor women sitting at a door, in the sun, talking about the things of God; and being now willing to hear their discourse, I drew near to hear what they said, for I was now a brisk talker in the matters of religion; but I may say, *I heard, but understood not;* for they were far above, out of my reach. . . .

"Methought they spake as if joy did make them speak; they spake with such pleasantness of Scripture language, and with such appearance of grace in all they said, that they were to me, as if they had found a new world; as if they were *people that dwelt alone, and were not to be reckoned among their neighbors.*"

"When I had heard and considered what they said I left them, and went about my employment again, but their talk and discourse *went with me,* . . . for I was greatly affected with their words, both because by them I was convinced that I wanted the true tokens of a truly godly man, and also because by them I was convinced of the happy and blessed condition of him that was such a one.

"Therefore I would often make it my business to be going again and again into the company of these poor people; for I could not stay away; and the more I went among them the more I did question my condition: and . . . presently I found two things within me, at which I did sometimes marvel. . . . The one was a very great softness and tenderness of heart, which caused me to fall under the conviction of what by Scripture they asserted; and the other was a great bending in my mind, to a continual meditating upon it, and on all other good things which at any time I heard or read of."

"About this time the state and happiness of these poor people at Bedford was thus, in a kind of vision, presented to me. I saw as if they were on the sunny side of some high mountain, there refreshing themselves with the pleasant beams of the sun, while I was shivering and shrinking in the cold, afflicted with frost, snow, and dark clouds; methought also, betwixt me and them I saw a wall that did compass about this mountain. Now through this wall my soul did greatly desire to pass; concluding that if I could I would even go into the very midst of them, and there also comfort myself with the heat of their sun.

"About this wall I bethought myself to go again and again, still praying as I went, to see if I could find some way or passage by which I might enter therein; at the last, I saw, as it were, a narrow gap, like a little doorway in the wall, through which I attempted to pass. . . . With great striving, methought I at first did get in my head, and after that by a sidelong striving, my shoulders and my whole body: then I was exceeding glad, went and sat down in the midst of them, and so was comforted with the light and heat of their sun.

"Now this mountain, and wall, etc., was thus made out to me: The mountain signified the church of the living God; the sun that shone thereon, the comfortable shining of his merciful face on them that were therein; the wall I thought was the world, that did make separation betwixt the Christians and the world, and the gap which was in the wall, I thought, was Jesus Christ, who is the way to God the Father. But forasmuch as the passage was wonderful narrow, even so narrow that I could not but with great difficulty enter in thereat, it showed that none could enter into life but those that were in downright earnest, and unless also they left that wicked world behind them; for here was only room for body and soul, but not for body and soul *and sin.*"

This passage from the story of his religious experience, in "Grace Abounding," is interesting for several things. It is interesting in itself for the truth it contains; for its illustration of the benefit that a seeker after God may receive from the conversation and society of pious people, no matter how poor and humble; and for the disclosure it makes of Bunyan's native bias and imaginative faculty of translating his religious experiences, of various sorts, into clear and picturesque allegories, attractive and illuminating to the mind and convincing to the heart. We shall have other interesting examples of this. They all go to show by what steps, by what spiritual conflicts and agony of soul, and by what Providential teaching and discipline the immortal dreamer became qualified to write "The Pilgrim's Progress." In "Grace Abounding" we have the preliminary rehearsal that prepared the way for it. It was based in actual fact, and distressful as are the facts of real life. It was no such stuff as ordinary dreams are made of—the fictions of fancy. Its production was by conditions and processes analŏgous to those by which a diamond or some other precious gem is produced through the intense heat of internal fires, and the tremendous pressure of the weight of mountains. "Those poor people in Bedford, to whom I began to break my mind," he says, told Mr. Gifford, their pastor, a dissenting minister, about him, who "took all occasion to talk with me," and "whose doctrine, by God's grace, was much for my stability." Mr. Gifford himself, after leading a wild, wicked, and stormy life, as soldier, gambler, and criminal, had experienced a remarkable conversion, which, combined with unusual gifts of mind, gave him skill in the treatment of souls.

"This man [says Bunyan] made it much his business to deliver the people of God from all those hard and unsound tests that by nature we are prone to. He would bid us take special heed that we took not up any truth upon trust; as from this, or that, or any other man or men, but cry mightily to God that he would convince us of the reality thereof, and set us down by his own Spirit in the Holy Word; 'for (said he) if you do otherwise, when temptation comes (if strongly) upon you, you not having received them (the truths of religion) with evidence from heaven, will find you want that help and strength now to resist that once you thought you had.'

"This [says Bunyan] was as seasonable to my soul as the former and latter rains in their season; for I had found, and that by sad experience, the truth of his words. . . . Wherefore I found my soul, through grace, very apt to drink in this doctrine, and to incline to pray to God, that in nothing that pertained to God's glory and my own eternal happiness, he would suffer me to be without the confirmation thereof from heaven; for now I saw clearly, there was an exceeding difference betwixt the notion of the flesh and blood, and the revelation of God in heaven; also a great difference betwixt that faith that is feigned, and according to man's wisdom, and that which comes by a man's being born thereto of God.

"But, oh! now, how was my soul led from truth to truth by God!"

This leading of his soul "from truth to truth by God," over which he thus exclaims, and which is graphically described by him in "Grace Abounding," has great interest and value for the illustration it gives concerning the help afforded by the Sacred Scriptures, when accepted and firmly believed in as the revelation of God and an infallible authority as to religious truth, in the guidance and confirmation of the soul seeking to know this truth. Led by the influence of "those poor Bedford women" to new diligence in its study, "I began to look into the Bible with new eyes," he says, "and read as I never did before; especially the Epistles of the Apostle Paul were sweet and pleasant to me; and, indeed, then

I was never out of the Bible, either by reading or meditation; still crying out to God that I might know the truth and the way to heaven and glory." It is interesting to observe, from his case, how the Bible so studied may light up the way, step by step, of an earnest inquirer until he arrives at a state of peace and settled joy from the happy assurance of God's forgiveness and unchangeable love.

We give the following two examples, selected from many:—

"One day as I was walking in the country, I was much in the thoughts of this question, 'But how if the day of grace is past?' And to aggravate my trouble, the tempter presented to my mind those good people of Bedford and suggested to me: that these being converted already they were all that God would save in these parts, and that I came too late. Now I was in great distress thinking this might well be so; wherefore I went up and down bemoaning my sad condition . . . crying out, 'Oh that I had turned sooner!' When I had been long vexed with this, these words broke in upon my mind, 'Compel them to come in, that my house may be filled; and yet there is room.'

"Those words, especially these, 'And yet there is room,' were sweet words to me, for I thought by them I saw there was place enough in heaven for me, and, moreover, that when the Lord Jesus did speak these words, he then did think of me; and that he knowing that the time would come that I should be afflicted with fear that there was no place left for me in his bosom, did before speak this word and leave it upon record that I might find help thereby against this temptation."

Another question that greatly troubled him was, "How can you tell that you are elected?"

"It may be that you are not, said the tempter; it may be so indeed, thought I. Why then, said Satan, you had as good leave off, and strive no farther. . . . By these things I was driven to my wits end, not knowing what to say, or how to answer these temptations."

He obtained relief from his distress, chiefly, from John vi. 37: "And him that cometh to me I will in no wise cast out."

"This scripture [he says] did most sweetly visit my soul. Oh! the comfort that I had from this word, 'in no wise!' As who should say, 'By no means, for nothing whatever he hath done.' But Satan would greatly labor to pull this promise from me, telling me, 'That Christ did not mean me and such as I, but sinners of a lower rank that had not done as I had done.' But I would answer him, 'Satan, there is in these words no such exception; but him that comes, *him, any him.*' If ever Satan and I did strive for any word of God in all my life, it was for this good word of Christ; he at one end, and I at the other. Oh! what work we made! It was for this in John, I say, that we did so tug and strive; he pulled and I pulled; but God be praised! I overcame him! I got sweetness from it."

Time and space forbid our citing other instances from this interesting chronicle of Bunyan's various experiences. It contains passages of sublime religions sentiment and pathos, and sheds by its vivid pictures of alternating religious despondency and exaltation, of fear and hope, of remorse and ecstatic joy, considerable light upon a subject that is attracting much attention in our day—the subject of Psychotherapy. It has a psychological as well as religious interest, and, carefully studied, will afford the Christian minister and the physician alike valuable suggestions as to right methods of dealing with troubled souls.

Most of Bunyan's prolonged darkness of mind and spiritual distress arose, we think, from his morbid self-consciousness, due in great part to the habit of introspection (practised by religious people to excess in those times), which led him to fix his thoughts on himself and the feelings of his heart for the evidence of acceptance with God, instead of fixing them on Christ and the true evidences of God's grace given in the Scriptures. He had a profound sense of sin and of the estrangement of the heart from God, and he intensified this feeling of sin, and added unnecessary weight to its natural burden of remorse, by reckoning as mortal sins the various idle thoughts and strange fancies that flitted through his mind. For instance, Satan suggested to him, he says,—

"after the Lord had set me down so sweetly in the faith of his holy gospel, and had given me such strong consolation and blessed evidence from heaven touching my interest in his love through Christ, . . . 'to sell and part with this most blessed Christ.' . . .

"This temptation did put me in such scares, lest I should at some time consent thereto and be overcome therewith, that by the very force of my mind, in laboring to gainsay and resist this wickedness, my very body would be put into action or motion, by way of pushing or thrusting with my hands or elbows; still answering, as fast as the destroyer said, 'Sell him,' 'I will not, I will not, I will not; no, not for thousands, thousands, thousands of worlds'; thus reckoning lest I should, in the midst of these assaults, set too low a value on him; even until I scarce well knew where I was, or how to be composed again. . . .

"To be brief: one morning as I did lie in my bed, I was, as at other times, most fiercely assaulted with this temptation, to sell and part with Christ; the wicked suggestion still running in my mind, 'Sell him, sell him, sell him, sell him,' as fast as a man could speak; against which also in my mind, as at other times, I answered, 'No, no, not for thousands, thousands, thousands,' at least twenty times together; but at last, after much striving, even until I was almost out of breath, I felt this thought pass through my heart, 'Let him go, if he will'; and I thought also that I felt my heart freely consent thereto. Oh! the diligence of Satan! . . .

". . . Down fell I, as a bird that is shot from the top of a tree, into great guilt and fearful despair!"

The "guilt" was a delusion, but his "despair" was real. This passage and others like it suggest that his mind at times was near to insanity. His persistent fear that he had committed the unpardonable sin, and his imaginary struggles with Satan attempting to mislead his soul and oppose his spiritual good when he tried to pray were like the hallucinations of a crazy man. But he was preserved from total madness by the soothing influence of God's Word. Its pervading tone of love and its divine wisdom proved an effective antidote. Though he reeled and tottered on the brink, he did not fall over. The outstretched hand of Christ that rescued Peter when sinking beneath the waves was stretched out to him also and upheld him. His dialogues with Satan amuse us, but him they terrified.

"The tempter [he says] hath come upon me with such discouragements as these: 'You are very hot for mercy, but I will cool you; this frame shall not last always; many have been as hot as you for a spirit [of prayer], but I have quenched their zeal' . . . but thought I, I am glad this has come into my mind; well, I will watch, and take what care I can. 'Though you do [said Satan], I shall be too hard for you; I will cool you insensibly, by degrees, by little and little. What care I, though I be seven years in chilling your heart, if I can do it at last? Continual rocking will lull a crying child asleep; I will ply it close, but I will have my end accomplished. Though you be burning hot at present, I can pull you from this fire; I shall have you cold before it be long.'"

These fancied dialogues and struggles with Satan were similar to those of Martin Luther in like circumstances. They were consonant also with the theological ideas of those times and the doctrine of the Reformers in the century preceding. "His [Bunyan's] doctrine," says Froude, "was the doctrine of the best and strongest minds in Europe. It had been believed by Luther, it had been believed by Knox. It was believed at that moment by Oliver Cromwell as by Bunyan." Bunyan may be said to have sat at the feet of Luther, as he himself in effect confessed. Like John Wesley, a century after him, he fell in with Luther's "Commentary on Galatians," and received from it similar spiritual enlightenment and relief.

"When I had but a little way perused it [he says] I found my condition in his experience so largely and profoundly handled, as if his book had been written out of my heart. He doth most gravely also in that book debate of the rise of these temptations, namely, blasphemy, desperation, and the like, showing that the law of Moses, as well as the devil, . . . hath a very great hand therein; the which, at first, was very strange to me, but considering and watching I found it so indeed. But of particulars here I intend nothing, only this methinks I must let fall before all men; I do prefer this book of Martin Luther upon Galatians (excepting the holy Bible) before all the books that ever I have seen as most fit for a wounded conscience."

But thanks to the advice of his pastor, Mr. Gifford (already quoted), his chief reliance was upon the teaching of the Bible.

"It would be too long here to stay [he says] to tell in particular how God did set me down in all the things of Christ, and how he did, that he might do so, lead me into his words; yea, and also how he did open them unto me, and *make them shine before me, and cause them to dwell with me, talk with me, and comfort me*, over and over, both of his own being and the being of his Son, and Spirit, and Word, and Gospel."

The method, so to speak, of his use of Scripture is thus set forth by him:—

"I would in these days, often in my greatest agonies, even *flounce toward the promise*, as the horses do towards sound ground that yet stick in the mire, concluding, though as one almost bereft of his wits through fear, 'On this will I rest and stay, and leave the fulfilling of it to the God of heaven that made it.' . . .

"Often when I have been making to the promise, I have seen as if the Lord would refuse my soul for ever: I was often as if I had run upon the pikes, and as if the Lord had thrust at me, to keep me from him as with a flaming sword. Then would I think of Esther, who went to petition the king contrary to the law. . . . The woman of Canaan also, that would not be daunted though called dog by Christ, and the man that went to borrow bread at midnight, were also great encouragements to me.

"I never saw those heights and depths in grace, and love, and mercy, as I saw after this. Great sins do draw out great grace, and where guilt is most terrible and fierce, there the mercy of God in Christ, when showed to the soul, appears most high, and mighty."

What the old theologians called the "law work" in religious experience, and which they deemed a necessary and essential precedent to the "work of grace" in the heart (without which indeed there could be no relief for it from its burden of sin), had the most thorough and complete operation upon Bunyan's soul. Bunyan believed that by reason of this experience he was given not only a wholesome fear of sin that kept him from backsliding, but a power and skill in dealing with troubled souls which greatly enhanced his usefulness as a preacher and pastor. "It was for this reason," he says, "I lay so long at Sinai, to see the fire, and the cloud, and the darkness, that I might fear the Lord all the days of my life upon earth, and tell of all his wondrous works to my children" (in the faith).

He was ordained to the ministry when he was twenty seven years old. Gradually and with much diffidence he entered upon the work, encouraged thereto by

"the most able for judgment and holiness of life [who] did perceive that God had counted me worthy to understand something of his will in his holy and blessed word, and had given me utterance in some measure to express what I saw to others for edification." "Wherefore, though of myself of all the Saints the most unworthy, yet I, but with great fear and trembling at the sight of my own weakness, did set upon the work"; —"which when the country understood, they came in to hear the word by hundreds, and that from all parts."

His development as a preacher was rapid and most extraordinary. Of his great eloquence and ability in preaching we have the fullest proof. "No such preacher to the uneducated English masses," says Froude, the historian, "was to be found within the four seas." "With the thing which these people meant by inspiration he was abundantly supplied." His fame as a preacher was not confined to the limits of Bedfordshire, where most of his ministry was spent: it extended to London, and in London, where he occasionally preached, the attraction of his eloquence drew great crowds to hear him. Mr. Doe, a warm contemporary admirer and citizen of the metropolis, says: "When Mr. Bunyan preached in London, if there were but one day's notice given there would be more people come together to hear him preach than the meetinghouse could hold. I have seen to hear him preach by my computation about 1200 at a morning sermon by 7 o'clock on a working day in the dark winter time. I also computed about 3000 that came to hear him one Lord's day in London at a town's end meetinghouse, so that half were fain to go away again for want of room, and then himself was fain at a back door to be pulled almost over people to get up stairs to his pulpit."

And not only "to the uneducated English masses" was he an acceptable preacher, but to the noble, the learned, the rich, and those of high social station. The learned Dr. John Owen was one of his frequent hearers, embracing eagerly every opportunity to hear him and inviting him to preach to his own select congregation in Moorefields; saying to King Charles II., who asked him, "how he could go to hear that tinker preach?" that he "would willingly exchange his learning for the ability to preach as well as the tinker."

It is interesting to know what were the particular personal qualities of Bunyan which gave him this eminence as a preacher, since, were it not for the fact that his fame as an allegorical writer eclipsed his fame as a preacher, he might fairly be regarded as one of the most eminent lights of the pulpit in his time. This judgment is warranted not only by his contemporary reputation, but by his published sermons that have come down to us.

Among the personal qualities that distinguished him as a preacher were the following:—

1. *He had a deep, unwavering conviction of the truth and importance of his message.* The "accent of conviction" was never lacking in it. He had thoroughly tested that truth by his own experience. "I preached what I saw and felt," he says. He could sincerely say, therefore, with the first preachers of the gospel, we "speak the things which we have seen and heard." He was an actual witness to their verity, not merely a repeater of things reported by others. He believed with all his heart that men needed an almighty saviour from sin and that in Christ Jesus only they could find him. As a result of this conviction he manifested an enthusiasm and earnestness in his preaching which seemed like a heavenly inspiration.

"I have been in my preaching [he says], especially when I have been engaged in the doctrine of life by Christ without works, as if an angel of God had stood at my back to encourage me. Oh, it hath been with such power and heavenly evidence upon my soul, while I have been laboring to unfold it, to demonstrate it, and to fasten it upon the consciences of others, that I could not be contented with saying, I believe and am sure; methought I was more than sure, if it be lawful so to express myself, that those things which I then asserted were true."

2. *He was direct and unflinching in his preaching of what he believed to be the truth.* "I did labor so to

speak the word," he says, "as that thereby, if it were possible, the sin and the person guilty might be particularized by it." Though by his plain preaching he condemned himself, he was not to be deterred by that fact.

"When, as sometimes, I have been about to preach upon some smart and searching portion of the word, I have found the tempter suggest, 'This condemns yourself; of this your own soul is guilty. Wherefore preach not of it at all; or if you do, yet so mince it as to make way for your own escape, lest instead of awakening others, you lay that guilt upon your own soul as you will never get from under.'

"But I thank the Lord [he says] I have been kept from consenting to these horrid suggestions, and have rather, as Samson, bowed myself with all my might, to condemn sin and transgression wherever I found it, though therein I did bring guilt upon my own conscience. Let me die, thought I, with the Philistines, rather than deal corruptly with the blessed word of God."

3. He combined with the earnestness and directness of address that we have spoken of a *marvelously clear, picturesque, and simple style.* Bunyan's style is the wonder of all students of rhetoric, and writers upon the subject. Macaulay says of it: "The vocabulary is the vocabulary of the common people. Yet no writer (or speaker as well) has said more exactly what he meant to say. For magnificence, for pathos, for vehement exhortation, for every purpose of the poet, the orator and the divine, this homely dialect—the dialect of plain working men, is sufficient." A. C. Benson compares his style to that of Cardinal Newman and says: "It was not so much the expression of a thought as the thought

itself taking shape in a perfectly pure medium of language."

Besides its simplicity and lucid plainness, the style of Bunyan had a persuasive warmth that touched men's hearts. "Let him write on what subject he may," says Dr. John Brown, his biographer, "he writes not long before he melts with tenderness, or glows with fire." His published sermons, "The Jerusalem Sinner Saved," "The Barren Fig Tree," "Come and Welcome to Jesus," and "The Greatness of the Soul," though enlarged considerably beyond the limits within which they were confined when preached, preserve the talking, animated style with which they were orally delivered, and are indeed full of tenderness and fire. The act of committing them to writing did not essentially change their mode of expression, but embalmed it.

Take the following example from a discussion on "Christ our Advocate":—.

"This consideration will help thee to put by that visor (*i. e.* mask) wherewith Christ by Satan is misrepresented to thee to the affrighting thee. There is nothing more common among Saints than thus to be wronged by Satan: for he will labor so to present Him to us with so dreadful and direful a countenance that a man in temptation and under guilt shall hardly be able to lift up his face to God. But to think really that He is my advocate, this heals all. Put a visor on the face of a father and it may perhaps for a while fright the child, but let the father speak, let him speak in his own fatherly dialect to the child, and the visor is gone, if not from the father's face, yet from the child's mind: *yea, the child, notwithstanding that visor, will adventure to creep into the father's bosom.* Thus it is with the Saints when Satan deludes and abuses them by disfiguring the countenance of Christ to their view; let them but hear their Lord speak in his own natural dialect—and he doth so when we hear him speak as an advocate—and their minds are calmed—their thoughts settled, their guilt vanished, and their faith revived."

4. The passage just quoted suggests that *a rare gift of imagination was another qualification* that gave Bunyan his eminence as a preacher. "Similes were ever coming to his mind like ripples over a stream," says Dr. Brown. These were of every kind and variety, so that all classes of hearers found pleasure in them. There were homely figures for the common people and exquisite ones for those of more refined taste.

The following are examples of both kinds:—

"Sins go not alone, but follow one another as do the links of a chain."

"The sinner, when his conscience is fallen asleep and grown hard, will lie like the smith's dog at the foot of the anvil, though the fire sparks fly in his face."

"Strike a steel against a flint and the fire flies about you; strike the law against a carnal heart, and sin appears, sin multiplies, sin rageth, sin is strengthened."

"Truths are often delivered to us like wheat in full ears, to the end we should rub them out before we eat them, and take pains about them before we have the comfort of them."

"Prayer is as the pitcher that fetcheth the water from the brook, therewith to water the herbs: break the pitcher and it will fetch no water, and for want of water the garden withers."

"He that comes to Christ cannot always get on as fast as he would. Poor coming soul, thou art like the man that would ride full gallop, whose horse will hardly trot. Now the desire of his mind is not to be judged by the slow pace of the dull jade he rides on, but by the hitching, and kicking, and spurring as he sits on his back. The flesh is like this dull jade; it will not gallop after Christ, it will be backward, though thy soul and heaven be at stake."

By the two following beautiful illustrations he shows the advantages and mutual benefits resulting from the united labors and fellowship of Christians in a well-ordered church:—

"When Christians stand every one in their places and do the work of their relations, then they are like the flowers in the garden that stand and grow where the gardener hath planted them, and then they shall both honor the garden in which they are planted, and the gardener that hath so disposed them. From the hyssop on the wall to the cedar in Lebanon, their fruit is their glory."

"Christians are like the several flowers in a garden, that have upon each of them the dew of heaven, which being shaken by the wind they let fall their dew at each other's roots, whereby they are jointly nourished and become nourishers of each other."

The imperfection of our purest and holiest desires, arising from the imperfection of human nature, never was more aptly expressed than in the following:—

"This is the cause of the coolness, of the weakness, of the flatness, and of the many extravagances that attend some of our desires; they come warm from the Spirit and grace of God in us, but as hot water running through cold pipes, or as clear water running through dirty conveyances, so our desires gather soil."

5. Another quality in him which made Bunyan eminent as a preacher was *the remarkable productiveness of his mind in regard to religious subjects.* His mind in itself was a mine of wealth while he worked on that particular vein. And its opulence was not due to any enrichment it had received from wide reading. Henry Ward Beecher, whose productiveness excited the wonder and admiring comment of Abraham Lincoln ("the most productive mind of ancient or modern times," he said), was a diligent

reader of all kinds of books, fertilizing his mind with their various elements of quickening power; but Bunyan's reading was chiefly confined to one book—the Bible. His thoughts were his own, or such as were suggested to his mind by his own experience, the outward world of nature, which he attentively observed, and the Bible. "I have not fished," he says, "in other men's waters: my Bible and Concordance are my only library." But few men ever studied the Bible as he did. As in his early religious experience, soon after meeting "those poor Bedford people," he said: "I never was out of the Bible, either by reading or meditation," so always. He saturated his mind and heart with it. It was his constant support in weakness, his daily food, the never-failing tonic of his spiritual life. Through all his changing moods, it was fitted to his various needs. Placing such dependence upon it, he extracted from it all its enriching, stimulating power. When dragged to prison for preaching the gospel, this affliction was mitigated by the fact that his insight into the Scriptures was enhanced thereby. "I never had in all my life," he says, "so great an inlet into the word of God as now. I could pray for greater trouble, for the greater comfort's sake."

We can easily believe that the Bible thus constantly studied and fed upon and made an elixir of life to his soul stimulated to extraordinary productiveness Bunyan's mind. It yields to such a student of its pages an equivalent to the best books in the world's literature. Bunyan found it so. It wonderfully quickened, strengthened, and purified all his mental faculties: it gave them for their use an inexhaustible treasure of thought and suggestion, and it gave him also his power of expression, the remarkable style of which we have spoken, in which the language of prophets, psalmists, evangelists, and apostles, as given in the Authorized Version of the Scriptures, is heard in its great range of thought and feeling.

6. One other thing which contributed greatly to Bunyan's success and eminence as a preacher was *his homiletic skill.* His sermons are worthy of any preacher's study for their valuable hints in this respect. The art of preaching finds in him some of its most important principles admirably exemplified. While we do not by any means regard him as a model preacher in all respects, and readily admit that he had great faults, as those of prolixity, frequent digression, excessive division, rambling, and others, we still maintain that he had great excellencies, which went far towards redeeming those faults, and which make him, because of them, always worth a preacher's time to observe and in some measure to imitate. We mention these four: (1) a picturesque and lively manner of addressing his hearers or readers by reason of which he is never dull, however prolix or rambling; (2) such a full and complete *explanation* of the text and different points touched upon, that there is no possibility of anyone mistaking, or of not getting a clear understanding of his meaning; (3) a remarkable and very successful use of the dialogue for the sake of answering objections or supporting and clinching a point by a short, telling argu-

ment; and (4) an earnestness to convince and win those addressed, which leaves no available means of persuasion untried, and which rises continually into expressions of tender appeal and passages of natural, unaffected eloquence.

Of these four excellencies, the third (*the use of the dialogue*) is perhaps the most unique and notable. As used by Bunyan it is very effective. No modern preacher that we can recall surpasses him in this respect. The only one that we can think of who approaches, and perhaps equals, him in the skilful use of this rhetorical weapon is the late Professor Edwards A. Park of Andover.* It is a dangerous weapon to use. One may easily wound himself rather than overcome his imaginary antagonist with it. But having the ability and skill to use it, as it was used by Bunyan and Professor Park, one may achieve wonders with it.

The story of Bunyan's imprisonment for the mere offense of preaching the gospel to a small company of religious people, dissenters from the established church, is too familiar to be dwelt on long by us. For the period of twelve years and upwards, his incarceration was prolonged, most of it, excepting occasional absences, spent in the larger jail of the county located in Bedford; to which was added, later, another short term in the small municipal jail placed midway on the bridge that spanned the river Ouse dividing the town. At the present time not a relic remains of either one of those prisons.

* See, for example, the sermon "The Prominence of the Atonement," in his Discourses (Andover: Warren F. Draper).

In the smaller jail tradition reports that the first part of "The Pilgrim's Progress" was written. To those two jails in Bedford was given the great honor of being each the place where a great book originated. In the jail on the bridge, Bunyan conceived and composed the first part of his immortal allegory: in the county jail, in the next century, John Howard, then the sheriff of Bedfordshire, whose official duty it was to inspect the prison of his county, and whose heart was profoundly stirred by what he found there of abuses and a wretched condition from which Bunyan had suffered, was started on his philanthropic career as a prison reformer, and incited to write his famous book on "The State of Prisons in England."

Bunyan took to his prison for his solace two books —the Bible and Fox's "Book of Martyrs." He needed all the support they could give him.

The following extracts from "Grace Abounding" describe his mental and spiritual distress over his situation:—

"Notwithstanding these helps, I found myself a man encompassed with infirmities. The parting with my wife and poor children hath often been to me, in this place, as the pulling of the flesh from the bones . . . because I would have often brought to my mind the many hardships, miseries, and want that my poor family was like to meet with, should I be taken from them; especially my poor blind child [his daughter Mary], who lay nearer my heart than all I had beside. Oh, the thoughts of the hardship my blind one might undergo would break my heart in pieces! . . . In this condition I was as a man who was pulling down his house upon the heads of his wife and children; yet, thought I, I must do it, I must do it."

JOHN BUNYAN

"Being but a young prisoner, and not acquainted with the laws, I had this laid much upon my spirit, that my imprisonment might end at the gallows for aught that I could tell. . . . Therefore Satan laid hard at me to beat me out of heart by suggesting thus unto me: 'But how, if, when you come indeed to die, you should be in this condition; that is, not to savour the things of God, nor to have any evidence upon your soul for a better state hereafter?' . . . I thought, if I should make a scrambling shift to clamber up the ladder, yet I should either with quaking or other symptoms of fainting give occasion to the enemy to reproach the way of God and his people for their timorousness. This lay with great trouble upon me, for methought I was ashamed to die with a pale face and tottering knees for such a cause as this. . . . Thus I was tossed for many weeks, and knew not what to do. At last this consideration fell with weight upon me, that it was for the Word and way of God that I was in this condition, wherefore I was engaged not to flinch a hair's breadth from it. Wherefore, thought I, I am for going on and venturing my eternal state with Christ, whether I have comfort here or not. *If God doth not come in, I will leap off the ladder even blindfold into eternity.* Lord Jesus, if thou wilt catch me, do; if not, I will venture for thy name!" "Now was my heart full of comfort. I would not have been without this trial for much; . . . and I hope I shall bless God forever for the teaching I have had by it."

Bunyan's long imprisonment, and that of the Quakers, George Fox and Whitehead, and others in that age of intolerance, with the physical sufferings and mental anguish that accompanied it, was a part of the great price paid for the liberty to worship God according to the dictates of the individual conscience, which is our precious inheritance. Incalculable is the debt of gratitude we owe them on account of it.

Froude defends the English government and the

magistrates of that time from the charge of cruelty, as if he had received a special retainer to do it. He declares, in substance, that Bunyan had only himself to blame; that his preaching was in violation of law; that the magistrates repeatedly told him and his wife that if he would promise not to preach, he should go free; but that to all their expostulations and warnings he opposed a stubborn and lawless attitude. "If you let me out today," he said, "I will preach again tomorrow"; and his wife, "He dare not leave preaching as long as he can speak." At this, one of the judges exclaimed: "Why should we talk any more about such a fellow? Must he do what he lists?" To which the poor woman might truthfully have answered: "Yes, my lord, God bids him do so. Take heed, what ye intend to do as touching this man, lest haply ye be found even to fight against God." This is the conclusion to which the world has now come.

The labored defense of Froude is no vindication of the magistrates or government. It was in clear violation of the promise of the king (Charles II.) at Breda, before his return to England, that if restored to the throne of his father, he would grant "liberty and consideration for tender consciences"; and that "no man should be molested for differences in opinion in matters of religion."

While in prison Bunyan busied himself in various ways: in the making of tagged laces, by which he earned something for the maintenance of his family; in preaching and ministering to his fellow-prisoners; and in writing works for publication.

One who heard him preach in prison says: "In the midst of the confusion (of the prison) I have heard Mr. Bunyan both preach and pray with that mighty spirit of faith and plerophory [*i. e.* assurance] of Divine assistance that has made me stand and wonder."

The most of the works written and published during his imprisonment were amplifications of sermons he had preached. Among these were the delightful treatises on "Christian Behavior" and the "Holy City," which bear clear marks of the genius that culminated in "The Pilgrim's Progress."

The "Holy City," the New Jerusalem, as he interpreted it, is not the abode of the Church of God in the life to come; it rather symbolizes the Church itself, that great community of redeemed men which shall eventually bring heaven's glory and happiness to the earth. Enraptured by the vision, he thus expresses his longing for the time of its fulfillment: "Never was fair weather after foul, nor warm weather after cold, nor sweet and beautiful spring after a heavy and nipping and terrible winter, so comfortable, sweet, desirable, and welcome to the poor birds and beasts of the field as this day will be to the Church of God." The wonderful suggestiveness and fertility of his mind in ideas is well exhibited in the interpretation he gives to the several features of the Holy City. Its twelve gates, three to each point of the compass, indicate that "God hath a people in every quarter of the world, and that from what quarter of the world soever men come for life, for those men there are the gates of life right before their doors."

Its foundations with the names of the twelve apostles on them indicate "that neither Christ nor any of his benefits can be profitable unto thee unless thou receive him alone upon the terms that they do offer him to sinners in their word and doctrine."

Its twelve gates of twelve pearls—"every several gate one pearl"—indicate "that as none can enter in but by Christ, so none can enter in but by a whole Christ: . . . thou must enter in by every whit of Christ, or by never a whit of him."

Its one "street of pure gold, as it were transparent glass," indicates that "at last the saints shall walk in *one way*. It is Anti-Christ that hath brought in all these crossings, by-lanes, and odd nooks that to this day many an honest heart doth greatly lose itself in. Men must have pure hearts for that golden street,—golden hearts with graces that are much more precious than gold."

That "the city was pure gold" indicates "how invincible a spirit the people of God are possessed of. Gold is a metal so invincible that no fire can consume it." Fire may melt it, and consume its dross, but instead of destroying it the fire refines it. "The church in the fire of persecution is like Esther in the perfuming chamber, but making fit for the presence of the king."

Holding a conspicuous place among these prison writings was "Grace Abounding," written for the spiritual good of those to whom he formerly ministered, "whom God hath counted him worthy to beget to faith by his ministry." "The remembrance of my great sins, of my great temptations, and of my great fears of perishing forever bring afresh to my mind the remembrance of my great help from heaven. He would therefore incite them to "search also for the hid treasure of their first and second experience of the grace of God."

Of the style in which he wrote it, which is essentially the style of all his works, adopted for the reason here given, he says: "I could have stepped into a style much higher than this in which I have discoursed, but I dare not." God did not play in dealing with him, he said, neither did he himself play when he sank as into a bottomless pit and the pangs of hell caught hold of him. Therefore he may not play in telling the story, but "be plain and simple and lay down the thing as it was. He that likes it may receive it, he that does not, let him produce a better."

No better rule for the formation of a good style could be given than that thus adopted by Bunyan and contained in the words *"be plain and simple, and lay down the thing as it was."* So Lincoln acquired his wonderful style. It was the result of his honest endeavor to tell the exact truth—to express and "lay down the thing as it was."

This rule does not exclude proper use of the imagination. It indeed requires this sometimes. Many times it is not possible "to lay down the thing as it was" without the aid of apt illustration. Subjects that are obscure to the common intelligence, like those of religion and its ideals, and the abstruse themes of philosophy, require the illumination given by the imagination. As visitors to Mammoth Cave would get no adequate conception of the magnitude and wondrous beauty of its jeweled chambers, except by the illuminating light of their torches, so explorers of all dark subjects would have no clear ideas in regard to them, no perception of their full meaning and real charm, but for the imagination's help. The writings of Bunyan are good examples of this truth. The attractive charm possessed by them is largely due to the imaginative light thrown upon them.

The most famous of his writings, "The Pilgrim's Progress," was conceived and largely composed in the last year of his imprisonment. Like all his works, its thought, lessons, and inspiration were derived from the Bible. Comparing it with Dante's great work, Dr. John Brown truly says: " 'The Pilgrim's Progress' is an English flower, as the 'Divina Commedia' is a Tuscan flower, grown on Jewish soil." One is as much a work of genius as the other. Their immortality, their unfading popularity with all classes of people, place them in the same rank. It is interesting to know how it originated and was composed.

The idea of it came to him while engaged with another work. It came to him as an inspiration, like Mozart's Requiem. It took possession of his mind, captivated, and engrossed it completely until it was finished.

He wrote it to please himself, without any thought, at first, of its publication or of the fame it was to bring him. Indeed he tells us in his homely "apology" for it, that when finished he hesitated to give it to the world and in his doubt consulted his friends about it.

> "Some said, John, print it; others said, Not so.
> Some said, it might do good; others said, No.
> Now I was in a strait, and did not see
> Which was the best thing to be done by me;
> At last I thought, since you are thus divided,
> I print it will; and so the case decided."

It cost him no painful effort to produce it. It sprang from his fertile mind like a spring flower from its native soil when quickened by the sunshine. In the doing of it there was no conscious elaboration. His thick-coming thoughts and fancies were, he says, "like sparks from coals of fire," spontaneous, unforced, and eager to find expression.

> "Thus I set pen to paper with delight,
> And quickly had my thoughts in black and white."

Concerning its characteristics little need be said, because they are so well known. Few there are of English stock but have read and appreciated its imaginative picturesqueness, its graphic descriptions, its genial humor, and childlike naturalness. It charmed and instructed us in childhood and still retains its spell over us in our adult years even to the end of life. Dean Stanley has truly said of it: "The pilgrimage Bunyan described is the pilgrimage of every one of us, and the combination of neighbors, friends and enemies whom he saw in his dream are the same as we see in our actual lives."

No other book depicts so vividly our varied

religious experiences, our spiritual needs, our fears, and our hopes, and the exaltation of mind granted to us in our better moments. In short, it has the elements of universality and stability characteristic of the highest works of genius, which make it agreeable to all classes and creeds, "a religious bond to the whole of English Christendom," and acceptable to the people of all time. Though the peculiar theology of Bunyan's day has become obsolete in most churches, and been supplanted by another whose doctrinal statements differ widely from it, strange to say, this change has hardly touched the truth and power of "The Pilgrim's Progress." It is vital still with the essential truth of Christianity. This has remained and will remain as invulnerable to attack from such changes as the teaching of the New Testament. With the good in them it accords; the error like a touchstone it reveals. Written after that remarkable "inlet into the word of God," which came to him in prison, in consequence of which he said: *"The Scriptures that I saw nothing in before are made in this place to shine upon me. Here I have seen Jesus Christ, and felt Him indeed,"* the Christian truth with which his mind was thus imbued, and which he endeavored to embody in his story, was well-nigh free—purged as by fire—from error, so that Dean Stanley's words at the unveiling of Bunyan's statue in Bedford, in 1874, are forever true of the situations and experiences described in the transparent, lifelike allegory: "All of us need to be cheered by the help of Greatheart and Steadfast and Valiant for the Truth, and good old Honest.

Some of us have been in Doubting Castle, some in the Slough of Despond, some have experienced the temptations of Vanity Fair: all of us have to climb the Hill Difficulty, all of us need to be instructed by the Interpreter in the House Beautiful; all of us bear the same burden; all of us need the same armor in our fight with Apollyon; all of us have to pass through the dark river; and for all of us (if God so will) there wait the Shining Ones at the gates of the Celestial City, which when we see, we wish ourselves among them."

The first part of this immortal work was published in imperfect form in 1678. Three editions were called for and published within a year (the last, only, having the completed form), showing that it leaped at once into the popularity which it has ever since enjoyed. Nathaniel Ponder at the sign of the Peacock was its publisher. "A modern artist," says Dr. Brown, "has painted a picture to indicate the instant popularity of it. A scholar is coming out from under the sign of the Peacock, and a peasant, whip in one hand and money in the other, going in, while near the shop-door are a gay gallant and a fair lady, schoolboys and grave men, all intently reading that story of the 'Pilgrim' they have purchased over the counter within. The picture is true of the time then, and true to the time now."

The second part, with the story of the pilgrimage of Christiana and her children with their companions, was given to the world early in 1685. The spelling of the book was the spelling of an uneducated man, calling for correction, but the style of it was Bunyan's own style, incapable of much amendment. An English clergyman, Joshua Gilpin, Vicar of Wrockwardine, in 1811, published "a new and corrected edition, in which the phraseology of the author is somewhat improved," but the alleged improvement was not accepted by the public as such. The vicar, though a highly educated man and with the best intentions in the world, was not a good judge of style and "the phraseology" best suited to the work.

Bunyan survived the completion of his great work about three years and a half, dying in London, August 31, 1688, having journeyed thither to place the MS. of a new book, "The Acceptable Sacrifice," with his publisher. His death was owing to a fever contracted from exposure to a drenching rain encountered on the way from Reading to London. He had visited Reading, which lay considerably out of his way, on an errend of mercy—happily successful. It was to bring about the reconciliation of an angry father with his wayward son. Before his fever had developed he was able to preach, of a Sunday, near White Chapel. The concluding words of his sermon, and the last words heard from his lips from the pulpit, were: "Consider that the holy God is your father, and let this oblige you to live like the children of God, that you may look your father in the face with comfort another day."

He was buried in the heart of London, in Bunhill Fields, "the *Campo Santo* of Dissenters," as it has been called, where the bodies of John Owen, George Fox, Isaac Watts, Daniel Defoe, Susannah Wesley, and many other notable persons have been buried. Such was the reverence felt for his piety that many of his contemporaries desired with their dying breath that their bodies might be buried near his in the expectation of being associated with him in the Resurrection Day. Such respect for a man's goodness and sanctity by his contemporaries is not always enduring. Time and research into the hidden things of his life often discover flaws in his character which change contemporary renown into later disrepute. Not so with Bunyan. Lapse of time and the survey of his work and character, unbiased by religious prejudice, have only added luster and new respect to his name. An interesting proof of it is seen in a recent item of news that has come to us from England. It is this, that a movement has lately been started there to place in Westminster Abbey a memorial window to John Bunyan, which has been heartily favored by the Archbishop of Canterbury and other dignitaries of the Anglican Church as well as by distinguished men of various dissenting religious bodies; and a committee has been appointed to raise the required sum of five thousand pounds for the fulfillment of the plan.

Such a memorial, in that place, inaugurated with appropriate religious ceremony, will be a beatification of John Bunyan by the Anglican Church and other Protestant bodies as worthy to be reckoned, despite the persecution and scorn heaped upon him when living, among the saints and heroes of the Christian faith, and among the noblest exemplars of its sanctifying power.

VII

FREDERICK W. ROBERTSON

VII

FREDERICK W. ROBERTSON

Born in London, February 3, 1816: Died in Brighton, August 15, 1853.

Robertson, all things considered, we regard as the most remarkable English preacher of the nineteenth century. He died at the early age of thirty seven, and his active ministry covered a period of only thirteen years; but in this brief period he did a work and fulfilled a ministry that, for depth and extent of its ultimate influence, was scarcely equaled by any contemporary in the labors of twice this length of time. Notable is the fact that this great influence was mainly a posthumous influence, scarcely recognized while he was living, and then only by a limited portion of the English religious public, but wrought by his published sermons and by the publication of his "Life and Letters," prepared by Rev. Stopford Brooke, and given to the world twelve years after Robertson's death. Those sermons, widely read by ministers of all denominations and Christian laymen throughout the English-speaking world, excited the profoundest and most lively interest by their freshness and originality of thought, their novel statement of Christian truth and their impressive style. As the writer recalls the impression

233

which those sermons made on his own mind when a Seminary student reading them as they first appeared, it seems to him now that they made upon him a deeper impression than the published sermons of any preacher he ever read. They awakened a sustained interest by their suggestiveness and originality, so that one did not soon tire of reading them; they stirred and purified the heart by their noble sentiments; they fructified the mind with seed thoughts which yielded an abundant harvest. They were the work of a man endowed with a rare genius perfected by careful training and self-culture, and refined by piety and suffering.

I. His Family and Early Home Environment

He belonged to a military family. His grandfather, Colonel Robertson, in whose house in London he was born, was a distinguished officer in the English army, and wounded in the service. His father was a captain in the Royal Artillery. Of his three brothers, two, Charles and Harry, won frequent honorable mention in the Kaffir war, and Struan was a captain in the Royal South Lincoln militia. The first five years of his life were passed at Leith Fort, near Edinburgh, where his father was stationed, and where he says "he was rocked and cradled to the roar of artillery." The conversation of home was of war and its exploits. Thus he was fed and nurtured from infancy through childhood and youth upon the anecdotes and associations of a soldier's life. Heredity and early environment contributed to produce in him a martial spirit, and make him eager for a soldier's career. This martial spirit gave a tone to his ministry and was one of the elements of power in his pulpit eloquence as in that of Chrysostom.

His father and mother were pious devout people of the evangelical type. The atmosphere of his early home was made sweet and wholesome by the best influences of religion. They were also people of culture and refinement and moved in a social circle of the best class.

II. EDUCATION AND MENTAL DEVELOPMENT

The father was his children's earliest teacher, and he superintended their instruction for several years after he had ceased personally to give them lessons. At sixteen, after having become well grounded in the classics and French languages, Frederick entered the New Academy, Edinburgh, where he at once took a high place in his class. He possessed the qualities of a superior scholar, extraordinary power of attention, quickness to learn, and a retentive memory, which enabled him in later years to "recall page after page of books which he had not read since his boyhood." He was also an intense worker and early formed the habit, which remained with him, of mastering fully whatever he studied. Besides studying at the Academy, he attended classes at the University and gave himself eagerly to studies in natural science, especially chemistry and physics. Returning home he wished to enter the army, but

his father, believing that this promising son **was**
better fitted by nature for the Church than for the
army, proposed to him that he should study for the
ministry. He answered, "Anything but that; I
am not fit for it." He was accordingly placed in
a solicitor's office and stayed there a year until his
health became impaired by his sedentary work, and
the galling influence of his secret disappointment.
His father then consented that he should follow the
bent of his mind, and an application was made for
a commission in the army. There was then no
vacancy, but his name was placed on the list for a
cavalry regiment in India. Two years he waited,
giving himself enthusiastically, meantime, to pursuits that would fit him for his anticipated career.
He became an expert rider, a good shot, and an
excellent draughtsman. He omitted nothing likely
to make him a good cavalry officer. His father,
believing from the long delay that his application
had been forgotten and would never be successful,
again proposed to this son to enter the Church, and
was met again with the same decisive refusal; until
other friends and a chain of circumstances united
to strengthen the father's persuasions, and his son
at length yielded. In one of his sermons in after
years, to illustrate how God's providence shapes our
course in life, he says: "If I had not met a certain
person, I should not have changed my profession;
if I had not known a certain lady I should not probably have met this person; if that lady had not had
a delicate daughter who was disturbed by the bark-
ing of my dog; if my dog had not barked that night,

I should now have been in the dragoons or fertilizing the soil of India." The decision made, he promptly acted upon it and entered Brasenose College, Oxford University, being matriculated May 4, 1837. Five days afterwards, the long-expected letter came from the military secretary of the English government, offering him a cavalry commission in the Second Dragoons with the option of exchange in the third just embarking for India. Had the letter arrived three weeks sooner, he had never entered the Church. He was then twenty-one years old.

Though with characteristic submission of spirit he resigned himself to what he believed to be God's will, the disappointment nevertheless saddened his whole life. He never ceased to think of what might have been had his wish for a soldier's career been gratified, and he indulged a secret, but sometimes expressed regret that he had not been permitted to realize it. "All his life long," his biographer says, "he was a soldier at heart." In the height of his popularity as a preacher, he said: "I would rather have led a forlorn hope than mount the pulpit stairs."

The time covered by his life as a student at Oxford, 1837–1840, was one of great interest. Among his contemporaries were Arthur Stanley and Ruskin; among his teachers were Buckland, the geologist, and Thomas Arnold, illustrious both as the great teacher of Rugby School and as lecturer upon history in Oxford. He speaks of Arnold as "every inch a man"; and has given us a picture of his appearance at his opening lecture on Modern History when, after years of obloquy, he was received then with great honor. "He walked up to the rostrum with a quiet step and manly dignity." Few, however, exercised much influence over Robertson; he was rather the magnet that drew others to himself.

The Tractarian movement was nearing its culmination. He shared the excitement produced by the writings of Newman, Pusey and Keble. He heard J. H. Newman preach some of his most famous sermons and was deeply impressed by his preaching. But he never adopted the distinctive opinions and ideas of the Tractarians. On the contrary, he resisted and actively combatted them. He read carefully the literature bearing upon the subject and formed from these studies a conviction from which he never swerved, that the Tractarian leaders were in error as to the principal things they contended for.

His biographer, speaking several years later of his attitude of mind toward the views of the High-Church piety, says: "It may be well here to set that question at rest. He had no sympathy with their views; but he had a great deal of sympathy with the men who held them, with their self-devotion, and with their writings. He reverenced the self-sacrificing work they were performing among poor and neglected parishes. He said that, as a body, they had reasserted the doctrine of a spiritual resurrection, which had been almost put out of sight by the 'Evangelical' party. He read Newman's sermons with profit and delight till the day of his death. There was no book which he studied more carefully or held in higher honor than the 'Christian Year' (of Keble). It seemed to him that some of its poems were little short of inspired. He saw in the importance which the Tractarians gave to forms a valuable element which he never lost sight of in his teaching. Only, while they seemed to say that forms could produce life, he said that forms were necessary only to support life; but for that they were necessary. To use his own illustration: 'Bread will not create life, but life cannot be kept up without bread.' On the subject of baptism he felt no sympathy with the Evangelical view, which left it doubtful whether the baptized child was a child of God or not; but because the Tractarian view declared that *all baptized* persons were children of God, he could so far sympathize with it. But on all other points, starting as he did from the basis that baptism *declared*, and did not create the *fact* of sonship, his difference was radical."

In his endeavor to get at the Scriptural teaching upon the questions discussed he studied the Bible most diligently and thoroughly. "It was his habit when dressing in the morning to commit to memory daily a certain number of verses of the New Testament. In this way, before leaving the University, he had gone twice over the English version and once and a half through the Greek. With his extraordinary power of arrangement, he mentally combined and recombined all the prominent texts under fixed heads of subjects. Owing to this practice, as he declared afterwards, no sooner was any Christian doctrine or duty mentioned or suggested to him by what he was writing than all the passages bearing on the point seemed to array themselves in order before him."

This incidental benefit, due largely to the Tractarian agitation, was of priceless benefit to him. There was another result, however, which he rightly or wrongly, much deplored. It was that of desultory discoursive reading. Instead of "reading for honors" *i.e.*—confining his attention to the few books and topics recommended in the college curriculum, and by thorough mastery of them according to a definite plan seeking to win class honors, he was led by the excitement of the controversy, questions of the day, "gleams and flashings of new paths of learning," to desert the prescribed course and follow whithersoever they might draw him, having no plan to guide him. Ten or twelve years after he left the University he says: "I now feel that I was utterly, mournfully, irreparably wrong. I would now give £200 a year to have read on a bad plan, chosen for me, but steadily."

But though his reading was thus somewhat miscellaneous, he did not fall into the fault of that "careless, multifarious reading," which, he says, "is an excuse for the mind to lie dormant whilst thought is poured in and runs through a clear stream, over unproductive gravel on which not even mosses grow," and which he reprobates as "the idlest of all idlenesses, and leaves more of impotency than any other." "I know what reading is," he said, when shattered health forbade close reading, "for I could read once and did. I read hard (at the University), or not at all, never skimming, and Plato, Aristotle, Butler, Thucydides, Jonathan Edwards passed like the iron atoms of the blood into my mental constitution." Besides these writers he read much and attentively Coleridge, Shelley, Shakespeare and Wordsworth. Though not a writer of poetry himself he had a poet's sensitiveness to the attractions of nature, and the appeal of human life in its different phases of heroic sublimity, romance, and touching pathos. He did not make many friends at Oxford and was not widely known, his dispositon inclining him to seclusion and solitariness. He was by nature shy and diffident. Except to his intimate friends he was reserved and taciturn, at the same time preserving a proud independence of spirit, which made him pursue his own course rather than be a follower of others.

III. His Ministry

The thirteen years and a few weeks of his ministerial life were passed in four places: Winchester, two years; Cheltenham, five years; Oxford, three months; Brighton, six years.

At Winchester, he began his work at twenty-four years of age, being ordained deacon July 12, 1840: he served as curate, or assistant, of Mr. Nicholson, rector of a large parish located among a very poor population, where there was much infidelity and immorality. His rector was an earnest, devoted man, in whom he found "a faithful friend whose sympathy cheered, and whose experience guided him." The work was hard and beset with difficulties, but "the difficulties of his position were his stimulus." They appealed to the soldier spirit in him. He labored with all his heart among the poor, and the working men, and was "so earnest, courteous and eager to serve that in a great measure he overcame their prejudices." His way of life, as described by one of his Winchester friends, was regular and simple: "Study all the morning, getting up early and eating almost no breakfast in order to be able to apply himself to work; in the afternoon, hard fagging at visitation of the poor in the dirtiest streets of Winchester; evenings, spent sometimes alone, but often with his rector." "He devoted much of his time to the Sunday school and made the teaching system attractive and useful by training the teachers himself." "A vein of melancholy ran through his character." Not much society was offered to him and he did not wish for it. "He was disposed to regard general society as a waste of time." He found devotional reading profitable and inspiring, especially the lives of eminently holy persons whose tone was one of communion with God. "It made his sense of the reality of religious feeling more acute when he found it embodied in the actions of men who expressed it." "Brainerd's Life," written by Edwards, he greatly valued. "To my taste," he said, "it stands alone as a specimen of biography." He gave much time to prayer and this gave tone to his preaching. "His sermons touched men to the quick. They were delivered with great ease and self-command, with vivid action, and an impassioned earnest manner that made every word tell." Though his biographer says: "The sermons preached at Winchester do not exhibit much power, are startlingly inferior to those delivered at Brighton, and do not, to the reader, even foretell his future excellence"; one of his constant hearers says: "His sermons *did* prophesy his future excellence. I am disposed to say that they were never at any time more impressive."

This difference of opinion can be reconciled, we think. The sermons of Winchester were of the common evangelical type; their doctrine, that of the traditional theology of the Evangelical School in which he had grown up. They sound a familiar note, which the widely diffused literature of that school has made trite and almost commonplace. Those of Brighton, however, were the product of a mind that had, through study and personal conviction, so changed and modified his earlier opinions of the Evangelical School, that a new and startling note is heard in them and a note of stronger personal passion and conviction, because the preacher knew that his teaching was likely to encounter prejudice and an opposition such as new statements or modifications of religious truth and departures from the beaten paths of theological statements and belief are certain to create.

Robertson's health broke down under the system of austere regimen, hard study, and unrelaxing toil which he had adopted. Toward the end of the first year a distressing pain in the side and an alarming cough developed. His spirits sank, he became despondent and his physicians ordered him to leave his work and go to Switzerland. Before his departure, he passed the examination for priest's orders, at which he presented so remarkable a paper upon the duties and work of the diaconate, in connection with the personal narrative of his own experience in the office, that the bishop "retained it and gave it to future candidates to read as a noble example of the spirit and mode in which the diaconate should be fulfilled." And yet, such was Robertson's morbid spirit and disposition to depreciate his work, that he looked back upon it with shame and a sense of failure.

Proceeding to the continent he traveled on foot up the Rhine, through portions of Germany on to Switzerland. Through the excitement of healthy exercise and change of scene his sadness gradually passed away and his health was partially restored. He keenly appreciated the beautiful and sublime in nature and the interesting traditions of the Rhine Valley, so that every step of the storied way was a delight to him.

Arrived in Geneva, having introductions to some of its people of social eminence, he soon formed a circle of valuable acquaintance. He entered eagerly into the discussions, social and religious, which then agitated the city. His brilliant powers of conversation, his intelligence and enthusiasm charmed all whom he met. Under the quickening influence of his improved health, he became much altered for the better, as if actually transformed.

He met there in Geneva the illustrious Cesar

Malan, and had more than one eager discussion with him over religious and theological questions, in regard to which they differed. Malan, sagaciously discerning in these conversations the excitable and despondent nature of the young man, said to him: "My dear Brother, you will have a sad life, a sad ministry." He met there also, in Geneva, his future wife, Helen Denys, the daughter of an English Baronet, and after a short acquaintance married her, and soon returned to England. But owing to still lingering traces of ill health, he was forbidden to take a ministerial charge for several months. At length, he was given a curacy in Cheltenham, and he entered upon its duties in the summer of 1842 at the age of twenty-six. Here, as at Winchester, he was happy and fortunate in being associated with a rector, Rev. Archibald Boyd, whom he greatly respected and admired. Mr. Robertson usually preached in the afternoon, and "he soon began to exercise upon his congregation his peculiar power of fascination." It was the fascination, not merely of an entrancing voice and pleasing delivery, but of a powerful, inspiring mind, rich in thought and animated by deep spiritual cravings and moral earnestness to do good. One who heard him at the beginning of his ministry in Cheltenham says: "I was not merely struck, I was startled by the sermon. The high order of thought, the large and clear conception, the breadth of view, the passion held in leash, the tremulously earnest tone, the utter forgetfulness of self in his subject, and the abundance of the heart out of which the mouth spake, made me feel

that here, indeed, was one whom it would be well
to miss no opportunity of hearing." "From the
first," says this informant, "he largely swayed those
minds which had any point of contact with his own.
In spite of what he says of Cheltenham, he had very
many hearers there, who knew how to rate him at
his proper value, before a larger public had indorsed
it. Nor was it among the laymen and women of
Cheltenham alone that he made his influence felt.
At the clerical meetings he attended, he would for
the most part remain silent, but sometimes when
many of his brethren were in difficulty about the
meaning of a text he would startle them by saying
a few simple words, which shed a flood of new light
upon the passage. He never put himself forward,
but his talents were none the less recognized and
held in honor by the foremost of his brother clergymen."

He exercised his peculiar fascination not only in
the pulpit and upon gatherings of clergymen, but
by his conversation in social circles. "He was a
marvelously bright and eloquent talker," his biographer says, and "he was cordially welcome everywhere." "Perhaps his influence on society was more
powerful, as more insensible, than his influence in
the pulpit." Society on the other hand greatly
stimulated and influenced him. "Some of his
highest and best thoughts were kindled by sparks
which fell from the minds of his friends. His intercourse even with inferiors in intelligence and culture
was always fruitful. He took their ideas and,
putting the stamp of his own mind upon them,

used them to serve his purpose. "It was not that he unfairly appropriated what belonged to others, but that he made it his own by the same tenure as property is first held, by the worth he gave to it." To such a man society is helpful and necessary that he may do his best.

Three things contributed greatly to the development and enrichment of his mind in Cheltenham: friends, the social atmosphere of the town, and the books he read. Prominent among his friends was Mr. Boyd, his rector. "The influence of this friendship," says his biographer, "was clearly marked. It bore fruit in his sermons. Under the impulse given by those of Mr. Boyd, they became entirely changed in character. Instead of writing them in one morning, without preparation, as at Winchester [which method is essentially that of mere improvisation, in which what is written is superficial, coming from the top of the mind, instead of from its richer depths], he studied for them on Thursday and Friday, and wrote them carefully on Saturday. . . . . Their tone was more intellectual, without being less earnest; their generalizations more daring and their practical teaching wider. Through the ideal which this friendship created, much of his peculiar intellectual power in preaching was drawn to the light."

Another friendship was formed with a gentleman well-read in metaphysics and acquainted with the results of recent theological and philosophical discussions in Germany. Their conversations were frequent and interesting and actuated by love of the truth; and "it was partially, at least, due to this friendship that Mr. Robertson escaped from the trammels which had confined his intellect and spirit."

The social atmosphere of Cheltenham was that of a fashionable watering place, or health resort like Saratoga. It was frequented, like Saratoga, by religious people, especially of the Evangelical sort. At that time it was a "hotbed of religious excite-ment." The controversy of the "Tracts for the Times" was at its height. There were the usual tests of orthodoxy applied to every new clergyman, and the usual ban placed on those who could not repeat the accepted Shibboleth. To hold certain doctrines and to speak certain phrases and to feel certain feelings was counted equivalent to a Christian life by many in the congregations. There was in all this talk much sham and religious pretense which voiced itself in hollow cant. At first, with unquestioning charity he believed that all who spoke of Christ were Christlike. "His truthful character, his earnestness, at first unconsciously and afterwards consciously, recoiled from all the unreality about him. So disgusted was he by the expression of religious emotion which fell from those who were living a merely fashionable life," that he gave up reading devotional books (which he afterwards confessed was a mistake), lest he should fall into the same habit. He was also shocked by the intolerance and harsh criticisms indulged in by the orthodox people and the religious papers of the Evangelical School, like the *Record* and the *Guardian*, which denounced suspected men without any regard to the truth of their charges. "They tell *lies* in the name of God," he said, and their dishonesty and bigotry shook his faith in the Evangelical system. The misrepresentations and impertinences of what he called "his muslin Episcopate" (the coterie of gossiping women who tried to shape his opinions and curb the freedom and honesty of his speech) added to his estrangement from the Evangelical party, until, in his strong reprobation of the faults of that party and reaction from their offensive dogmatism, he found himself gradually parting from the school in which he had been reared and with which he had so far worked. He unfairly charged upon the Evangelical system of doctrine the faults of its adherents and advocates. He forgot that the truth may have false adherents and faulty people that advocate it, as well as error. In his loss of confidence in a portion of the Evangelical School he was disposed to repudiate entirely their theology, notwithstanding the fact that it was held by his father and mother, and had been held by some of the most saintly people in the past, like Simeon, Wilberforce, Scott, Newton and Venn. "It must be said," admits his biographer, "that he himself showed but scant justice to the Evangelical party. He seems to have imputed to all its adherents the views of the *Record* newspaper. He sometimes forces conclusions upon them which the great body of them would repudiate. He unconsciously overstates, in his letters, some of their opinions." He went too far, no doubt, so far as to be unjust to the system he thus forsook. The influence of the social atmosphere of Cheltenham on Robertson's mind was, therefore, to a great extent baneful. It developed in him an antagonism and bitterness of spirit; a bewilderment of mind whose effect for a time was to make him severe and uncharitable in his judgments; an uncertainty in regard to the truth until emancipated from a narrow traditionalism by accession of new light and broadened and strengthened in other ways. "When he escaped from it," his biographer says, "he sprang from a dwarf into a giant."

But the break with the evangelical faith in which he had been reared, and which he held in the earlier years of his ministry at Cheltenham, did not come suddenly. It was gradual, and not complete for some time; not until he had ended his work in Cheltenham. During the process his mind was clouded, and he groped blindly for the truth. It was apparent in his preaching, so that his intimate friends perceived it by the uncertainty of his tone and the obscurity of his utterances—something unusual with him. "One of these," we are told, "who was with him at the English Lakes, said to him one day with some sharpness, pointing to the summit of Skiddaw, which was unseen the while for mist,—'I would not have my head like the peak of that mountain, involved, as we see it now, in cloud, for all that you would offer me.' 'I would,' rejoined Robertson, 'for by and by the cloud and mist will roll away, and the sun will come down upon it in all his glory.'"

His faith was justified. To another friend, later

on, he wrote: "A man ought to burn his own smoke if he cannot convert it into clear flame. I am quite willing to struggle on in twilight until the light comes. Manly struggle cannot fail. Only a man must struggle alone. His own view of truth, or rather his own way of viewing it and that alone, will give him rest."

It is not strange that, while his mind was in this state, and his pulpit utterances so affected by it, he was misunderstood, misrepresented, and criticised by some of his hearers. This was galling to his sensitive nature, and made him think that his work was an entire failure. "Through the mist which his own sensitiveness (and doubts) created he saw the misconceptions of a few magnified into a phantom of failure." But he struggled on to the end of his work in Cheltenham, doing faithfully what his pastoral office required. He was especially painstaking, here, as in every parish he served, in the preparation of his class of young persons for confirmation. "The labor which every year he bestowed upon this work," says his biographer, "was great. He personally interested himself in all the candidates. The heavier the clay, the more pains in his tillage."

The influence of his reading and studies was to expand and enrich his mind. He read widely and thoughtfully. Carlyle, Niebuhr, Guizot, works on natural science, Tennyson and Dante, he thoroughly studied and appreciated. Dante, he read daily and committed the whole of the "Inferno" to memory. Tennyson's poems were devoured as they appeared. Of Tennyson's "In Memoriam," he said:

"To me it has been the richest treasure I have had. It is the most precious work published this century."

"He had a useful habit of reading on the questions of the day. Owing to it he was always ready with a well-considered view of all the subjects which had agitated the country during his career." Most important of all, he read constantly and critically the Bible, the Old Testament and the New. He studied the Gospel until he made the mind of Christ his own and the personality of Christ as real as that of his most intimate friend. He read not only for the joy which knowledge gives, but to quicken his mind to creative power. To a friend he gave this counsel, basing his advice, no doubt, upon his own practice: "Receive, imbibe and then your mind will create. Poets are creators because recipients. They open their hearts to Nature instead of going to her with views of her already made and second-hand: they come from her and give out what they have felt and what she said to them. So with Scripture; patient, quiet, long-revering listening to it; then, suggestions."

He made one great mistake, that of neglecting to take regular outdoor exercise. In deference to what was thought suitable to a clergyman, "he allowed himself none of the healthful exercises which he loved except an occasional walk and ride into the country." To a person of his morbid, sensitive nature, smarting under criticism and given to brooding over and magnifying the import of what he heard said of himself, Nature's influence was especially needed as an antidote to his vexed and distempered soul. He needed the tranquil effect of her magnificence and calm, and when tired and exhausted with study; he needed the restorative invigorating effect of pure air and exercise amid her diverting scenes and beautiful objects. Happy would it have been for him had he acted upon the advice of his favorite poet, Wordsworth :—

> "Come forth into the light of things,
> Let Nature be your teacher.
>
>   *   *   *   *   *
>
> "She has a world of ready wealth,
> Our minds and hearts to bless,—
> Spontaneous wisdom breathed by health,
> Truth breathed by cheerfulness,
>
> "One impulse from a vernal wood
> May teach you more of man,
> Of moral evil and of good,
> Than all the sages can.
>
> "Sweet is the lore which Nature brings;
> Our meddling intellect
> Mis-shapes the beauteous forms of things,
> We murder to dissect.
>
> "Enough of Science and of Art!
> Close up those barren leaves;
> Come forth, and bring with you a heart
> That watches and receives."
>   Wordsworth's *The Tables Turned.*

Near the end of five years his position in Cheltenham became intolerable and he resolved that he must sunder his connection with the church he was serving and the Evangelical School with which he had been identified. "Within its pale, for him, there was henceforth neither life, peace, nor reality."

Acting upon this conviction he started for the continent in September, 1846, in the middle of the thirty-first year of his age, going directly to the Tyrol by way of Munich. and to the vicinity of Innsbruck; thence, later, on to Switzerland and then to Heidelberg, where, for six or eight Sundays in the absence of the chaplain of the English congregation, he occupied the pulpit to the great delight of the people.

In the six or eight weeks spent in the Tyrol and Switzerland he passed through the great spiritual crisis of his life. The sublime scenery of the Alpine region and the healthful exercise he took in exploring it afforded the medicine he needed. There he wrestled with his doubts and fears, and conquered. The stages of the conflict are veiled in mystery. His biographer does not describe them, nor does Robertson himself do more than hint at them. He kept no diary that has ever been found, by whose records we can trace them. The following passage, however, in a lecture to the workingmen of Brighton refers to this crisis in his religious faith: "It is an awful moment when the soul begins to feel the nothingness of many of the traditional opinions which have been received with implicit confidence, and in that horrible insecurity begins also to doubt whether there be anything to believe at all. In that fearful loneliness of spirit, when those who should have been his friends and counselors bid him stifle his doubts, to extinguish as a glare from hell that which for aught he knows may be light from heaven, and everything seemed wrapped in hideous nncertainty, I know of but one way in which a man may come forth from his agony scathless; it is by holding fast to those things that are certain still—the grand simple landmarks of morality. If there be no God and no future state, yet even then it is better to be generous than selfish, better to be chaste than licentious, better to be true than false, brave than a coward. Blessed beyond all earthly blessedness is the man who in the tempestuous darkness of the soul has dared to hold fast to those venerable landmarks. Thrice blessed, because his night shall pass into clear bright day, with a faith and hope and trust no longer traditional, but his own." Dr. Brastow's statement seems to be a good summary of the truth: "All such changes are likely to come gradually and the process is likely to be obscure. Without doubt in his case the transformation was more gradual and inward and silent than appears at the surface of his life, although the culmination was rapid, and seems to have been limited to the course of a few months, after which he emerged into a new and singularly sudden consciousness of power, and his growth thence onward is marvelous." ("Representative Preachers.")

After an absence of only three months he returned to Cheltenham, but to no more service there in the ministry, having resigned his curacy while at Heidelberg.

While waiting for another charge he said: "If I take work, it must be single-handed. I can no longer brook to walk in leading strings (as curate to a rector).''

He wrote to Wilberforce, then bishop of Oxford, and asked for employment. The bishop offered him the charge of St. Ebbe's, Oxford, a church in one of the worst parts of the town. He accepted the charge, and immediately his preaching there attracted attention. "The undergraduates, a sensitive touchstone of a man's worth, dropped in one by one at first, and then rushed to hear him in crowds." Here for the first time he was entirely free, able to say, without opposition from without, without a shadow of inward restraint, the thing in his own heart. Here, too, for the first time, perhaps, he rested firmly on principles which he had secured at the price of a terrible spiritual contest. He became more peaceful. The dark shadow of failure began to pass away."

Of the light into which he had come, and the resulting assurance henceforth enjoyed by him he thus speaks in his later letters: "I would not exchange the light I have for the twilight I have left for all that the earth can give. Clearer, brighter light every day and more assurance of what truth is and whom I serve. I walk not in doubt but in the light of noonday certainty." Of his pulpit teaching thenceforward he says: "I could not tell you too strongly my own deep and deepening conviction that the truths which I teach are true. Every year they shed fresh light on one another and seem to stretch into immensity. They explain to me life, God, and the Bible; and I am certain that

what fresh light I shall receive will be an expansion
and not a contradiction of what I have. The principles are rooted in human nature, God and the
being of things, and I find them at the root of every
page of Scripture."

The *chief* "principles" on which he taught were:

1. The establishment of positive truth instead
of the negative distruction of error.

2. Spiritual truth is descerned by the spirit instead of intellectually in propositions; and therefore truth should be taught suggestively not dog-
matically.

3. That belief in the human character of Christ's
humanity must be antecedent to belief in his divine
origin.

4. That Christianity, as its teachers should, works
from the inward to the outward, and not *vice versa*.

5. That truth is made up of two opposite propositions, and not found in a *via media* between the two.

6. The soul of goodness in things evil.

Mr. Robertson had been in charge of St. Ebbe's,
Oxford, only two months, when the rectorship of
Trinity Chapel, Brighton, was offered him. He
promptly declined it with its more ample salary and
larger prospect of influence, believing himself bound
in honor to stay where he was. He was induced,
however, by the trustees of Trinity to submit the
matter to his bishop, and the bishop advised him to
go. He accordingly entered upon his labors in
Brighton, August 15, 1847, in his thirty-second year.

Brighton is the great watering place of England.
If Cheltenham is like Saratoga, Brighton is like

Atlantic City. It had the attractions and difficulties of such a place. Some of the trials that had afflicted him at Cheltenham vexed him still at Brighton. People of all religious schools frequented it, and the new rector of Trinity quickly attracted their attention. The conservative, critical hearers of the Evangelical School detected a new strange note in his preaching. His views of religious truth, his modes of stating Christian doctrines, his interpretation of the Scriptures, seemed to them not only novel but at variance with the traditional belief of the Evangelical School, and they shook their heads in disapproval. Soon after his coming, early in the year of 1848, he began a course of lectures on the first book of Samuel. It will be remembered that those were exciting times in England, and the Continent of Europe was heaving with the throes of political and social excitement and of incipient revolution. In the exposition of that sacred book, and commenting upon the events recorded there, he had to treat of topics that were then engrossing much thought, and eagerly discussed in England; such topics as, the rights of rulers, the rights of property, the rights of labor, the brotherhood of man, etc. Says his biographer; "It was not his fault that these lectures, running side by side with the national convulsions and social excitements of Europe and England, had a double interest, an ancient and modern one." A cry was raised against him. He was spoken of as a revolutionist and a democrat. An anonymous letter was sent to the bishop accusing him of preaching on political subjects in a manner calculated to disturb still more the feelings of the workingmen of Brighton. He answered, that "if the principles revealed in the inspired history of Israelitish society happened to be universal, and to fit current events, it only proved the deep inspiration and universal character of the Bible, and he was not to be blamed."

He was charged with being a Radical in politics and in religion. To this charge he thus replies in a letter to a friend: "When I first heard the charge of radicalism, I was astounded. I had tried to *feel* the meaning of Christ's words and to make my heart beat with His; and so I became what they call a Radical. Nevertheless the Radicals and the Chartists refuse to own me as a brother, and call me a rabid Tory. However, of one thing I have become distinctly conscious, that my motto for life, my whole heart's expression, is, 'None but Christ'; not in the (so-called) evangelical sense, which I take to be the sickliest cant that has appeared since the Pharisees bare record to the gracious words that he spake, and then tried to cast him headlong from the hill of Nazareth; but in a deeper real sense, *the mind of Christ;* to feel as he felt; to judge the world and to estimate the world's maxims as he judged and estimated. That is to feel 'none but Christ.' But then in proportion as a man does that, he is stripping himself of garment after garment, till his soul becomes naked of that which once seemed part of himself; he is not only giving up prejudice after prejudice, but also renouncing sympathy after sympathy with friends whose smile and approbation was once his life, till he begins to suspect that he will be very soon alone with Christ."

Through his preaching and because of his friendly and sympathetic interest in the working classes, in common with Kingsley and Maurice, he was charged with Socialism, and heresy and general unsoundness. The *Record* newspaper, the organ of Evangelicalism, which had expressed suspicions about him when in Cheltenham, resumed its attacks. Referring to them in a letter to a friend he said: "God forbid they should ever praise me. One number alone contained four unscrupulous lies about me on no better evidence than that some one had told them, who had been told by some one else. They shall have no disclaimer from me. If the *Record* can put a man down, the sooner he is put down the better. The only time I have ever said anything about socialism in the pulpit' has been to preach against it. An evangelical clergyman admitted some proofs I had given of the *Record's* dishonesty, but said: 'Well, in spite of that, I like it, because it upholds the truth, and is a great witness for religion.' Said I, 'Is that the creed of *Evangelicalism?* A man may be a liar and slanderous, and still uphold the truth!' He felt an ineffable scorn for such a Christianity as that, and denied with indignation this claim that the *Record*, as the accredited organ of the Evangelical party, having been admitted by the confession of its own followers and supporters to be convicted of flagrant falsehood and dishonesty, could be said to "uphold the truth and be a great witness for religion." He insisted, and rightly, that it was untrue to Christ and false to its own past history, and hence said, rather harshly perhaps, "The evangelicalism (so-called) of the *Record* is an emasculated cur, snarling at what is better than itself."

If, in answer to his indignant inquiry, "Is that the creed of evangelicalism?" the supporters of that School assented, he did not hesitate to repudiate it. He was justified in doing so, as much as Luther and the Protestant Reformers were justified in seceding from the corrupt Catholic Church of their day. Dr. J. H. Jowett, in an admirable article (*The Congregationalist*, June 10, 1912) on "Trusting One's Instincts," rightly says, that in view of Christ's standard of judgment, "By their fruits ye shall know them": "We are not to be concerned with the label but with the fruit. Men are to be judged not by their professions, but by their character, not by their theology, but by their life." We lay the emphasis on the wrong thing, therefore, when we rate what has been reckoned a sound theology above a sound morality. Robertson, who had learned, as we have seen, the mind of Christ, by studying his teachings as few men of his time studied them, laid the emphasis where Christ laid it, and the religious world now reverences his memory for doing so.

It is distasteful to us to revive the memories of theological controversy with its bitter rancor and resentments after the period of more than sixty years, and when the participants in it have passed "to the world that will decide," as Baxter says, "all our controversies, and the safest passage thither is by peaceable holiness"; but we are justified, we think in doing so, since thus only can Robertson's violent break with "Evangelicalism" be excused, and the heated atmosphere of his environment at Cheltenham and Brighton be understood. His biographer speaks of "the intense sensitiveness which pervaded his whole nature" and says it was "the root of all that was peculiar in Robertson's character and correspondence." "His senses, his passions, his imagination, his conscience, his spirit, were so delicately wrought that they thrilled and vibrated to the slightest touch." Made morbid by disease, it was unquestionably an infirmity which sometimes betrayed itself especially in his letters to intimate friends. He tried, however, conscientiously to curb it, and he so schooled himself to patience and self-control that he rarely, in public, said or did anything unseemly. He *held on to himself*, that as a Christian, he might show "the meekness and gentleness of Christ."

But close observers discerned the truth. "His very calm," Lady Byron said, "was a hurricane." Rev. J. H. Jowett, D.D., calls this quality, however, a weakness that was like St. Paul's thorn in the flesh, which by God's grace turned to his advantage. "Robertson of Brighton," he says, "was extremely sensitive. He was easily jarred. His whole being was as full of feeling as the eye. He prayed for the removal of the infirmity, and the thorn remained. But his prayer was answered. His very weakness was made the vehicle of strength. His sensitiveness gave him his sense of awe and triumph in the presence of nature. It gave him his almost instinctive sense of the characters of men. It gave him his superlatively fine apprehension of the secrets of the Most High. God gave him a sufficiency of grace, and through his apparent infirmity God's power was made perfect." Falsehood and hypocrisy, cruelty and oppression, the sin of the strong against the weak, kindled his wrath, and his flaming indignation expressed itself in stirring eloquence. But we believe it was Christlike indignation, and that the eloquence it inspired was wholesome for men to hear. The people of Brighton soon realized it.

All classes were drawn to Trinity and it was crowded to the doors. Henry Crabbe Robinson, Lady Byron and other representatives of the literary class and of the aristocracy were there, and servants and workingmen. Thoughtful and eager-minded men came in from all parts of Brighton attracted not only by his eloquence but by his original thought, clear reasoning, and the affluence of his mind in illustrations of the truth. "His mind was crowded with images which he had received and arranged in a harmonious order. With these he lit up the subjects of his speech, flashing upon obstruse points the ray of an illustration, and that with a fullness of apt words, and with, at the same time, a reticence which kept the point clear. He united in a rare combination imaginative with dialectic power. He felt a truth before he proved it; but this felt, then his logical power came into play. He disentangled it from the crowd of images and thoughts that clustered round it. He exercised a serene choice over this crowd, and rejected what was superabundant. There was no confusion in his mind. Step by step he led his hearers, till at last he placed them on the summit whence they could see all the landscape of his subject in harmonious and connected order. He clothed in fresh brightness the truths which, because their garments were worn out, men had ignorantly imagined to be exhausted. He drew out the living inspiration of the Bible."

To his bishop he gave the following account of his mode of preparing his sermons: "The word *extempore* does not exactly describe the way I preach. I first make copious notes; then draw out a form (rough plan); afterwards write copiously, sometimes twice or thrice, the thoughts, to disentangle them and arrange them into a connected whole; then make a syllabus, and, lastly, a skeleton which I take into the pulpit."

The sermons thus carefully premeditated and prepared for delivery are, in the words of an intelligent judge: "The bloom and wonder of modern pulpit eloquence. They are charged so abundantly with arrows of lightning to flash home conviction on the conscience; they indicate such intense prophetic earnestness; they contain such fearless denunciations of evil, in high places and in low; they manifest such sympathy on the part of their author with the lowly, the hard working, the suffering and the poor; they display such a mastery of the latest European thought, so profound an acquaintance with both the letter and the spirit of the Scriptures,

as of the innermost secrets of the life which is 'hid
in God,'—its sorrows, its battling with doubts, its
triumph through clinging to the cross of Christ;
they disclose a creative ability to turn truisms into
living truths, or to convert the dry bones of orthodox
assertions into vital influences for the daily life, such
a grasp of great spiritual and historical principles,
such a power to sever the essential from the acci-
dental in the discussion of questions of Christian
casuistry, such wisdom and liberality in the treatment of subjects like that of the Sabbath, that
Robertson must be pronounced, of all later Christian
public speakers, *facile princeps*."

A wonderful thing about Robertson's sermons,
as we have remarked of those of some others, is
that they have not lost their interest and charm
because preached more than half a century ago.
They are not stale and juiceless; they are inspiring
and spiritually profitable still as the sermons of only
the greatest preachers are, like those of Chrysostom,
Cardinal Newman, Beecher and Brooks, and they
form a rich part of our literature.

His pulpit ministrations and his preaching are
thus described by persons who heard him: "I have
never heard the liturgy read as Mr. Robertson read
it. He carried its own spirit with him, and those
prayers, so often degraded by careless reading into
mere forms, were, from his voice, felt to be instinct
with a divine light and spirit. The grave earnestness and well-weighed emphasis with which he read
the Gospel of the day were absolutely an exposition
of its meaning."

In preaching, "so entirely was his heart in his words that he lost sight of everything but his subject. He not only possessed, but was possessed by his idea; and when all was over and the reaction came, he had forgotten, like a dream, words, illustrations, almost everything. But though he was carried away by his subject, he was sufficiently lord over his own excitement to prevent any loud or unseemly demonstration of it. His gesture was subdued. His voice, a musical, low, clear, penetrative voice, seldom rose; and when it did, it was in a deep volume of sound which was not loud, but toned like a great bell. It thrilled, but not so much from feeling as from the repression of feeling, and his face glowed as alabaster glows when lit up by an inward fire. And, indeed, brain and heart were on fire. He was being self-consumed. Every sermon in those latter days burnt up a portion of his vital power."

His congregation was often enthralled, as by a spell, by his preaching. One of his constant hearers says: "I cannot describe in words the strange sensation, during his sermon, of union with him and communion with one another which filled us as he spoke. I used to feel as if every one in the congregation must be thrilling with my emotion, and that his suppressed excitement was partly due to his consciousness of our excitement. Nor can I describe the sense we had of a higher Presence with us as he spoke, the sacred awe which filled our hearts, the hushed stillness in which the smallest sound was startling, the calmed eagerness of men who listened as if waiting for a word of revelation to resolve the doubt or to heal the sorrow of a life, the unexpected light which came upon the faces of some when an expression struck home and made them feel, in a moment of high relief from pain or doubt, 'this man speaks to me and his words are inspired by God,' and when the close came and silence almost awful fell upon the church, even after a sigh of relief from strained attention had ceased to come from all the congregation, I have often seen men so rapt that they could not move till the sound of the organ aroused them to the certainty that the preacher had ceased to speak."

Such witchery of speech, with its entrancing power, is a mark of the highest pulpit eloquence.

It is evident from these testimonies and a study of his sermons, that Robertson possessed to a remarkable degree the *personal qualities* of intensity of feeling, sensitiveness to the power of truth, and a receptive soul, responsive not only to truth's appeal but to the events and questions of the time. "His heart," says his biographer, "throbbed in response to the music of the march of the world, always to him a martial music. He spoke and thought best when great events encompassed him."

At the same time he was not hurried away by a hasty impulse; he was self-restrained and cautious. "Before he gave a public opinion on any subject, he studied it with care. He did not argue blindly on the outside, but sought to attain the central point of a question. But having come in this way to his opinion, he was bold to avow it. He was loyal to

God and his truth, though he might suffer reproach and ostracism because of it."

The conditions under which his ministry was exercised were peculiar and need to be considered, if we would clearly understand and appreciate this man's career and character.

(a) The External Contemporary Conditions of the Times

1. *It was a time of transition in theology.* Through the influence of German philosophy and Bible criticism, translated into English and interpreted by Coleridge and Carlyle and the Oxford scholars, the old doctrinal statements and theories were being questioned and discredited, and new theories and statements sought for and attempted. At such times there is usually much disquietude and alarm, and the religious world is divided between the liberals, who welcome inquiry and encourage discussion of the various points at issue in the belief that truth will be the gainer, and the conservatives, who would stifle inquiry and repress discussion, for fear that the truth will be the loser through decay of faith consequent upon the shock that is given to the popular mind concerning fundamental doctrines whose interpretation is changed and credibility thus shaken. Robertson, having passed through the crisis involved in this transition during the latter part of his stay at Cheltenham and the time of his visit to the Tyrol and the weeks of sojourn spent afterwards in Heidelberg just before going to

Brighton, and believing then that his own feet were planted on solid ground, which it would be in the interest of Christian truth and human happiness to disclose, he with characteristic courage straightway proclaimed his new views. "Thus," we are told "within the short space of six months he put himself into opposition with the whole accredited theological world of Brighton on the questions of the Sabbath, the Atonement, Inspiration and Baptism. He was not one who held what are called liberal opinions in the study, but would not bring them into the pulpit. He would not waver between truth to himself and success in the world. He was offered advancement in the Church, if he would abate the strength of his expressions with regard to the Sabbath. He refused the proffer. Far beyond all other perils which beset the Church, was, he thought, this peril, that men, who were set apart to speak the truth and to live above the world, should substitute conventional opinions for eternal truths. He respected his own conscience, believed in his own native force and in the divine fire within him. He endeavored to receive, without the intervention of commentators, immediate impressions from the Bible. To these impressions he added the individual life of his own heart and his knowledge of the life of the great world."

2. *It was a time of transition in politics.* It was the time of the volcanic outburst of February, 1848, in Paris, when Lamartine proclaimed a republic in France, and the cry of "Liberty," "Equality," and "Fraternity" reached across the English Channel,

and the demands involved in this outcry were being eagerly discussed in England; the time of the Chartist Movement and Kingsley's "Alton Lock" and "Yeast"; the time of Cobden's agitation for the abolishment of the oppressive Corn Laws, and the establishment of the principle of Free Trade. Robertson's spirit shared the hopes of the English common people. He rejoiced, we are told, in the prospective "downfall of old oppressions," and in the "young cries of Freedom" thought he discerned the sound of the Chariot of the Son of Man coming to vindicate the cause of the poor."

He was, however, by birth and education an aristocrat, like Wendell Phillips, and, therefore, conservative in his tastes and feelings; but also, like Phillips, he was by conviction and principle a democrat, and, notwithstanding his aristocratic leanings, advocated with all his powers of eloquence the cause of the poor and oppressed, and devoted himself to their welfare. By so doing he was denounced as a revolutionist. He foresaw that this would be the case. He says: "It brings no pleasure to a minister of Christ. It makes him personal enemies. It is ruin to his worldly interests and, worse than all to a sensitive heart, it makes coldness where there should be cordiality. Yet through life I am ready to bear this." He "was not, however, swept away into the alluring current of socialism. He systematically opposed socialism, on economical and Christian grounds, as dangerous to the state and destructive to the liberty it professed to confer. His aristocratic tastes made it impossible he should be a radical. The result was that, speaking at one time like a Liberal, and at another like a Conservative he was misunderstood, and reckoned an enemy by the extreme spirits of both parties." Conscious of this discord in himself, he thought it marred his usefulness. We think it caused him much unhappiness, but made him to a considerable extent *the reconciler of parties.* This belief is justified and witnessed to by the inscription on the monument erected to his memory in Brighton: "He awakened the holiest feelings in poor and rich, in ignorant and learned; therefore is he lamented as their guide and comforter by many who in the band of brotherhood have erected this monument."

3. *It was a time of transition in the style of preaching.* He marks a new epoch in the methods of the pulpit and in Homiletic literature. It is the epoch of textual analysis and interpretation. His sermons are worthy of special study because of the superior method of construction used in them. He may be said to have revived the old Scotch manner of preaching; he introduced into England and carried to a great degree of excellence, the textual and expository methods used by Maclaren and carried by him almost to perfection. We cannot help thinking that Maclaren was a careful student of Robertson's sermons, and adopted them as the models upon which he fashioned his own pulpit work. Robertson's preaching was textual preaching of the best sort. In it he adhered closely to the historic sense of the sacred writers; aimed to know precisely, and to convey to his hearers, their point of view and their

intention; and to set forth the full significance of their teaching.

Never was there a preacher who conveyed to his hearers a better or truer idea of the wealth of meaning contained in the Scriptures. He had what a German theologian calls "exegetical divination" and what Dr. Brastow thinks may more appropriately be called "homiletic divination," a power of insight into the ethical and spiritual suggestions of the Scriptures. This natural power of spiritual insight was aided and strengthened by his careful, accurate scholarship, and the rich stores of information garnered in his general reading. Everything in him, his imagination, his vigorous reasoning faculties, his opulant scholarship, his vivid apprehension of Christ, his personal experience of Christian truth, which vitalized his whole being, contributed to the Biblical suggestiveness of his sermons.

(b) PERSONAL CONDITIONS

1. *Broken health.* He performed his remarkable work in Brighton handicapped by poor health. His health was incurably shattered by his hard work at Cheltenham, by his neglect of needed exercise, and by the mental and spiritual distress caused by his loss of faith in, and his breaking away from, the traditional school of theology. He thus speaks of himself just before entering on his work at Brighton: "I have been very unwell, thoroughly done up, mentally and bodily." Though he could say that, by reason of the mountain air and hard exercise

found in the Tyrol, he had "got back something like calmness and health again," he never really recovered. He remained to the end of his days, through all those six years in Brighton, a sorely shattered man. He had been there scarcely six months when he wrote to a friend: "In outward success all looks well; consequently I work in good spirits. But Sunday night, Monday, and all Tuesday are days of wretched exhaustion, actual nervous pain." "The excitement is killing. I begin to fear I shall never keep it up." "Brighton air is wonderful, but even that fails." In vain he tried to allay and subdue this killing excitability by giving more attention to exercise, and by placing himself under the healing influence of Nature, by walking along the edge of the cliffs by the sea and sitting down where he could command a full view of sea and sky, to soothe and cure the fever of his heart. He could not get rid of it. It grew worse and worse. The reaction from preaching left him sleepless, despondent, wretched.

2. *A Chronic Morbid Condition of Mind.* The wonder is that his mind was not paralyzed or otherwise made incapable of work by his excitability. But it seemed to give him a preternatural power of thought and mental achievement. Some of his finest sermons were thought out when distress, it might be supposed, "only gave him leave to feel." He could concentrate his mind, however, upon his work in the wildest hours of nervous excitement, and the pain which racked his body and sensitive soul like a spur to his genius made him most crea-

tive. In these states of excitement he was most brilliant and his most startling eloquence was produced.

He might, perhaps, have recovered, had he been willing to favor himself; had he demanded, when he found himself breaking down, a long release from his work; or if, while continuing in the harness, he had worked with moderation. But his vacations were short, either from imagined necessity, or choice. He never took more than a few weeks, when, as he himself confessed, he was not fit for ministerial work and needed a protracted release from it. "I want years and years to calm me," he said, "My heart is too feverish—quivers and throbs as flesh recently cut by the surgeon's knife."

In this invalid state of shattered nerves, tortured body, and mental feverishness, he ought to have avoided every unnecessary draft upon his energies, and resolutely declined those extra burdens which regard for thoughtless friendship or the desire to do good prompted him to undertake. Had his friends and admirers understood his case, how much he needed rest, and how fatal every added task would prove, they would never have wished him to perform for them those acts of service which ultimately cost him and them so dear. But they did not understand, and he would not tell them, and so in the very time he was suffering from those dreadful reactions from preaching, he performed tasks that were destroying his chance to live and hurrying him to his grave. He wrote long letters to explain to inquirers the religious subjects he had discussed, but had not made quite clear in his sermons; he prepared literary lectures for the instruction or financial profit of the Working Men's Institute; he served on committees charged with framing the policy of the Institute, and he was their adviser when critical questions arose for their consideration. He projected courses of expository lectures upon different books of the Scriptures, which required much special study in preparation, gave extra time and labor in preparing a special Training Class of the Church for Confirmation and Church Membership; and, strangest of all, on Sunday evening, when spent and weary with the day's preaching, he wrote out for a friend from memory the sermons of Sunday morning. "It was peculiarly irksome to him," his biographer says, "but he did it freely and gladly because impelled by friendship. He forgot the toil, but the toil did not forget to produce its fruit of exhaustion."

The world has profited by that sacrifice of friendship. Those sermons thus reported, are most of them published as he wrote them, in the volumes that were given to the world after his death, and which created for him the world-wide fame as a preacher he had not till then attained; but the possession of this treasure, secured at such cost, is associated in us with a feeling of pain at the thought of the cruelty involved in lashing that jaded overworked spirit to the task. Not even our gratitude, nor the fame which thus accrued to him, can make that sacrifice seem right or an adequate compensation for the misery it cost him.

There is another thing he ought to have done. He should have lived more in the society of friends and his fellow men, instead of secluding himself from them. But he yielded to the isolating influences which one feels who is greatly misunderstood, misrepresented, disapproved of, and censured for deviating from the beaten track of opinion, and for advocating opinions that are new and supposed to be dangerous. His sensitive soul smarted under the harsh judgments pronounced against him as a teacher of error and a friend of socialists, and he withdrew more and more from society. This made him suspicious and lonely and a sufferer of the ills that visit a life of solitude. Instead of the strength and inspiration of Christian fellowship, he experienced the weakness and the depression of mind consequent upon the feeling of being deserted. The wonder is that this morbid conditon did not more infect his sermons with gloom. In them there is not much trace of it; his genuine piety preserved them from it, but in his letters it breathes a sadness and gloom which are painful. It is no wonder that his body and mind could not endure long the oppression of it; that he died prematurely in the middle of his thirty-eighth year, his death being preceded by symptoms of distress and breakdown most pathetic. "Somehow," he says in the last year of his life, "I cannot originate thoughts and subjects now, as I used." "I shall not be able to go on much longer if this continues; whole tracts of brain seem to be losing their faculty and becoming quite torpid and impotent; memory and grasp are both going, and with an incessant call for fresh thought, this feeling is a more than ordinarily painful one." These and other tokens of mental failure that might be gathered from his letters remind us of Luther's remark concerning his mind when it had begun through the long wear of theological conflict and ceaseless toil to lose its power: "It is like an old knife, the steel edge of which has been all worn away from much and constant whetting."

More pathetic even than these signs of creeping mental paralysis was his discouragement and depression of heart under the impression that his ministry was a failure. For this he himself was partly, if not entirely, to blame, on account of his manifested repugnance to hearing, or receiving any commendation of his preaching, through which he might have learned how much it helped and benefited his hearers. "If," says his biographer, "he hated one thing more than another it was the reputation of being a popular preacher." So he coldly repelled the grateful thanks of his hearers for the benefit they had received, as if they were empty compliments, fulsome flattery, which, as imputing · to him a childish vanity, no self-respecting preacher can bear to listen to. Such applause galled and stung him into galling words, and few cared to provoke such an answer a second time. Thus repelling and hushing the voices of praise with which his friends and hearers longed to express their gratification and gratitude for his sermons, he was wilfully blind to the unmistakable good they had wrought. We wish that the sadness which oppressed his heart could have been brightened by some prophetic foresight of the marvelous appreciation and world-wide enthusiasm those sermons were to produce when published after his death and the world enjoyed the benefit of his ministry. Dr. Brastow truly says: "He did not know how well he wrought. He did not know the full import, reach, or measure of his prophetic utterance. He did not know how deeply he spoke into the lives of men. Never was man more unconscious of what he was doing for others, for the Church, for the world. It was in much a sad history, but most precious for the multitudes of needy men whom he has helped. More fully than any other English preacher of his century has he spoken the true prophetic word for hungry and disquieted human hearts." (Brastow's "Modern Representative preachers.")

It ought further to be said that like all preachers who "have spoken the true prophetic word," Robertson was more than an eloquent preacher. He was a *seer;* he possessed the spiritual insight and the religious feeling which qualified him to be a pioneer in a new advanced age of theological teaching. Like Horace Bushnell and the two Beechers, besides the admirable sermons he and they gave to us, he is to be credited with the wholesome "modernism" that has characterized the Protestantism of this age as well as the Roman Catholicism, and which signifies the change in the religious ideas and spiritual apprehension of Christianity and its interpretation due to the fresh and more scholarly study of the Scriptures and the new light shed upon them by the development of modern science and the new psychology of today. The Christianity of our times is more practical than speculative; it emphasizes the ethical side of the religious life, and the importance of the ethical precepts of the New Testament, and of the example and spirit of Christ as matters of far more concern to Christians than the definitions and dogmas of theology which in times past have so much exercised the mind and interest of the Church. This shifting of emphasis, unmistakable in the thought of these times, and wholesome as most men think, is largely due to Robertson and other preachers of "the true prophetic word." As the Old Testament prophets, Isaiah, Amos, Hosea and others, saved ancient Judaism from the growing narrowness and false interpretations of the Scribes and Pharisees which were tending to falsify it as the truth of God, so Robertson and his successors in the same line have saved Christianity from errors of doctrine and practice that were tending to stifle its spiritual life and discredit it in the eyes of the world.

VIII

ALEXANDER McLAREN

VIII

ALEXANDER McLAREN

1826–1901

Dr. McLaren is one of the greatest and most interesting preachers of the last century. The recent biography by his sister-in-law, published by Hodder and Stoughton, gives us an interesting and seemingly just account of his life and personal character, which is both trustworthy and complete. "In this book," the author says in the preface, "Dr. McLaren's name is spelt as he signed it, not Maclaren as in his published works."

From the materials furnished by this biography we derive the particulars in regard to the subject of our sketch. He was born in Glasgow, February 11, 1826. He was the son of David and Mary McLaren, and the youngest child in their family of six. His parents were Christian people of the Puritan type. His father, David McLaren, was a business man but "eagerly devoted his leisure hours to Christian work"—especially to preaching the gospel. "He had many business anxieties," his son says, "but his children remember to have heard him say that when he began his preparation for Sabbath on the Saturday afternoon, all his troubles passed from his mind, and left him undisturbed till Monday morning, when the fight was renewed."

"His ministry," his son adds, "was marked by much intellectual vigor and clearness. It was richly scriptural, expository, and withal, earnestly evangelistic. Its key-note was: 'That which we have seen with our eyes—and our hands have handled of the word of life—we declare unto you.' His children set on his tombstone the two words 'steadfast, unmoveable.'"

The father, like his son, was a Baptist, and Alexander inherited from him, besides this denominational bias, mental and spiritual traits.

The mother, Mary Wingate, was a person, "whose patient fortitude, calm wisdom and changeless love were her husband's treasure for many years of mingled sunshine and storm," and left a memory "fragrant to her children."

Alexander went through the course of the High school of Glasgow, and entered its University in his fifteenth year, but he continued there only a year because of the removal of his family to London. In that one year, however, he distinguished himself by his superior scholarship, so that at its close he received several prizes. "He remembered all his life," we are told, "that prize giving. He was seated far back, and the first time his name was called he had to be waited for, so the Master remarked to the Lord Provost who presided, 'This young gentleman has to appear so often that he had better be accommodated with a seat nearer the table.'"

Cambridge and Oxford in those days were not open to Non-conformists, so after examination, he entered, in 1842, the Baptist College at Stepney, now transplanted to Regent Park, London. The committee before whom he appeared were struck with his boyish appearance and also with the excellence of his examination papers.

The principal of Stepney College at that time was Dr. Benjamin Davis. To him Alexander McLaren "owed his lifelong habit of patient, minute study of the original, not only in the preparation of sermons, but in his daily reading of Scriptures for his own spiritual life."

It is proper that here we should speak of the conscious beginning and development of his religious life. Of course, being the child of such Christian parents, he was the subject of early religious impressions, but these did not crystallize into definite shape until, in those years of his boyhood, he joined a Bible class taught by the Rev. David Russell, a Congregational minister and afterward his brother-in-law. In connection with this Bible class Mr. Russell held some revival meetings which he attended with the result that, "to him, under God," Dr. McLaren said in his old age, "I owe the quickening of early religious impressions into loving faith and surrender, and to him I owe also much wise and affectionate counsel in my boyish years." He joined the Hope St. Baptist Church, Glasgow, when fourteen years of age, and when, two or three years later, he entered the Baptist College at Stepney with its theological course of study, it was with the purpose of preparing himself for the ministry. Shortly before his death, he said: "I cannot recall ever having had any hesitation as to being a minister; it seems to me it must have been simply taken for granted by my father and mother and myself; it just had to be."

Before he had completed his twentieth year, he was sent by the authorities of Stepney College to preach one Sunday, November 16, 1845, at Portland Chapel, Southampton. His preaching gave such satisfaction that he was invited to preach there three months. The trial resulted in a call by the church to be its pastor. The place was not very inviting—the congregation was small and the salary meagre, and the chapel had a past history that was clouded with failure. But he accepted the call notwithstanding, saying: "If the worse comes to the worst, I shall at all events not have to reflect that I have killed a flourishing plant, but only assisted at the funeral of a withered one." He began his pastorate there, June 28, 1846, when he was but little more than twenty years of age, and he remained in it twelve years. For ten of those years he remained single, working strenuously to build up his "poor little congregation," which gradually but steadily grew in numbers and influence. Later in life, when he had become a famous preacher he said that he was "thankful that the early part of his ministry had been spent with such a church in a quiet corner of England where he had leisure to grow and time to think." "The trouble with most of you young fellows," he said to a company of young ministers, "is that you are pitchforked at once into prominent positions and have to spend your time in attending meetings, anniversaries, and even breakfasts, when you ought to be at home studying your Bible."

His conception of the Christian ministry was that it was preëminently a ministry of Christian truth, and he applied himself diligently to the study of the Christian Scriptures. He studied them not only as presented in the best English versions, but in the original Hebrew and Greek. This was evident from his manner of reading the Scriptures in public worship, from the emphasis given to the significant words, from the clear insight into their real meaning revealed and the sympathetic interpretation he gave of it because of his previous careful study. "Every day," we are told, "he read a chapter in the Hebrew Old Testament and one in the Greek New Testament." He was a careful exigete of the Bible and on his careful exegesis he based his illuminating expositions of its truth. "The best lesson," says Dr. Parkhurst, "which McLaren teaches the preachers of today is the necessity of direct and absorbing work upon the Bible, in order to be able to speak with interest and power; and that the Bible only needs hard, faithful study to yield that which will be most fresh, vivid and interesting and helpful to our congregations."

Those years of his young manhood with that small Southampton church were formative years, years determinative of his destiny, as the first years of a man's ministry usually are. In them his habits of study and his methods of work were formed and perfected; in them his conceptions and ideals of ministerial achievement were shaped and tested, and in them his powers of thought and communication were developed to a very high degree of excellence. He always endeavored to do his best. He lavished upon that small congregation of humble people the best efforts of a rarely gifted mind and earnest soul. His development and progress were therefore constant, rapid, remarkable. The people of that early Southampton congregation watched his growth with interest, and keenly enjoyed the benefit of it. Appreciating his worth, they forecast the eminence that awaited him in the ministry, and when he had reached the meridian of his power and fame thought his preaching did not surpass that of the days when he was their minister. His preaching then, like Beecher's early preaching in Indianapolis, had notes of eloquence that distinguished it in the glorious maturity of his later years.

From the beginning, his constant aim, perseveringly adhered to and strenuously labored for, was to perfect himself in the preacher's art, so as to make himself a successful preacher of the gospel.

In his ministry, he magnified the preacher's office and in his practice exalted it above the pastoral office and its duties. Not that he underrated and disparaged pastoral work; he commended and honored it, indeed, in those who were specially fitted for it; but he believed, that for himself preaching was his special vocation and he endeavored to fulfill it to the utmost of his ability.

In the fulfillment of it he adopted the following

method and principles of action, in preparation for the pulpit:

"I began my ministry," he says, "with the resolution that I would not write my sermons, *but would think and feel them*, and I have stuck to it ever since. It costs quite as much time in preparation as writing, and a far greater expenditure of nervous energy in delivery, but I am sure that it is best for me, and equally sure that everybody has to find out his own way." He "so *saturated* his mind with his subject that facing his congregation, looking into their eyes, his thoughts clothed themselves in suitable words."

But, as he further explains, though he resolved not to write his sermons, he did not entirely discard the help of the pen. "I write my sermons in part," he says. "The amount of written matter varies. When I can, I like to write a couple of sentences or so of introduction, in order to get a fair start, and for the rest I content myself with jottings, fragmentary hints of a word or two each, interspersed here and there with a fully written sentence. Illustrations and metaphors I never write; a word suffices for them. If I have *heads*, I word these carefully and I like to write the closing sentences. I do not adhere to what is written, as there is very little of it that is sufficiently consecutive. I make no attempt to reproduce more than the general course of thought and constantly find that the best bits of my sermon make themselves in preaching. I *do adhere to* my *introductory* sentences, which serve to shove me off into deep water; beyond that I let the moment shape the thing. Expressions I do not prepare; if I can get the fire alight, that is what I care for most." "This is my ideal," he says of the method thus sketched. "A sufficiently scrappy one you will think, but I am frequently obliged to preach with much less preparation. The amount written varies from about six or seven pages of ordinary note-paper to the barest skeleton that would go in half a page."

If we had only this sketch to judge by, we might fairly think him a careless workman. It seems to indicate that he left much to chance and the hope of a happy inspiration at the time of preaching, instead of guarding by the most careful preparation against the possibility of failure. But we should make a great mistake if we should form such an opinion of him or of his work. His seeming carelessness is that of conscious mastery of the conditions of success. As a matter of fact, he left little to chance; his preparation for preaching was so thorough and painstaking that there was only the smallest possibility of failure. Though he did not write out his sermons, though his preparation seemed limited to the making of a meagre outline, his *prevision* of their contents was usually clear and certain. He knew exactly what he wanted to say, though the precise language in which he was to express his thought was not previously settled upon and fixed in writing. He secured this unerring certainty of thought and expression by the unwearied patience and unstinted labor given to the previous study and meditation of his themes. He thus acquired an opulent mind, which never lacked good things to say, nor words, *the right words*, to express them.

In his preparation for the pulpit he observed the following principles, which are gathered from the interesting and instructive address, entitled "An Old Preacher on Preaching" delivered in 1901 at the City Temple in London at a joint meeting of the Baptist and Congregational Unions. The principles enumerated shaped his preaching through all his ministry.

(1) *Deference to the teaching of God's word and submission of mind to it as containing the truth which the Christian minister is summoned to proclaim.* "This teaching of God is found in the Bible," and makes its study supremely important. "A preacher," he says, "who has steeped himself in the Bible will have a clearness of out-look which will illuminate many dark things, and a firmness of touch which will breed confidence in him among his hearers. He will have the secret of perpetual freshness, for he cannot exhaust the Bible." "Our sufficiency is of God, and God's sufficiency will be ours in the measure in which we steadfastly follow out the purpose of making our preaching truly Biblical."

At his Ministerial Jubilee he said of his own endeavor: "I have tried to make my ministry a Ministry of Exposition of Scripture. I know that it has failed in many respects, but I will say that I have endeavored from the beginning to the end to make that the characteristic of all my public work. I have tried to preach Jesus Christ, and the Jesus

Christ not of the Gospels only, but the Christ of the Gospels and Epistles; He is the same Christ."

(2) *Every preacher by independent study of the Bible should ascertain for himself the truth of God to be found in it.* Dr. McLaren condemns those ✦ who "get their opinions" of Christian truth from others instead of forming them for themselves. "These opinions do not grow, are not shaped by patient labor, but are imported into the new owner's mind, ready-made in Germany or elsewhere, but not in his own workshop." "We have need to remember," he says, "the woes pronounced on two classes of prophets; 'those who stole the word, every man from his neighbor, and those who prophesied out of their own hearts, having seen nothing and heard no voice from on high.' We have to be sure that we stand on our own feet and see with our own eyes; and on the other hand we have to see that the Word, which is in that sense our own, is in a deeper sense not our own but God's. We have to deal at first hand with Him and to suppress self that He may speak."

(3) *The habit of brooding over a text or passage of Scripture in a devout spirit to ascertain its teaching is illuminating and profitable.* "This is sometimes ✦ called the 'incubation of a text' and often results in rich and surprising disclosures of meaning. As one reads or listens, he says, 'Yes, that was all in the text. Why had no one discovered it before?' We need for the prophet's office much secluded fellowship with God, who 'wakens' his servant's ear morning by morning and gives him 'the tongue of

them that are taught.' No man will ever be the Lord's prophet, however eloquent or learned he may be, unless he knows what it is to sit silent before God and in the silence to hear the still, small, most mighty voice that penetrates the soul, and to the hearing ear is sweet as harpers harping with their harps and louder than the noise of many waters."

His power of productive thinking became at length spontaneous. The subject definitely fixed upon, whether of sermon or address, "it goes simmering through my head wherever I am."

At the request of his friend, Prof. T. H. Pattison, Professor of Homiletics in the Rochester Theological Seminary, he wrote to the students there this word of counsel: "I sometimes think that a verse in one of the Psalms carries the whole pith ✗ of homiletics—'While I was musing the fire burned, then spake I with my tongue.' Patient meditation, resulting in kindled emotion and the flashing up of truth into warmth and light ('I must give it red-hot,' he said) and then, and not till then, the rush of speech 'moved by the Holy Ghost'— these are the processes which will make sermons live things with hands and feet, as Luther's words were said to be. May I add another text, which contains as complete a description of the contents as the psalm does of its genesis? 'Whom we preach' there is the evangelistic element, which is foundation of all, and is proclamation with the loud voice, the curt force, the plain speech of a herald; and there is, too, the theme, namely, the Person, not a set of doctrines, but a Person whom we can know only by doctrines, and whom, if we know, we shall surely have some doctrine concerning. 'Warning every man'—there is the ethical side of preaching; and 'teaching every man'—there is the educational aspect of the Christian ministry. These three must never be separated, and he is the best minister of Jesus Christ, who keeps the proportion of them most clearly in mind and braids all the strands together in his ministry into a 'three-fold cord, not quickly broken.' "

(4) *The minister needs to bring the truth thus found to the test of his own experience.* This was not only a fine theory with him, it was confirmed and acted upon continually by him in his practice. His preaching was that of a spiritually-minded *witness* to the truth he proclaimed. "I have always found," he says, "that my own comfort and efficiency in preaching have been in direct proportion to the frequency and depth of my daily communion with God. 'I have tried to preach Christ' as if I be-lieved in him. The root of all is that we ourselves should feed on the truth we preach to others. The preacher has need of the personal element in his message; he has to speak as one who has felt the rapture of the joyful news which he proclaims."

This principle, we have repeatedly said, is essential to the preacher's greatest success. It cannot be too often or too strongly insisted upon. "Some preachers fail in the pulpit," says a thoughtful and sagacious observer, "because the truths uttered are not first *vitalized* in the seed-plot of a living experience. Such preachers are dry and unimpressive. What they have to teach is truth perhaps, but truth second-hand, with no stamp of individuality, or certification of its genuineness derived from the preacher's own verification of it. On the other hand, the simplest truth drawn fresh from the well-head of a living experience carries with it an unmistakable stamp of personal attestation and genuineness. It has a strange power of attraction and impression. Even the most captious cease to cavil when they hear it, silenced and awed by the demonstration of the spirit thus given it.

A sermon from a preacher of this sort is what Alexander Knox says every sermon should be, "a cordial communication of vitalized truth." The sermons of McLaren were of this kind. We have the proof of it in his conception of the work of the ministry and the qualifications he demanded of the preacher. Besides declaring, as just quoted, that "the preacher has need of the personal element in his message," he says, "The preacher is spoken of in the New Testament as a 'herald'; this title implies that his proclamation be plain, clear, assured. He is not to speak timidly, as if diverse winds of doctrine had blown back his voice into his trumpet. He needs to deliver his good news with urgency, as if it was of some moment that people should know and accept it. Is that note of urgency audible, as it should be, in our preaching?

"The evangelist has also need of tenderness. 'We entreat as though God did beseech by us.' What outgush of sympathetic yearning can be too great fitly to bear on its current the message of a love which died to save? Are we not too little accustomed to preach with our hearts?"

(5) *He took scrupulous care in his preaching to convey to his hearers the exact truth of God which he had learned.* "The preacher is not to bring an ambiguous message in cloudy words," is one of his pithy sayings. He therefore aimed to be just to the sense of his text. Dr. John Brown says that in his earlier ministry Dr. McLaren's fastidiousness in the choice of words led him sometimes, when preaching, to pause until he found fitting expression for his thought, refusing to accept any but the best language in which to clothe his ideas. Practice after a while gave him readiness and skill in the use of that choice, flexible, clear English style, which distinguishes to a remarkable degree his published sermons, none of which he permitted to be published until he had reached his full maturity.

(6) *He bestowed much labor and pains upon the plans of his sermons.* The basis of his sermon plan is usually a careful textual analysis with a large element of exposition. His introductions are generally models of careful, skillful exposition. His topics and divisions are solidly based upon the results of his analysis and careful exegesis. In his handling of the text, "you may be sure that the meaning he gives is, so far as he can find it, honestly derived from the Scripture passage used and not unfairly forced upon it." There is often great felicity in his interpretation and statements of the teaching of his texts. Examples: sermons 1,

19, 21 of the first series of "Sermons preached in Manchester."

The *partitioning* of his discourse on the lines made by his textual analysis is the work of a master-workman. It is at once evident that we have no careless bungler here. On this account when he had attained the maturity of his powers and perfection of his skill, because of the value of his work as affording the best models of homiletic skill and achievement, McLaren was called" the Preachers' Preacher," *i. e.*, a preacher such as they especially appreciate, and whom they find it profitable to study for the superiority of his method and the inspiring excellence of his work.

Preparing himself for his pulpit by this method and in accordance with these working principles he became, even while in Southampton, a marked man in the Baptist religious body; so that when the important church in the Union Chapel, Manchester, was left without a pastor, in 1858, he was called to its service, and ministered to it until 1903, a period of forty-five years. Entering upon his pastorate there at the age of thirty-two and continuing in it to the age of seventy-seven, his long ministry to that church and congregation had, of course, its different stages: its stage of early increasing splendor, of meridian glory, and of slowly waning brightness like that of the late afternoon; but from first to last it was a great and most successful ministry. "Perhaps no preacher," said Sir William Robertson Nicoll concerning him when near the end of it, "has ever ploughed so straight and sharp a furrow across the field of life, never looking aside, never turning back, maintaining his power and his freshness through all the long years that stretch between his early beginning and the present day." Other testimonies as to his greatness as a sermon-maker and preacher might be quoted by the score. At his Ministerial Jubilee it was the general opinion expressed by the letters received and the addresses heard, that Dr. McLaren had "enriched the pulpit literature of our times with treasures which the Christian Church will not willingly let perish."

Especially striking and specific is the testimony of an eminent American preacher, Dr. Parkhurst of New York. He says: "Roaming about a theological library, a volume of 'Sermons preached in Manchester' caught my eye. We opened by chance and began to read. The sermon was upon Heb. 12: 1. (19th sermon, first series of the "Sermons in Manchester"). Surely it was a find to us! It brought just the message which we had long needed and been unconsciously seeking. That sermon wrought a revolution in our apprehension of Christianity, and in our preaching. When we planned to cross the Atlantic, we said, 'We will see and hear McLaren,' and we did it, going two hundred miles for the purpose. 'The Union Chapel' was a brick building seating fifteen hundred people. Two thousand were packed into it that day, the people crowding in chairs close up to and back of the pulpit. The preacher then was in his sixty-first year. In personal appearance he was thin, tall, spare, with an attractive face. When young he must have been a handsome man. He did not look clerical. He wore no pulpit gown, not even the ministerial white cravat. In preaching he had no manuscript or notes before him. In the introduction he clearly announced his subject, and told his hearers how, *i. e.*, in what order, he proposed to present it. Soon his subject possesses him and he takes fire. His thought transforms him. His voice becomes resonant, tender, impressive. It seems as if God was speaking to you. Every person in the house is held in solemn and impressive awe of the truth. 'That is preaching,' I said, 'and we have not heard the like in Europe.' "

Further evidence of his greatness is found in *his skillful application of the gospel to men.* He wrought out for himself, and for the use of the ministry, in his published sermons, the best explication we know of the plan of salvation disclosed in the New Testament. "It is here," says Dr. John Brown, "that Dr. McLaren's distinctive excellence as a preacher shows itself. Through a long public life he has been a continuous, profound, accurate and prayerful student of God's revelation, and at the same time a close observer of the actual facts of religious experience as found in the living men and women of the church of God. In this way he has attained to something like a clear and coherent science of that spiritual life which is derived from Christ and maintained by the spirit of God; and as we might expect from the character of the man this science underlies all his teaching." (See "Puritan Preachers and Preaching," Yale Lectures by John Brown D.D.)

Examples of Dr. McLaren's doctrinal teaching are found in sermons 8, 9, 10, 11 and 20 of the third series of "Sermons preached in Manchester." In these sermons, and others, we are shown how "the law of the spirit of life in Jesus Christ sets us free from the law of sin and death"; and how "the word of Gods' grace is able to build men up and to give them an inheritance amongst all them that are sanctified." For a clear and succinct statement of this "Science of Spiritual Life," as formulated by Dr. McLaren, we refer to Dr. Brown's instructive study of him. Though possibly called "obsolete theology" by some, it is, to many others, nevertheless as vital and enduring as the teaching of the New Testament and of human experience.

What were the personal qualities which have made Dr. McLaren so great a preacher? We find the following spoken of or clearly indicated by his published sermons:

(1) *An impressive personal presence and delivery in the pulpit.* "He has a face," says Professor Pattison, "which, in its profile, at times suggests that of Dante; eyes of wonderful luster and depth; a tall lithe figure; appropriate and effective gesture; and a varied voice, which, while retaining enough of the Scottish accent to make it pathetic, is more remarkable for its power to give a sharp and crisp accentuation to certain words."

An Australian journalist, describing his preaching, when Dr. McLaren visited that continent, says:

"A wondrously pathetic little bit in the sermon about Abraham and Isaac going up Moriah will not soon be forgotten. Here the voice changed, softened and seemed to linger over the words: 'Where is the lamb?' While the answer, 'My son, God will provide himself a lamb,' was like the wail of a breaking heart."

Such power of managing the voice, so as to give to striking situations and utterances a deep, lasting impression and a haunting lodgment in the memory, is rare in public speakers and of great value.

(2) *Sanity of mind.* By reason of this, his views of Christian truth and its application to human needs and diverse situations were always marked by justness and sobriety. The truth has received no distortion, or refraction, or false coloring, in its passage through his mind because of any morbid tendency or eccentricity. His estimates and statements are fair and trustworthy, and his hearers are inspired with confidence in him because of his obvious candor and justness. They do not think it necessary to discount and modify what he says, to obtain the real truth.

(3) *Penetration, whereby he discerned the hidden treasures of truth and its manifold implications.* His natural power of penetration was doubtless increased and quickened by his constant study of the Bible, and his much thinking upon its truth. "The entrance of God's word giveth light," and "in His light we see light."

(4) *Keen religious sensibility.* This gave warmth and intensity to his religious feelings and his utter-

ances of Christian truth, caused him to kindle easily in the presence of a congregation for whom he had, as he thought, an important divine message, and made his sermons aflame with energy and persuasive appeal. This sensibility to truth and eagerness to impart it to men and persuade them to heed it, is the orator's distinctive gift, and Professor Pattison says of McLaren: "He has what is rare in the preacher, the scholar's mind coupled with the orator's heart." It is a quality, however, that distinguishes all great preachers.

(5) Another quality, which he possessed in common with other great and popular preachers, was *a lively and fruitful imagination*, with which to illustrate and glorify the Christian truth he presented. "In freshness and fertility of illustration," says Professor Pattison, "he is unexcelled by any contemporaneous preacher." We find ample proof of this in his published sermons. Metaphors and similes of a striking and beautiful kind abound in them. You can scarcely find a sermon, in which there is not found, pictured in full, or suggested, some impressive image that adorns and makes memorable the truth set forth. Read over the 8th, 9th, 20th, and 21st sermons of the first series of the "Sermons Preached in Manchester"; or the 1st, 2d, and 20th of the third series, for examples. Note the variety and the originality of his illustrations and the different fields from which he derives them. He makes nature, art, history, and the scenes of man's common toil, all tributary to his purpose to explain and exalt the truth. We

here give a few specimens: "You and I write our
lives as if on one of those 'manifold' writers which
you use. A thin filmy sheet *here*, a bit of black
paper below it; *but the writing goes through upon the
next page*, and when the blackness that divides two
worlds is swept away, *there*, the history of each
life remains legible in eternity."

"The only question worth asking in regard to
the externals of our life is, 'how far does each thing
help me to be a good man?' And to care whether
a thing is painful or pleasant, is as absurd as to care
whether the brick layer's trowel is knocking the
sharp corner off a brick, or plastering mortar on
the one below it before he lays it carefully on its
course. 'Is *the building getting on?*' That is the
one question that is worth thinking about."

"If we have once got hold of the principle that
all which is, summer and winter, storm and sunshine, possession and loss, memory and hope, work
and rest, and all the other antitheses of life, is
equally the product of His (God's) will, equally
His means for our discipline; then we have the
amulet and talisman which will preserve us from
the fever of desire and the shivering fits of anxiety
as to things that perish. As they tell us of a Christian Father (Bernard of Clairvaux), who, traveling by one of the great lakes of Switzerland all
day long on his journey to the church council that
was absorbing his thoughts, said toward evening
to the deacon who was pacing by him, 'Where is
the Lake?' So you and I, journeying along the
margin of this great flood of things when wild

storm sweeps across it or when the sunbeams glint upon its waters and "birds of peace sit brooding on the charmed wave," shall be careless of the changeful sea, if the eye looks beyond the visible and beholds the unseen, the unchanging real presences that make glory in the darkest lives and 'sunshine in the shady places.' " ✳

The greatest value of such imaginative power in the preacher combined with his religious sensibility and emotion to intensify it, is that *by it he is able to invest familiar and commonplace truths with fresh charm and potency*, and thus renew or keep perpetually alive their practical influence over the heart. Most religious truth after a while becomes trite and commonplace; on this account men are in danger of neglecting it, But if men neglect it, before they have acted upon it and wrought its saving and sanctifying virtue into their hearts and lives, they do so at their peril. Happy and most useful, therefore, is the preacher who has the power of rescuing men from that peril by preserving through his imaginative charm the practical influence of the truth. Example; 2d sermon, third series of "Sermons Preached in Manchester"; "The Bitterness and Blessedness of Brevity of Life."

(6) *He possessed a thoughtful and suggestive mind.* Dr. Joseph Parker, speaking of him, says: "*He always says something to his people, something that sticks.* In this respect he is much superior to Spurgeon. He thinks more and better." He is not merely a preacher, occasionally, of great sermons, like Professor Park and Robert Hall; but an in-

exhaustively productive preacher of good sermons; sermons which as a rule made a powerful impression, and made it for the truth he preached and not chiefly for the preacher. His native capacity for strong, rich thoughts was strengthened by his habits of brooding over his truth and of careful elaboration of it in preparation for preaching. Schooling himself, as he did, to "use, as his first and chief organ of expression of thought, not the pen but the tongue," the wonder is that he was able in the premeditation of his sermons to exact from his mind so much genuine, prolonged, consecutive thinking. It implied great native mental ability perfected by the discipline of education and held to its work by the most determined will. As examples of clear, admirable and just thinking, study the 13th and 23d sermons, of the third series of the "Manchester Sermons." Because of this quality we do not know of any sermons that better deserve, or would better repay careful study than Dr. McLaren's. They are valuable for their wealth of Biblical truth adorned with great learning and a chastened imagination; for their exemplification of the highest homiletic skill, and for the convincing proof they afford to any intelligent, fair-minded reader, that a sermon, ideally considered, instead of being a dull, vapid talk, or a heavy essay, as is commonly supposed, may be, and often is a delightful, uplifting, profitable discourse well worth a man's thoughtful attention.

(7) *He possessed an invincible faith in the permanent value and importance of the preacher's office.*

As God had appointed that men should be saved by the preaching of the gospel, Dr. McLaren could not be made to think that this office would ever become useless and the pulpit effete. "The teaching office of the preacher is depreciated," he said, "as being superseded by the hundred-voiced press. But granting the influence of the press, if this supersedes the pulpit, it is the fault of the occupant thereof. A certain minister once told a shrewd old Scotch lady that he was engaged to deliver an address on the power of the pulpit, and asked what her views on the subject were. She answered: 'The power of the pulpit! That depends on wha's in it,' which is a truth to be laid to heart by all preachers. No man is superseded but through his own deficiencies. There must be weakness in the wall which the storm blows down. The living voice has all its old power today, when it is a voice and not an echo, or a mumble. If a man has anything to say, and will say it with all his heart, and with all his soul, and with all his strength, he will not lack auditors. Books have their province, and preachers have theirs, and neither can efface the other, or supply the place of the other."

In this confidence he worked on with unflagging zeal. His wife, who was his cousin, Marion McLaren, contributed much to his success. They were married March 27, 1856, while he was yet in Southampton. She gave to the last two years of his ministry there its crowning grace, and in Manchester for more than a quarter of a century she greatly helped him.

ALEXANDER McLAREN

Writing in his old age to Sir William Robertson Nicoll in regard to a sketch of his career in the British Monthly, he said of his wife: "I would fain that in any notices of what I am, or have been able to do, it should be told that the best part of it all came and comes from her. We read and thought together, and her clear, bright intellect illumined obscurities and 'rejoiced in the truth.' We worked and bore together, and her courage and deftness made toil easy and charmed away difficulties. She lived a life of nobleness, of strenuous effort, of aspiration, of sympathy, self-forgetfulness and love. She was my guide, my inspirer, my corrector, my reward. Of all human formative influences on my character and life hers is the strongest and best. To write of me and not to name her is to present a fragment."

Their union was ideal. When she was taken from him December 21, 1884, he was stunned at his loss, and life seemed robbed of its chief charm. In the words of Browning: "The soul of his soul had been taken from his side."

The first of the three stages of McLaren's Manchester ministry was from 1858 to 1875, when he was chosen president of the Baptist Union, the highest dignity that a Baptist minister can attain in England. He was then but forty-nine—younger than anyone ever previously chosen. The office was never given to anyone but a man of first rank. What had been the achievements which won for him this honor? Besides the good work done in Southampton that had attracted the attention of Union Chapel, Manchester, the following things in Manchester: In the first place he soon gained there a great increase of reputation as a preacher. Before long it became noised abroad through the city that a remarkable preacher had come to them. "Very soon," says his biographer, "the congregation ceased to be drawn from the immediate neighborhood. Listeners came from all parts of the city and beyond it. Some came in carriages, very many came on foot. There were no tram cars or bicycles in those days, but many a young clerk or student who worked hard through the week found his way by 10.30 a. m. to Union Chapel, and left it refreshed in spirit and resolved to come again."

The church grew in numbers and vitality. On account of the increase of numbers the chapel which he found there became much too strait for them and a new chapel of much larger capacity and superior equipment for their flourishing work was built after he had been with them eleven years. His people felt the pressing need of it long before its erection, —but he rather discouraged the undertaking. He feared that the new chapel "would be half-empty." The chapel was opened, however, for worship in November, 1869, and from the first it was crowded. "The congregations," we are told, "were as remarkable for their composition as for their size. They contained men of all classes and creeds, rich and prosperous merchants, men distinguished in professional life, and others working their way toward success. Young men from the offices and warehouses of the city sat side by side with artisans. Strangers were attracted in large numbers, among them clergymen and dignitaries of the Established Church, Non-conformist ministers, literary men, artists and students from the theological colleges."

As a result of the growth and "vitality" of his church, missions sprang up in the neighborhood like offshoots around a flourishing tree. These were "chiefly staffed and supported by the Union Chapel congregation." His influence was so great and inspiring that volunteers for the work in every case and ample funds to sustain it were easily raised. He only needed to point out a good chance for Christian service to have it embraced by those he deemed fit to undertake it and able to support it. Besides having a kind of oversight of these offshoots from his church he showed such an interest in the small and feeble churches in his vicinity that they began to flourish under the stimulating consciousness of his regard for them. "Gradually without his even thinking of it," says his biographer, "he did very much the work of a 'bishop,' and his diocese was not a small one." He became first of "the three mighties" of his ministerial association. "No one was so frequently elected to preach the association sermon, to write the circular letter or to take a prominent part in the meetings as Dr. McLaren. Ministerial recognition services were considered sadly incomplete if he could not be present, and the joy of the opening or re-opening of a chapel was sensibly diminished when he could not preach one of the sermons." He was in demand for special occasions there in Manchester, and in London.

NINE GREAT PREACHERS

In the great Free Trade Hall of Manchester he first spoke at the annual meeting of the City Mission in 1860 at the same time that Joseph Parker made his debut there. The two men, we are told, were striking contrasts to one another in appearance and in what they said, but both arrested attention from the very first and retained it. It was not long before he became an object of enthusiastic love and admiration for the whole city—its pride, as giving distinction to Manchester. "He never, perhaps, took part in a meeting in the Free Trade Hall when the large building was not filled to its utmost capacity, and for years before the close of his career almost invariably the immense audience rose to receive him and cheer enthusiastically."

He was invited to preach before the London Missionary Society, at its annual meeting held in old Surrey Chapel, the scene of many noted gatherings. The sermon given had for its subject "The Secret of Power." Though it was more than fifty years ago, there are some still living who were present on the occasion and remember "the awed attention of the great congregation." Among those who came into the vestry to greet him after the service was Dr. Binney, who, when McLaren was a young minister at Southampton had visited and preached for him, and given him such an insight into the art of preaching by his talk and the example of his sermon, that he said many years afterwards, "it was Binney taught me to preach." McLaren, noticing his entrance, came forward to meet him, and they silently clasped each other's hands, both faces eloquent with emotion. The pupil had surpassed his master; for Binney felt, as he afterwards told a friend, that he himself "had fallen so far short of the ideal that had been placed before him, he had never even seen it as an ideal." The sermon gives the title to one of McLaren's published sermons. It is a remarkable sermon. Few Christians can read it without being thrilled by its thought and spiritual "power," though such was his humility that he never would have thought of himself as an example of it.

By the end of the first stage in his Manchester ministry, McLaren's manner and style of preaching had become formed. We may therefore now picture him to ourselves as a preacher having the qualities ascribed to him in full action and about to enter upon its second stage, extending from 1875–1890, when J. Edward Roberts became his assistant. Everything involved in and contributing to the power of his preaching—"that wondrous preaching, that made one's heart vibrate with infinitude," as an intelligent hearer said of it, is important. Sabbath morning he desired "to be invisible from the time he left his study till he was in his pulpit." His bearing in the pulpit was that of one so engrossed with the subject of his message that thought of himself did not disturb him. This made him the more impressive. The reading of the Scripture and the prayer "helped" him, he said, and really prepared the way for the sermon. His reading interpreted the sense, and in the prayer "I try to remember," he said, "that I am speaking to God

for others and for myself and that He is listening."
The tone of his voice as he prayed unmistakably
indicated that *he did remember* God was listening.

When he rose to deliver his sermon he appeared
as one whose soul was full of the message he brought.
His colleague and successor, Mr. Roberts, says of
him with indubitable truth: "The power that holds
the congregation spellbound is not only the power
of a splendid intellect and of a skilled orator, though
these are there; it is the power of one who has
come straight from the presence of God into his
pulpit and who speaks as he is moved by the Holy
Ghost." Another of his hearers says of him: "His
two most striking peculiarities are his utter simplicity and his intense earnestness; he literally quivers
with the intensity of his feeling and his desire to
give it expression. He looks at you, and you see
and hear a soul gripping yours and holding it.
There is no opportunity for criticism. This man
is a prophet and you must either listen and swallow
or flee."

In accord with the two foregoing testimonies
is that of a plain farmer's wife. Nine years after
she had heard him preach, she said: "I can hear
him now; and the strange thing was I never at the
time thought about its being Dr. McLaren that
we all knew and liked; it just seemed listening· to
a message from God." A message from God! This
reminds us of the apostle's words, "As though God
did beseech you by us, we pray you in Christ's
stead." That was the impression he endeavored
to make. Sometimes his entreaty had an *individu-*

alizing personal note, and a profound stillness pervaded the assembly as each hearer felt the grip of the preacher's soul laid upon and holding him. His radiant look assisted his appeal. "The address created an atmosphere," another listener said. "The preacher this morning lifted us into the region of the spiritual, into the presence of Jesus Christ."

We can scarcely realize what this preaching of McLaren meant to him; what an expenditure of all the forces of his being—body, mind and spirit. Early in his ministry he spoke of each Sunday service as a "woe." "This feeling continued through his life," his biographer says, "and only those who were with him when he was anticipating, not only special services, but his weekly preparation for his own pulpit, can know the tear and wear of spirit which that preparation involved." "In retrospect," she says, "it seems little short of a miracle that his life of strenuous preparation for each sermon preached was continued for nearly sixty years."

Notice the words, "for each sermon preached," for he could not relieve the "tear and wear" of this weekly preparation by occasionally preaching an old sermon. "He had to revivify it to his own mind by hours of thought and prayer. A sermon to him needs to be not what he had prepared weeks, months or years before, but what filled his mind now, as he faced his congregation."

Though "he had singular nerve power which quickened and intensified his thoughts and set fire to his words," the wonder is that this "nerve power" freely and constantly drawn upon in the preparation for the Sabbath and in the two services preached on that day was not completely exhansted long before its failure. The secret of its unfailing recuperation and remarkable conservation through all those years lay in *his command of sleep*—"tired nature's sweet restorer." Like John Wesley he could successfully invoke sleep when needed. For its interest as a physiological fact and for the benefit of other preachers, we quote the entire paragraph in which his biographer speaks of it: "On Sundays, and indeed week days, too, he always rested for an hour or more in the afternoon. The whole time was spent in sleep. He had a most remarkable power of being able to sleep at will, a power without which he could scarcely have continned the strenuous life he led for so many years. He could say that, notwithstanding life-long perturbation before each sermon and public engagement of any kind, he had never lost a night's sleep either before or after even those he dreaded most. During the last year of his life he said: "Very early in my career as a minister I resolved that when my head reached the pillow and 'I will both lay me down to sleep,' or its equivalent had been said, I would try to make my mind a blank, and I thank God I have been able very successfully to do so through my long life."

The popularity and success of a preacher depends much upon the personal impression he makes upon the community in which he lives and upon men generally. If he is conceited and "puts on airs," he repels men, no matter how great his gifts; if, on the other hand, he is a modest, friendly, approachable man, shows a kindly heart, and withal is possessed of a genial humor, so that he can tell a good story and is ready to laugh appreciatively at the stories of other men, he is liked by all and his brilliant pulpit gifts will win the more admiration. Dr. McLaren was a man of the latter kind. There was nothing stiff, austere, or clerical about him. His dress and manner were those of an unpretentious, ordinary gentleman. He usually wore what the Scotchmen call a soft hat and the light-colored suit of the business man and he had the rapid, springy walk of a "lay"-man. His biographer tells two anecdotes in regard to his appearance to strangers who saw and met him on his vacations. An old woman, when informed that the gentleman to whom she had been "tellin' the road" was a minister, said firmly, "I dinna think it, he's ower light in his walk and he loupit ower the burn like onything."

A copy of his photograph placed in the photographer's window was recognized by tourists from Manchester and Liverpool. Many copies of it were called for by would-be purchasers. The artist, finding that the negative had not been preserved, sulkily remarked: "That man micht hae tellt me he was famous, and I would hae keepit him— he didna look like it."

In 1877 the University of Edinburgh conferred upon him the degree of Doctor of Divinity, an honor which, though accepted with hesitation because of his modesty, he ultimately appreciated and enjoyed.

"After the ceremony was over Professor Blackie said to a friend, 'Commend me, among all the faces there, to McLaren, with his clear-cut features and eagle eyes.'"

Towards the end of 1880, after he had been in Manchester twenty-two years he showed signs of impaired health. Work was difficult and preaching impossible. He became depressed and thought of sending in his resignation. His church responded with promptness to what was clearly demanded, that he should be released from work as long as necessary for his recovery. No time was fixed but he took a year for rest and recuperation. Toward the end of 1881 he resumed his work—"but with a difference. Up to this time he had had no assistant, but now the Rev. J. G. Raws was chosen for that office. And after this time Dr. McLaren only preached once each Sunday, while Mr. Raws supplied that which was lacking on his part and greatly added to his peace of mind." His interrupted work, taken up again, was carried on with renewed vigor and sustained energy until his wife died in December, 1884. What her loss meant to him and his children cannot be described. "For a time he could not face meeting friends, however sympathetic," and he hid himself from them. But he felt that he still had his work to do and he was only three Sundays away from his pulpit. The shadow of his great affliction, however, remained, "seen in the lines of his face, heard in the pathetic ring of his voice, and, above all, felt in the chastened, tender, but always manly tone of his mature teaching."

ALEXANDER McLAREN

His fame as a preacher had reached to the antipodes, and in 1888 he was earnestly invited to come to Australia and New Zealand as the representative of the English Baptist Union, and on September 21, he and his two unmarried daughters sailed from London. His reception and entertainment in Adelaide, Melbourne and Dunedin, N. Z., were enthusiastic and the tour through the islands was one of repeated ovations—a triumphal progress. "Everywhere," he wrote, "we have met with the truest kindness. I have felt the unflagging attention of the great audiences (3,000 they tell me) most inspiring and I feel thankful that good has been done. . . . The butter has been laid on with a spade, but the heat has melted it and it has mostly run off." "I have never spoken to more sympathetic and more responsive audiences. They have helped me greatly." The stimulus of such interest and enthusiasm led him to overdo. "I feel as if I had come to an end," he said before the end of a month, and a pause was necessary.

On his way back to England he doubted being able to begin work again and he thought of resignation. During his absence his assistant, Mr. Raws, had received a call to a pastorate elsewhere and was only awaiting Mr. McLaren's return to leave. This gave him anxiety. After several months, in January, 1890, Mr. J. Edwards Roberts, still in college, was chosen for his assistant and "so began the long connection (of thirteen years)honorable to both."

We come now to the third (and last) stage of Dr.

McLaren's ministry in Manchester, from 1890–1903. It was a stage of declining physical strength, but of little less mental vigor.

In 1896 he completed the fiftieth year of his ministry, and interest in the event was widely felt and signally manifested. "An address handsomely bound" signed by three hundred and fifty fellow ministers was presented to him. On the occasion of its presentation, "he most truly received an ovation" from the large audience assembled. With evident emotion he said, "I can only render from my heart of hearts thanks, largely mingled with wonder, at the place which you allow me to feel that I hold in your regard."

"In Manchester the desire to commemorate Dr. McLaren's Jubilee finally took the form of asking him to sit for his portrait, which was to be presented to the city and placed in the art gallery." The formal presentation of the portrait was accompanied by speeches from the Lord Mayor, Bishop Morehouse, and Dr. McLaren's friend, Sir William Crossley, who was in the chair.

The testimonies of the bishop and of the chairman in regard to the eminence and power of Dr. McLaren as a preacher are so impressive as to justify quotation. Said Bishop Morehouse: "Thirty years ago I was studying with great profit the published sermons of the gentleman we honor today; and I will say this, that in an age which had been charmed and inspired by the sermons of Newman and Robertson of Brighton, there are no published discourses which for profundity of thought, logical arrangement, eloquence of appeal and power over the human heart, exceed in merit those of Dr. McLaren."

Sir William Crossley said: "Dr. McLaren's writings are well known and have made him friends all over the world. Those who have heard him preach know him better still, and those who have known and loved him for many years and have enjoyed his friendship know him best of all. But all are are deeply indebted to him not only for his high scholarship, but for the marvelous power he has of getting round men's hearts, elevating their desires and making them think more and more about spiritual things."

Another notable occasion during the period we are now considering was the joint meeting of the Baptist and Congregational Unions held in the City Temple, London, April, 1901, when Dr. McLaren gave his famous address (above referred to), "An Old Preacher on Preaching." The Temple was densely crowded and many could not get in. Contrary to his custom he had written out the address fully and read it. But notwithstanding the restraint it was heard throughout with rapt attention. Sir W. R. Nicoll said of it, "Considering its design and its speaker and its audience, it was simply perfect and will never be forgotten by those who heard it." But strange to say, we learn from his biographer that Dr. McLaren's own verdict was, "A failure because I read it. Again and again I was tempted to fling the paper from me and *let myself go.*"

In October of 1901 still another notable occasion was the autumn meeting of the Baptist Union in

Edinburgh, at which he again occupied the chair, and as president gave the usual address. The subject of his address was "Evangelical Mysticism," which, he said, "though theoretically recognized by all does not enter in its due proportion into either the creed or the experience of most of us, to the great detriment, as I believe, of both experience and creed." A passage toward the end, "when," we are told, "his radiant look told even more than his words" gives us probably a just idea of his subject and his own conception of it. "Consider how the consciousness of the higher life in Christ brings with it an absolute incapacity of believing that what men call death can effect it. Christ in us *is* 'the hope of Glory.' The true evidence for immortality lies in the deep experience of the Christian spirit. It is when a man can say 'Thou art the strength of my heart,' that the conviction springs up inevitable and triumphant that such a union can no more be severed by the physical accident of death than a spirit can be wounded by a sword, and that, therefore, he has the right to say further, 'and my portion forever.' "

On the last Sunday in June, 1903, at the completion of the forty-fifth year of his Manchester ministry he ended his pastoral labors with Union Chapel, having previously informed his congregation that the time had come when he had no longer the "physical strength for the continuous discharge of the joyous duties" thereof.

But though he scarcely preached again, there or elsewhere, he does not wish to resign himself

to entire idleness. Years before this he quotes with
approval Whittier's "My Psalm" and its lines,

> "I break my pilgrim staff, I lay
> Aside the toiling oar,"

as appropriate to the anticipated close of his pastoral
work. He now has got beyond that feeling and has
John Wesley's desire "to cease at once to work and
live," and says that "to enjoy a well earned rest is a
delusion." The habit of creative work and the habit
of doing it constrains him to exercise his faculties as
his diminished strength may permit for the remaining
seven years of his life. It was very good work too,
such as his Expositions of the American Sunday-
school lessons in the Sunday-School Times, and
"The Expositions of Holy Scripture," though at
times he would ask, "Is it not foolish for an old
man to imagine he can do good work?"

But best of all, those last years were years of
growing fitness for heaven. Writing to a friend he
said, "You will get patience increased if you 'practice the Presence of God.' I feel for myself that
that is what I need most. Call the attitude by any
name you like, it is the life of all our religion. Christ's
name for it is the best, 'Abide in Me.' "

Writing to another friend, he says, "You ask
me about my thoughts when they are free. I think
I can say that they do often, and with a kind of
instinct, turn Godward. Many times they glide
thither, perhaps because age diminishes wish to work
and indolence as much as devotion determines the
set of the current. I do not wish you to think that

my thoughts invariably turn Godward. It is often difficult to keep them fixed on God or Christ, but I am quite sure the more we make the effort to penetrate all our life with conscious contemplation of the Divine Presence and Love, the more peaceful we shall be and the better able to accept His will and to find it right."

His attending physician asks "Who could be for any time in his company without feeling that his presence and his words were at once an inspiration and a benediction?" Talking with him concerning the future, he said: "I cannot perhaps always, but sometimes I can say (with Richard Baxter)

> "But 'tis enough that Christ knows all
> And I shall be with Him."

"On the afternoon of May 5, 1910, very quietly the end came." His ashes were laid beside those of his wife, where years before a stone cross had been erected with the words, *In Christo, in Pace, in Spe.* The trustful words express his state of mind as he approached that grave in the beautiful sunset of his life, when we fancy Tennyson's lines may have often recurred to him:

> "Sunset and evening star,
>   And one clear call for me!
> And may there be no moaning of the bar,
>   When I put out to sea.
> *   *   *   *   *
> "For tho' from out our bourne of Time and Place
>   The flood may bear me far,
> I hope to see my Pilot face to face
>   When I have crossed the bar."

IX
HENRY WARD BEECHER

IX

HENRY WARD BEECHER

1813–1887

This man may be regarded as the greatest of American preachers. This is the opinion of many judges of the highest eminence. Let the estimates of two of these stand for the substance of the expressed opinions of a score. "That is true of him as a pulpit orator," Professor G. B. Willcox says, "which never has been true before of any other preacher in this country and will never be true again; if in any company of intelligent persons you should speak of the foremost preacher on this continent without mentioning his name, nine persons in every ten would know whom you meant."

The second judge is Dr. Armitage, a distinguished Baptist preacher of New York, who says of him: "His sermons exhibit a larger reading of human nature, a broader use of philosophical inquiry, a fresher application of Gospel truths, a clearer induction of common sense, and a more independent rectitude than can be found in any other modern preacher."

In our inquiry as to the influences contributing to make him great, we find that heredity is to be reckoned among the chief. His father and mother were both superior persons. His father, Lyman

Beecher, was one of the greatest preachers of his generation. Dr. J. H. Barrows, who denominates him "the King of the New England Pulpit" at the time, describes him as "a man of magnetic eloquence, restless energy, and great evangelical fervor!" His name is associated with important reforms, as that against dueling, in regard to which he preached a notable, widely-read sermon called out by the death of Alexander Hamilton through his duel with Aaron Burr; and especially the Temperance reform, in regard to which he preached a series of powerful sermons that did much to check the flood of intemperance which then was desolating the land.

Lyman Beecher was a man of indomitable spirit, whom no difficulties could daunt, and a tireless worker for the promotion of good. His illustrious son said of him: "My father always had the angel of hope looking over his shoulder when he wrote." He was an earnest believer in and advocate of the "New Theology," as it was then called, as contrasted with the old, fatalistic hyper-Calvinistic theology, which denied free agency and the sinner's ability to repent and embrace the salvation of Christ revealed in the Gospel. He was a sanguine, self-reliant man. He believed that if he could have talked with the poet Byron, he could have so clearly explained to him the truth of the Gospel that all his mental difficulties would have been removed, and he would have been converted from his misanthropy and become a joyful Christian. He was withal a frolicsome man with his children; he used to dance with them in his stocking feet to the music of his own violin and the great damage of his stockings. He familiarized them with the questions of the day, set his boys to arguing with him concerning them, and "thus," says Dr. Abbott, "developed their mental muscle, taught them to do their own thinking and to stand by their convictions and defend them. He had a delightfully naïve, childlike egotism, quite free from self-conceit, yet inspiring him with a kind of self-assurance which is often the precursor of victory." He became through his oratorical ability the champion of Orthodoxy. "He was by nature a warrior and delighted in battle," and in Boston, whither he was called in 1826 to be the pastor of the Hanover Street Congregational Church, where he remained six years and a half, he achieved great distinction by his successful defense and vindication of evangelical Christianity from the attacks of Unitarianism, through which the tide of unbelief was stayed and large gains were made by revivals of great power to the ranks of the orthodox faith. Wendell Phillips was one of his converts. "I was made for action," he said, "the Lord drove me on; but I was ready. I have always been going full speed." Having such a father, Henry Ward Beecher inherited from him zeal for God's truth and righteousness, independence of mind and a gift of convincing speech.

His mother, Roxana Foote Beecher, was no less remarkable as a woman than her husband among men. The testimonies of her children, Catherine, Harriet and Henry Ward, have wreathed her character with a crown of womanly virtues that make it saintly. (She was an ardent lover of nature and good literature, of painting and music. "There was a moral force about her," says Mrs. Stowe, "a dignity of demeanor and an air of elegance which produced a constant atmosphere of unconscious awe in the minds of little children." She had also "one of those strong, restful and yet widely sympathetic natures in whom all around seemed to find comfort and repose." "She possessed," says Abbott, "that peculiar strength which comes from close and intimate communion with God," and "her piety of spirit and her placidity of temperament combined to give her an equipoise which made her the trusted counselor of her husband, on whose judgment he depended, and in whose calm his own turbulent spirit found rest." Henry Ward Beecher inherited from his mother those qualities which were most characteristic of her and which constituted his social charm. She died when he was but little more than three years old, but she remained all his life a potent influence. "No devout Catholic," he said, "ever saw so much in the Virgin Mary as I have seen in my mother, who has been a presence to me ever since I can remember."

(Having such parents, to whom he was born in Litchfield, Conn., June 24, 1813, and brought up in the companionship of sisters and brothers richly endowed with native genius, he derived from home and family the best and most inspiring impulses.)

And yet there was nothing precocious, or intellectually remarkable in him, as a child or boy. On the contrary, he was rather dull and backward in his studies, and chiefly remarkable for his love of fun and good-natured mischief, his abounding animal health and spirits. This was true of him in Litchfield and in Boston, to which city his father removed when Henry was thirteen years old.) He was sent to Boston's famous Latin School, the educational nursery of so many distinguished men; he entered it soon after Charles Sumner had left it, and while Wendell Phillips was still in it; but its classic atmosphere and splendid traditions did not kindle in him any ambition or fondness for study.) It "was to him a Sinaitic desert." "He became moody, restless and irritable." In this condition of mind he was set by his wise father to reading biographies of great sailors and naval heroes. From his reading, the desire to go to sea was kindled in him. His father did not object, but advised him first to qualify himself by further study to be something more than a common sailor. Henry confessed that he aspired to be a captain or a commodore, and that it would be well for him to study mathematics and navigation. So he consented to go to Mt. Pleasant School, near Amherst, where boys fitted for college, and his shrewd father still hoped in this way that his son would finally enter the ministry.

At this school he found two teachers that had the faculty of stimulating him to good work in study by showing him how to study and what benefit he might gain from application to it. They were John E. Lovell, who taught him elocution, of whom he afterwards said: "A better teacher in his department was never made," and W. P. Fitzgerald, the teacher of mathematics, who taught him to conquer in studying, and to be sure of his ground by making him defend and prove the correctness of his solutions. While at Mt. Pleasant a revival occurred and he was numbered among the converts and united with his father's church in Boston.) The awakening of his mind to study and the quickening of his religious life wrought by the revival, led him to give up the idea of a sailor's life and to turn his thoughts toward the ministry.)

In 1830, his eighteenth year, he entered Amherst College.) "To college," says Dr. Abbott, "he carried with him a nature of strange contradictions. A masculine robustness of nature mated to a feminity of spirit—a habit of hard work (formed at Mt. Pleasant), but a habit of working according to his own mood, not according to rules prescribed to him by others." This disposition, as might be supposed, prevented him from winning a high grade in his class. His college standing is indicated by his later remark, that he once "stood next to the head of his class, but it was when the class was arranged in a circle." But though he gave no more attention to the allotted studies than was necessary to enable him to pass, he was a diligent reader of books and an investigator of subjects that interested him,) and he gained among his fellow-students a reputation for uncommon ability as a writer, a debater and public speaker.) Among the subjects debated was the question of the African colonization of American negroes. He was given the negative, and fifty years after he said: "In pre-

paring that speech, I prepared for my whole life."
Through his growing fondness for public speaking
and the reputation he thus acquired, he was repeatedly invited during his course to conduct prayer-
meetings, to preach, to lecture on temperance and
phrenology and other topics, by which he earned
some money and in which he acquitted himself with
growing distinction.) In the winter vacations he
taught school in various places to assist in his college
support, and in every place was he forward to speak
on subjects of moral reform and religious duty.

During his college course at Amherst his father
was called to the Presidency of Lane Theological
Seminary, Cincinnati, where Henry entered in 1834,
at twenty-one, immediately after his graduation
from college. His Seminary course was similar to
his college course in its miscellaneous reading and
the studies given to topics outside the prescribed
curriculum. From only one part of the regular
seminary work did he get much benefit by devoting
himself to its study; that was in the Bible studies
taken under Professor Calvin E. Stowe, who later
married his sister Harriet. "By him he was led
into a thorough study and analysis of the Bible as a
body of truth, instinct with God, warm with all
divine and human sympathies, clothed with language
adapted to their best expression and to be understood
as similar language used for similar ends in everyday
life."

These studies, especially those relating to the
Gospels and the Epistles of St. Paul, were fruitful
studies, which in later years gave to his preaching,

to a remarkable degree, a rare insight into the mind
of Christ and a comprehensive and sure grasp of the
essentials of Christian truth.) To systematic, tech-
nical theology he paid but little attention, and he
never showed much interest in or knowledge of it.
In fact he was lamentably and discreditably lacking
in his acquaintance with its definitions, conflicting
theories, and discussions. But his repugnance was
not without some justification. He had grown up
in an atmosphere of theological discussion and controversy, and Lane Seminary then was a veritable
storm center of theological controversy, between the
old-school and the new-school theologies. (His
father, who warmly championed the teachings of
the new school, was fiercely assailed,—so fiercely
that he was compelled to leave his wife's death bed
to defend himself before Presbytery and Synod from
the charge of heresy.) Thus "Henry Ward Beecher
learned," says Dr. Barrows, "that however earnest,
unselfish and consecrated the life of a Christian
minister, like his father, might be, he was not safe
from persecution and deposition from the ministry,
unless he assented and conformed to the literal
teachings of what he deemed an irrational, misleading and obsolescent theology." The spectacle
filled him with perplexity and disgust. He had,
therefore, no taste for theological study and inquiry.

He was not idle, however. He "taught a Bible
class of young ladies, making the most careful preparation for his work"; for a time he acted as editor
of the Cincinnati *Journal*; he lectured on temperance;
he preached as he found opportunity. But the

bewilderment of mind produced by the theological controversies of that time naturally resulted in a feeling of uncertainty and mental doubt. The future looked dark and his prospects dubious. Could he ever get a license to preach, or a church willing to hear him? "I must preach the gospel as it is revealed to me," he said, but he had no clear revelation for a while upon which he could plant his feet with any degree of assurance. But at length such a revelation came. The account of it is given in the first chapter of Dr. Lyman Abbott's "Henry Ward Beecher," a remarkably interesting book; also in the seventh chapter of Dr. John Henry Barrows' valuable biography. A portion of the account of Dr. Abbott we here give, for the bearing it has upon a proper understanding of Henry Ward Beecher's ministry:

"I was a child," he says "of teaching and prayer: I was reared in the household of faith: I knew the catechism as it was taught: I was instructed in the Scriptures as they were expounded from the pulpit and read by men, and yet, till after I was twenty-one years old, I groped without the knowledge of God in Christ Jesus. I know not what the tablets of Eternity have written down, but I think that when I stand in Zion and before God the brightest thing I shall look back upon will be that blessed May morning when it pleased God to reveal to my wondering soul the idea that it was His nature to love a man in his sins for the sake of helping him out of them; that He did not do it out of compliment to Christ, or to a law, or a plan of salvation, but from

the fulness of His great heart; that He was a being
not made mad by sin, but sorry; that He was not
furious with wrath toward the sinner, but pitied
him: In short, that He felt toward me as my mother
felt toward me, to whose eyes my wrongdoing brought
tears and who would fain with her yearning love
lift me out of my trouble. . . . And when I
found that Jesus Christ had such a disposition and
that when his disciples did wrong he drew them closer
to Him than He did before, and when pride and jealousy and rivalry and all vulgar and worldly feelings
rankled in their bosoms, He opened His heart unto
them as a medicine to heal these infirmities, I felt
that I had found a God. . . . Time went
on and next came the disclosure of a Christ ever
present with me, a Christ that was never far from
me, but was always near me, as a companion and
friend, to uphold and sustain me. This was the
last and the best revelation of God's spirit to my
soul. It is what I consider to be the culminating
work of God's grace in a man; and no man is a Christian until he has experienced it. I do not mean
that a man cannot be a good man until then, but he
has not got to Jerusalem till he has seen the King
sitting in his glory, with love to him individually."
This vision colored and shaped his whole after-life
and ministry. He regarded it as an epitome of
the gospel, as the sum and substance of Christianity,
and he was eager to proclaim it to the world. Its
effect upon him was like that wrought upon Luther
by the heavenly voice: "The just shall live by faith";
or that produced in John Wesley, when his burden

of sin rolled off as he listened to the interpretation of Paul's letter to the Romans given by a devout Moravian at an Aldersgate Street meeting in London. He felt that he now had a message, a real gospel message for mankind, and his heart burned to tell it.

The opportunity came in 1837, when, at his graduation from the seminary, he received a call to a small Presbyterian church in Lawrenceburg, Indiana, at a nominal salary of $400, including what he received from the Home Missionary Society. The church was composed of twenty members, nineteen women and one (poor stick of a) man. He served it two years, performing the duties of both preacher and sexton. He says: "I swept the church and lighted my own fire. I took care of everything connected with the building." Upon this meager salary he ventured to marry. The young man and his wife began housekeeping in two rooms over a stable, furnished with borrowed furniture. Surely no minister ever made a humbler beginning! He entered upon his work with some definite ideas as to the *conditions of success*. In his journal these entries are found: "Remember you can gain men easily if you get round their prejudices and put truth in their minds; but *never* if you attack prejudices." "My people must be alert to make the church agreeable, to give *seats* and wait on *strangers*." "*Secure a large congregation;* let this be the first thing."

The young minister made a favorable impression at the very start by his genial sociability and friendliness and his good sermons, so that the "large congregation"—as large as the little church could hold—which he had deemed as of first importance, was soon secured.

Of his preaching he says: "I preached some theology; as a man chops straw and mixes it with Indian meal in order to distend the stomach of the ox that eats it, so I chopped a little of the regular orthodox theology [picked up while in the seminary and in the discussions at home with his father] that I might sprinkle it with the meal of the Lord Jesus Christ. But my horizon grew larger and larger in that one idea of Christ."

As his horizon of truth enlarged his field of influence widened. In 1839 he was called to the Second Presbyterian Church, Indianapolis, at a salary of $600; which call, after twice declining it, he at length accepted at the request of the synod. Indianapolis then had a population of only 4000, and its distinguishing features, Dr. Barrows says, were "mud and malaria." It possessed all the crudeness and ugliness of a new Western town. Hogs and pigs ran at will in its streets, or wallowed in the muddy pools. "With the exception of two or three streets," he says, "there were no ways along which could not be seen the original stumps of the forests. I bumped against them too often in a buggy not to be sure of the fact."

Here, as at Lawrenceburg, a large congregation equal to the utmost capacity of the new church erected for it, was soon gathered. His originality, his freshness of presentation of gospel truth and his personal magnetism charmed all who heard him.

Dr. Abbott says: "From the first his church was a church of strangers. The members of the legislature attended it almost in a body. His presentation of God as a Father of infinite compassion, whose character is revealed in the earthly life of Jesus Christ, was, in that time and place, extraordinarily novel. Men knew not what to make of it and curiosity commingled with higher motives to attract audiences eager to hear this strange gospel." "Here I preached my first real sermon," he says. He means that not till then did he have a true idea of the aim and purpose of a sermon, or did he know how to adopt his gospel, "the Gospel of Christ as he had learned it from a careful study of the Evangelists and as it had been burned into his soul by the heat of a great experience," to the various needs of men. The true idea of a sermon he saw was this: It is a means to an end, and everything in it—text, exposition, argument, illustrations—all are to bear upon this definite end. "How to adapt his truth to his hearers was a discovery made by a careful study of the teaching and practice of the Apostles, and especially the Apostle Paul. He learned, as John Knox and Jonathan Edwards had done before him, that they laid "a foundation first of historical truth common to them and their auditors; that this mass of familiar truth was then concentrated upon the hearers in the form of an intense application and appeal; that the language was not philosophical and scholastic, but the language of common life." He tried this method and it met with immediate success, which filled him with joy. "I owe more to the Book of Acts and the writings of the Apostle Paul than to all other books put together," he said. These principles which he speaks of are axiomatic in Homiletics. We see them exemplified in the preaching of Jonathan Edwards, Robertson and McLaren, as well as in that of Beecher. From the application made of them. great success attended his ministry in Indianapolis. His preaching in those eight years was especially evangelistic in character, and large revivals resulted from it, his church increasing eightfold. With great joy and wonder he witnessed the work. "He stands upon the shore to see the tide come in. It is the move of the infinite ethereal tide. It is from the other world."

He took particular interest in young men and they responded to his interest. His church was full of them, and for their sakes he prepared a series of "Lectures to Young Men," which became famous and were republished in England. The pictures of vice and sin, which he portrayed in these lectures, are most graphic, not to say realistic. The denunciations poured out upon the sins depicted were scathing and terrible, so terrible that once a man, who thought that he was particularly aimed at, met him on the street with pistol in hand and said: "Take it back right here or I will shoot you on the spot." "Shoot away," Beecher replied and coolly walked on, to the bully's discomfiture.

He steadily grew in preaching power. His style in those days was pictorial, concrete, more florid than in later years. But his illustrations, which were profuse, were original and ever fresh. He never repeated one. His store was inexhaustible, gathered from all fields, nature, science, history, literature and the occupations of men, and his application of them was most apt and striking.) His reputation for eloquence spread throughout the land, and calls were extended to him from the Park Street Church, Boston, and the newly organized Plymouth Church, Brooklyn. The latter, after some considerable hesitation, he accepted for the sake of his invalid wife, whose health the malarial atmosphere of Indianapolis had greatly shattered.)

On the journey east, Mr. Beecher, then thirty-six years of age, but appearing younger, was very attentive to his wan and sad-faced wife. An old lady, whose compassion was touched by her miserable countenance, said to her, encouragingly, while he was gone to procure something for her refreshment and comfort at a halting place, "Cheer up, my dear madam. Whatever may be your trial, you have cause for great thankfulness to God, who has given you such a kind and attentive son."

The change happily restored her to health, and she survived him several years. His ministry to Plymouth Church, Brooklyn (October 10, 1847 to March 8, 1887) covered a period of nearly forty years. An infant enterprise of twenty-one members when he came to it, it became under his ministry, the largest and the most notable church in the land, conspicuous not only for its size, but for its splendid munificence in charity and great achievements in every form of Christian enterprise. It is numbered among those few historical churches in our country that have gained a world-wide reputation, due chiefly to the *éclat* and success of the work of their ministers.

The ministry may be thought of as a kind of business, great in its aims and difficult of accomplishment. What were Mr. Beecher's personal equipment and spiritual capital for the important business now entered upon in which he was to achieve such splendid success?

(1) *A magnificent physique with perfect health.* Dr. Barrows speaks of his "enormous physical vitality." Fowler, the phrenologist, called him "a splendid animal," and Dr. Abbott says, "vigor of health was characteristic of him all his life. He had a good digestion and an excellent nervous system." He inherited this fine strong physique from his paternal ancestors, two of whom had been blacksmiths strong enough to pick up a barrel of cider and drink from its bunghole. Having such an inheritance he took good care of it. He was temperate in diet and studied to take such food as was suited to his particular needs. He took daily outdoor exercise and was always a sound sleeper, and had the faculty of "throwing off cares and anxieties, whether they belonged to him or others, when he believed that further carrying them would do no good."

(2) *He had had a unique preparation or apprenticeship for his business.* In this apprenticeship were included not only the ten years spent in Lawrenceburg and Indianapolis, with their varied experiences of life as then existing in those new Western towns, in editing horticultural and floricultural

journals, and in lecturing, but the years of his seminary and college life, with their miscellaneous reading and atmosphere of theological discussion and doubts and perplexities, ending in the extraordinary spiritual visions of God and of Christ which had filled him with eagerness to tell men what he had seen and proved.   In that varied experience and strenuous life his mental and spiritual powers had been wonderfully developed, and he had learned how to use and profit by them.

(3) *Extraordinary power of expression.* Whatever aids expression—imagination, feeling, oratorical ability—was his in largest measure.   Charles Kingsley, hearing him some years later when in the maturity of his strength and preaching power, said: "Mr. Beecher has said the very things I have been trying to say ever since I entered the Christian pulpit." No thought, however profound, delicate, elusive, grand or beautiful surpassed his power of expression. It was equal to the clear and impressive utterance of whatever might come into his mind or stir his heart.   "It is his transcendent gifts of expression, his diction," says Dr. Brastow, "that has won for him the title, 'The Shakespeare of the Modern Pulpit.' His nimbleness and fertility of mind, vividness of imagination and passionate intensity of feeling were all tributary to this linguistic faculty.   He was an artist in speech.   His diction is a distinct gift and he cultivated it with ceaseless assiduity.   It is notable for its ease and affluence, its wealth and variety. It combines all the qualities of an effective pulpit style."

(4) *A voice of remarkable compass and melody.* "His voice," says Dr. Cuyler, "was as sweet as a lute and as loud as a trumpet. In its tenderest pathos, that witching voice touched the fount of tears. When he rose into impassioned sublimity 'they that heard him said that it thundered.'" This remarkable voice was not natural; it was the result of careful culture and training, which dated as far back as the Mt. Pleasant School of his boyhood, when he came under the instruction of Professor John Lovell, whose praise he never ceased to speak. When he was a child he had a serious defect in his speech, which made it almost unintelligible, so that his Aunt Esther said: "When Henry is sent to me with a message, I always have to make him say it three times. The first time, I have no manner of an idea, any more than if he spoke Choctaw; the second I catch now and then a word, and the third time I begin to understand."

Dr. Lovell's training enabled him to get the better of this defect, and he studied continuously to perfect his voice and his mastery of it.

(5) *An extraordinary and peculiar genius to which he gave free play.* He belonged to a peculiar family. Though himself the most richly endowed and distinguished of them all, all of his father's children were persons of mark because of their rare natural gifts and ability. Another such family, so richly endowed and so eminent, each and all, can hardly be found in our American history. There was in him a peculiar personal strain, inherited partly from his father and mother, and partly original with

himself, which gave him the preëminence among
his brethren as a preacher and made him eventually
the prince of the American pulpit. It was a kind
of prophetic capacity for inspiration and rare spiritual exaltation. "I am what I am by the grace of
God through my father and mother," he said.
"I have my own peculiar temperament; I have my
own method of preaching, I am intense at times on
subjects that deeply move me. I feel as though all
the oceans were not strong enough to be the power
behind my words. There are times when it is not
I that is talking, when I am caught up and carried
away so that I know not whether I am in the body
or out of the body, when I think things in the pulpit
that I never could think of in my study, and when
I have feelings that are so different from any that
belong to the normal condition, that I can neither
regulate nor understand them."

It was through this peculiar religious genius that
he sometimes spoke as if really inspired. "He
seemed," Hon. Andrew D. White says, "to have a
deep insight into the great truths of religion and to
be able to present them to others, opening up at
times great new vistas of truth by a single flash."
At such times he exhibited a combination of pulpit
power and charm scarcely equaled by any other
preacher of his day.

(6) *Extraordinary fertility of mind.* His mind
was in itself a mine of wealth. Its opulence, apart
from any enrichment it received from his studies
and much reading, was marvelous. Upon any
subject that he touched he had much of great value

to say. Mr. Lincoln spoke of him as "the most productive mind of ancient or modern times," and Dr. Joseph Parker in his eulogy of him said: "My sober impression is that Mr. Beecher could preach every Sunday in the year from the first verse in Genesis without giving any sign of intellectual exhaustion or any failure of imaginative force." Surely, this was an important item in his capital in view of the long ministry that lay before him in Brooklyn. It never failed him. To the very end he maintained the interest of his church and of the Christian public in his preaching.

(7) *(A natural style in preaching.)* His ordinary preaching was in the conversational style. "In a sense," says Dr. Abbott, "every sermon was a conversation with his audience. In the phrasing of it, always, in the figures employed, often in the structure of it, sometimes the audience took an unconscious part." His sermons were unwritten, except a few introductory sentences, which served "the purpose of shoving him off into deep water," as McLaren says of a similar practice of his own. His preaching was topical rather than textual. "A text," he says, "is like a gate; some ministers swing back and forth upon it. I push it open and go in." His topics, such as "The Hidden Christ," "What Christ is to Me," "The Crime of Degrading Men," were topics adapted to his peculiar temperament. He followed a carefully prepared outline, usually rapidly sketched Sabbath morning. But those few Sabbath hours by no means represented all the work he put upon his sermons. They, with the

time occupied in delivering his sermon, represented only what may be called his *creative work.* He was a constant student in his own way. Scores of his notebooks, filled with thoughts and points for sermons, prove this. The sermons themselves, with their evidences of careful study and extensive survey of the fields of thought treated, prove it. The fact is, that before the Sabbath his mind was carefully stored with the materials for his sermons, and these he was able, through his remarkable powers of concentration and productive effort, quickly to crystallize into a suitable form, or plan, and vitalize for effective delivery. He was unique in his method as well as his genius, and is not a safe example for any other man except in the general spirit of his work. It was "a singular feature of his productive power," we are told, "that it seldom lasted more than two or three hours." But in those two or three hours, on Sabbath morning, before and during the public service, which stimulated and exalted his powers to the utmost, he performed wonders.

Such a style in preaching, unfettered, conversational, free from artificial monotonous declamation, brings the preacher close to his hearers, keeps them wide-awake and makes the preacher vividly dramatic as well as more genuine and lifelike in his speech. It is the style of the best preachers. In the case of Mr. Beecher with his fine flexible voice, his imaginative power, and natural ease upon the platform, it was carried almost to perfection. As he warmed to his work and his soul was kindled to a blaze by his theme, he became transfigured.

(8) *(Joyousness of spirit.)* Mr. Beecher in his
ministry felt himself to be a messenger of good tid-
ings. It was a natural consequence of that
wonderful vision in which God was revealed to him
as a loving father and Christ as a potential daily
friend. God was to him a perpetual presence; he
lived in the sunshine of his countenance; he walked
in the companionship of Jesus Christ, and he believed
and taught that the same privilege was offered to his
hearers. Therefore his preaching was a message of
hope to the despondent, and of good cheer to the
sad-hearted. Similar was the effect of his public
prayers. These were as remarkable as his sermons.
In them he voiced the spiritual aspirations, the
adoration and the conscious needs of his hearers as
few preachers ever did or could do. He carried
them into the felt presence of God, and their souls
were purified and strengthened by the visions they
had of his grace and glory. For years those public
prayers were reported by an excellent stenographer
and published with his sermons in the *Christian
Union*. Subsequently a selection of them was
published in book form. Dr. Abbott says: "If there
is any collection of prayers which surpasses these
prayers of Mr. Beecher in spiritual eloquence, in
the self-revelation of childlikeness of heart and familiarity of fellowship with the Everlasting Father,
and in understanding and interpretation of the wants,
simple and complex, superficial and profound, of
the human heart, I have not seen it." From such
sermons and prayers, his hearers went forth from
the service radiant with hope and trust. A gifted

lady of his congregation says of the mood in which she usually left Plymouth Church: "The sun was always shining for me whatever the weather."

(9) *An evangelical passion for bringing men to God through faith in Christ.* Under the stimulus of this passion he was unwearied and tireless in his labors. At one time in his ministry, in Indianapolis, "he preached seventy nights in succession." Through the incitement of it, his first years as pastor of Plymouth Church were full of religious activity, and the joy of ingathering was great for both pastor and people.

(10) The last item I speak of in my summary of Mr. Beecher's equipment for the great business of ministering to Plymouth Church, upon which he entered at his coming to Brooklyn, was *good sense.* His genius was not marred or crippled by the proverbial eccentricities of genius. Though one of the most brilliant of men, he was sane, temperate and judicious in his utterances. He had the mark of a wise man, which the homely conundrum, that asks "why such a man is like a pin?" gives in its answer to the question. "Because his head keeps him from going too far." It kept him from going too far in the heated discussion that arose in the antislavery agitation preceding the Civil War, in the general anxiety and perplexity over the policy of government during the war and in the debate over the settlement of the question of the Reconstruction period. In those discussions his opinions and utterances were those of a wise and calm statesman. Such likewise were his opinions and counsels upon

the various civic and ethical questions which concern society and individuals.

His good sense was manifest also in his not venturing to rely too much upon his inventive genius
and ready eloquence and such happy productive
moods as might come to him in preaching. "No
man can preach well," he said, "except out of an
abundance of well-wrought material." And so, as
Dr. Barrows says, "he was always industriously
filling in or getting his accumulations into shape,
vitalizing them with conscious and unconscious
thought."

Having such an equipment for his work, we now
are to think of him entering upon this great work at
thirty-four years of age. Though his stock of systematic theology was small, for reasons that have
been given, he knew by heart what was most essential in the theology of a preacher and he knew well
how to use it. He believed that "no man lives who
does not need to repent of sin and turn from it";
"that turning from sin is a work so deep and difficult that no man will ever change except by the help
of God"; that "the Gospel is the power of God unto
salvation"; that "in the person and work of Christ
this power is centered," and that "success in preaching depends on the power of the preacher to put
before men the Lord Jesus Christ."

"The new preacher," Dr. Abbott says, "at first
drew but moderate congregations. Not until after
six months did the church building begin to fill so as
to be crowded, but from that time on it was unable
to accommodate the congregations." People came

to hear him from all parts of Brooklyn, from New York on the other side of East River, and from all parts of the land. For more than a quarter of a century it was common for people coming to New York for business or pleasure and spending the Sabbath in the city, to cross the ferries to Brooklyn to hear Beecher, and if, on stepping off from the ferryboat, these strangers asked a policeman the way to Plymouth Church, the answer usually received was: "Follow the crowd."

It was the writer's great privilege as a young man often to hear him in Plymouth Church and to share the feelings and impressions there made upon the great throng by this remarkable preacher then in the zenith of his power and fame. I wish I could give my readers some just conception of his eloquence. But no description can convey it. Even his sermons, as reported by the best of stenographers can give but a most inadequate idea of it. "The difference between the sermon as he preaches it," Dr. Storrs once truthfully said, "and the sermon as it is printed and published to be read afterward, is like that of fireworks as they appear at night in all their brilliance and glory and the blackened smoking framework which the boys stare at the next morning." In the last chapter of Dr. Abbott's interesting book, "Henry Ward Beecher" there is an interesting and instructive comparison of Beecher's pulpit and oratorical power with that of other great preachers and pulpit orators. Dr. Abbott says: "In particular elements of charm or power he was surpassed by some; in combination of charm and power by none.

If the test of the oration (or sermon) is its perfection, whether of structure or of expression, other orators have surpassed Mr. Beecher; if the test is the power of the speaker to impart to his audience his life, to impress on them his conviction, animate them with his purpose, and direct their action to the accomplishment of his end, then Mr. Beecher was the greatest orator I ever heard; and, in my judgment, whether measured by the immediate or the permanent effects of his addresses, takes his place in the rank of the great orators of the world."

The Plymouth Church pastorate of Mr. Beecher may be conveniently divided into three periods: the ante-bellum period with its intense excitements growing out of the agitation of the subject of slavery, in which Mr. Beecher took a prominent part as preacher, platform speaker, and editor; the period of the Civil War, when his fame as a preacher and orator was at its maximum; and the period covered by and following the Tilton scandal with its dire effects upon his reputation and influence.

Eloquence is dependent upon the man, the occasion and the theme of speech. It is not enough for its highest exhibition that a man have all the gifts and accomplishments of the orator to the highest degree. There must be worthy occasions and topics to stimulate the man to the utmost. Slavery and its aggressions and wrongs furnished Mr. Beecher these occasions and topics. From the time he went to Brooklyn to the outbreak of the Civil War, the atmosphere of our country was heated and stifling and reverberant with the signs of the gathering tempest. Beecher's whole soul with all his magnificent powers of conscience and love of righteousness, hatred of wrong, imaginative sympathy and generous sensibilities, were stirred and enlisted in the conflict of opinion. He was irresistible in his advocacy of the cause of the slave and in his plea for his emancipation. Even those who supported slavery and were strongly biased by its commercial interests were subdued to better sentiments when they came under the spell of his eloquence. Dr. Abbott gives this striking instance: "It is 1858. A Southern slaveholder is at my side. The preacher has declared, as he often did, that he has no will to interfere with slavery in the States. No wish to stir up insurrection and discontent in the slave. But he will not obey the Fugitive Slave Law. Thereupon he pictures the discontented slave escaping, portrays him stealthily creeping out from his log cabin at night; seeking a shelter in the swamp, feeding on its roots and berries, pursued by baying bloodhounds; making his way toward liberty, the north star his only guide; reaching the banks of the Ohio river; crossing it to find the Fugitive Slave Law spread like a net to catch him. And I see the fugitive, and hear the hounds and my own heart beats with his hopes and fears; and then the preacher cries: 'Has he a right to flee? If he were my son and did not seek liberty I would write across his name 'Disowned,'" and he writes it with his finger as he speaks, and I see the letters of flaming fire; and the slaveholder at my side catches his breath while he nods an involuntary assent; and as we walk out together he says: "I could not agree with all he said, but it was great, and he is a good man."

The second period in Mr. Beecher's Brooklyn pastorate, that of the Civil War, was marked by two extraordinary efforts: He first endeavored by tongue and pen to bring public opinion up to the point of demanding the abolishment of slavery, which was done by President Lincoln's Emancipation Proclamation of January, 1863. To us at this distance, it does not seem possible that this could have required any extraordinary effort. Had not slavery caused the war with all its cost of blood and treasure? Was it anything other than a just retribution upon the Confederate States in rebellion, to destroy the hateful institution that had wrought such mischief? Furthermore, it was demanded as a wise war measure. As long as the President stayed his hand from signing the proclamation that set the slaves free, those slaves were made the unwilling but valuable helpers of the rebellion. They tilled the fields and raised the crops that supported its armies in the field. They were their body servants and teamsters and the custodians of their homes, while their masters were battling at the front to resist and destroy the United States government. Strike off their fetters and proclaim their freedom and they would become the government's helpers, reinforce its armies and otherwise render it invaluable service.

But these considerations, so obvious to us now, were strangely inoperative then. The Union statesmen and the President himself were slow to perceive their force and act accordingly. It required an immense volume of argument and a flood of eloquent exhortation from those who appreciated the situation to bring about the decree of liberty to the slave. And Beecher was foremost among those whose voices pleaded for it, and at length prevailed.

The second extraordinary effort was put forth by Mr. Beecher while visiting England for needed rest in the fall of 1863, in the endeavor to create there a sentiment favorable to the North, to counteract the influence of Confederate emissaries and the English aristocracy in behalf of the South. This influence had become so powerful that the English government was more than half inclined to join Louis Napoleon, the French Emperor, in an act of forcible intervention for the recognition of the Confederate States. It wavered, because the English common people as distinguished from the higher classes, sympathized with the North. But the sufferings of the common people, produced by our great war through the suspension or stagnation of the great industries by which they earned their support, were chillingly discouraging these sympathies as year after year went by without ending the war and bringing them relief. When Beecher arrived there, on his way home after some weeks of recuperation and rest on the continent, the American cause was wavering in the balance; the critical moment, in fact, had come, and he was importuned by the friends of our country to speak on the issues of the war. Their entreaties prevailed, though he had thrice before refused, in the belief that any effort he might make would prove vain, and arrangements were made for a series of speeches at Manchester, Glasgow, Edinburgh, Liverpool and London.

No sooner was the announcement made than the Rebel sympathizers planned to thwart his purpose and prevent his being heard by vociferous interruptions and noise, by capturing, in short, the meetings advertized and turning them to their own advantage. "So long as physical violence is not resorted to," says Abbott, "this sort of tactics seems to be treated in England as a legitimate part of the game." Blood-red placards were posted in the streets of the cities where he was to speak. They called upon the mob to prevent his speaking by misreporting his past utterances and by gross libels of his character and purpose. No wonder that he was in an agony of depression before he entered upon his task and spent most of the morning on his knees. Like Jacob he wrestled with God, and like him he prevailed, so that before going to the meeting in Manchester "a great sense of repose" was given him. We will not undertake to describe each meeting nor is it necessary. He encountered a similar experience in them all. "It was like talking to a storm at sea," he says of his address at Manchester; and of his address at Liverpool, where the uproar was greatest and most prolonged, where for an hour and a half he fought the mob before he got control, "I sometimes felt," he says, "like a shipmaster attempting to preach on board of a ship through a speaking trumpet, with a tornado on the sea and a mutiny among the men."

Not to prolong our account, suffice it to say that

in every one of those five places he gained the mastery over his audience by his wit, his good-natured patience, his artful and subduing eloquence, and compelled them to hear him. The addresses were fully reported and widely published by the English press. Such unity pervaded them that they seemed like one connected speech and they presented and vindicated the cause of the North so well that the thought of intervention was abandoned. "Probably," says Mark Hopkins, "the world has seen no grander instance of the ascendency of eloquence and of the personal power of a single man, and he a foreigner, in the face of prejudiced and excited mobs."

When Mr. Beecher returned to America, he received such an ovation as few American citizens ever received from their grateful countrymen. Well had it been for his happiness and perhaps for his fame if then he had died in the fifty-first year of his age. But for his purification he must needs pass through a fiery furnace, in the heat and anguish of which he wished for death a thousand times before that boon was granted him. This brings us to the third notable epoch of his Brooklyn pastorate,— that covered by the Tilton scandal and its dire effects for a time upon his good name. We do not propose to enter upon a rehearsal of this strange and mysterious affair. It remains still an unsolved mystery, and perhaps always will remain so. If any one is curious to learn all that is now known about it, he can turn to the twelfth chapter of Abbott's book, or the fuller account given by Dr. Barrows' volume (chapters 37–40).   The writer's opinion is that there was no truth in the charges made against him.   He holds this opinion because of the published statement of Mr. Wm. A. Beach, Tilton's counsel: "I had not been four days on the trial before I was confident that he was innocent"; because Judge Neilson, who presided at this trial, was of this opinion; because of all the writer saw and heard as a member of the celebrated Plymouth Church council summoned to review the case after it had been passed upon by the courts, and which, after the fullest investigation, unanimously pronounced him still worthy of confidence as a Christian minister; and because his own church, the great Plymouth Church, whose charities and honorable men are widely known, remained steadfast in its confidence, solidly and unitedly so, to the end of his life.   This could not have been so, and *never is* the case, where there is any good ground of suspicion that the minister, who is accused of this particular sin alleged against him, is guilty.   For these reasons, and for the psychological reason that the writer repeatedly attended Plymouth Church during that period, and heard Mr. Beecher's public prayers, and could not believe it possible for a man to pray as he did if that man were an immoral man, or a hypocrite—he, therefore, agrees with Dr. Lyman Abbott in saying: "Personally I believe that future history will attach as little emphasis to this episode in the life of Beecher as history now attaches to analogous imputations, with far more to give them color, brought against John Wesley in his lifetime."

What now, in conclusion, shall we say of him?
Not that he was a perfect man; he had unquestionably his faults—trivial faults, however—faults which
he himself confessed and deplored more than did his
friends; but they were the faults of *a great man,*
whose greatness so impresses us that we are inclined to forget or condone these faults. He was also
a large-hearted, broad-minded, good man, whose
goodness remains unimpeachable in spite of the dark
cloud which for a while cast its shadow upon him.
It is safe to say that people of candor generally
believe this. Striking evidence of it is to be seen
there in Brooklyn, where he lived for nearly forty
years and was best known. As the people filed past
his coffin in Plymouth Church, "the suggestion was
made," says Dr. Abbott, "that a statue should be
erected by citizens of Brooklyn to his memory. In
less than two weeks after his death, a meeting of
citizens was held to forward this movement, and it
was so largely attended that many were unable to
gain admittance to the room. The money for the
purpose was easily obtained, rather it should be
said, was spontaneously offered, and in June, 1891,
the statue, designed by J. Q. A. Ward, was erected
in City Hall Square, facing the building where he
had been put on trial as for his life, and remaining
there a perpetual witness to the judgment of the
citizens of Brooklyn between him and his accusers."

It presents a good likeness of the man, as he appeared in his later years. It seems appropriate that
it should stand in that crowded city square surrounded by all sorts and conditions of men, for whom

his great heart beat in sympathy. He was a man of the people and lived for them. One may easily imagine those lips of bronze softening to flexible flesh and speaking once more in the tones of that "witching voice," which entranced men so often for their good. The memories of his compassion for the poor and oppressed, and of his terrific scorn for all unrighteous, conscienceless scoundrels, whom no appeal of weakness or misery can move to pity or compunction, it is good for men to have revived. They make this place a place for repentance and the beginning of a new life to some; to others a place of gratitude for God's gift of good men to this sin-stricken earth. Dr. Barrows says rightly, that Lowell's characterization of Lincoln "was equally true of Mr. Beecher."

> "His was no lonely mountain peak of mind,
>
> .   .   .   .   .
>
> Broad prairie rather, genial, level-lined,
> Fruitful and friendly to all human kind,
> Yet also nigh to heaven, and loved of loftiest stars."

X

PHILLIPS BROOKS

X

PHILLIPS BROOKS

1835–1893

In an interesting comparison of Henry Ward Beecher and Phillips Brooks as preachers, Dr. Lyman Abbott says: "I should describe Phillips Brooks as the greater preacher, but Mr. Beecher as the greater orator"; the distinctive function of the preacher being, in his opinion, "the unveiling of the invisible world, looking himself and enabling others also to look upon the things which are unseen and eternal." This was the exclusive mission of Phillips Brooks and in the fulfillment of this he is unsurpassed, Dr. Abbott thinks, by any American preacher. In this opinion we agree with him after a careful study of Brooks' life and ministry.

He was the second son, in a family of six boys, of William Gray Brooks and Mary Ann Phillips. He owed much to his parents, both of whom belonged to the best and most distinguished of the old New England families. "The consummate flower of nine generations of cultured Puritan stock," Dr. Brastow says. ("Representative Modern Preachers.") We can recall no public man of the last century who outranks him in this respect of ancestral worth. A long line of ancestors, eminent for piety, culture, learning, wealth and high social position, he was able to look back upon from both sides of his parental house. It is an interesting genealogical history which is presented to us in the first chapter of his "Life" by Professor Allen, his biographer—one replete with profitable suggestions and numerous anecdotes.

Phillips Brooks united in his own person and character the most remarkable traits and qualities of both parents. It was indeed a rich inheritance which he derived from them.

A friend of Phillips Brooks has given us the following account of them and of what they each bequeathed to their gifted son. "Mr. Brooks (the father) always gave me the notion of a typical Boston merchant, solid, upright, unimaginative, unemotional. Mrs. Brooks gave me the notion of a woman of an intense emotional nature; the very tones of her voice vibratory with feeling and deep spiritual life—the temperament of genius and the saintly character. I felt that Phillips Brooks owed to his father very much—the businesslike and orderly habit; the administrative faculty which worked so easily; the clear logical understanding (combined with powers of clear conception and statement) that framed so well the skeletons of those sermons, which the intuitive reason, the active imagination, the literary sense, the spiritual fire (qualities derived from his mother) so richly filled out and inspired afterwards; and the strong common sense that no fervor of feeling, no passionate outburst of soul, could ever sweep from its anchorage. But I never had a question that what made Phillips Brooks a prophet, a leader, a power among men, was from the Phillips (the mother's) side of the family. The stalwart form, the big heart, the shapely head, the changeful countenance, the voice that so easily grew tremulous with feeling, the eager look and gesture, the magnetism, the genius seemed to me, and I believe seemed to him, his mother's. The father saw things as they were; she saw things in vision, ideally as they should be. So Phillips Brooks knew the facts of life, seeing with his father's eyes, and all the hopes and possibilities of life through the eyes of his mother."

His biographer, commenting upon this fusion of the qualities of both parents in his personality, adds: "Had he received by transmission only the outlook of his father, without the inspired heroism of his mother, he would not have risen to greatness. But, on the other hand, had he inherited from his mother alone, he might have been known as an ardent reformer, not unlike his kinsman Wendell Phillips, but the wonderful fascination of his power for men of every class and degree, the universal appeal to a common humanity, would have been wanting."

Phillips Brooks was almost as fortunate in his birthplace as in his parentage. Boston at that time was, more than now, the highest seat of culture and refinement in our country. Its atmosphere was magnetic and stimulating from the social and public influences generated by its historic memories, its eminent citizens, its civic privileges, its constellation of brilliant authors, its enterprising publishing houses, its superior schools, libraries and educational advantages, its distinguished preachers and flourishing churches. All these advantages to the highest degree were enjoyed by Phillips Brooks through the high social position of his parents. Possessed of ample means they lavished upon their sons every educational advantage that could contribute to their welfare, besides devoting themselves at home to their happiness and culture. He was educated at Boston's famous Latin School and at Harvard College, receiving from the former excellent instruction and training in the principles of English Composition and the Ancient Classics, and at college having a taste for literature developed which he gratified by wide and diligent reading. He read with extraordinary speed. He was endowed, like Macaulay, with a marvelous gift of very rapidly taking in a printed page. "His record as a student," his biographer says, "shows that he possessed the capacity for exact scholarship, but also that he had no ambition to maintain a high rank in his class. He stood thirteenth in a class of sixty-six. He took his college course easily. He gave the impression of one who was not obliged to drudge in order to master his studies." His thorough training, his quick insight, his capacity for mental concentration enabled him to perform with ease and speed the required task, leaving him abundant leisure for discursive reading, the mastery of books, and the observation of life." "He gave no sign of being an orator. When he became known in after years as a pulpit orator, those who remembered him in his college days were surprised." But he disclosed in those college days uncommon ability as a writer. "In the occasional papers (presented to 'The Hasty Pudding' and the A. Δ. Φ. college societies of which he was a member), where he chose his own subject and was in sympathy with his audience, free to give full expression to his thought, his wit, or humor, he was unsurpassed."

Having thus sketched his mental development, it remains to speak of his spiritual and religious development. His mother was his first and most important religious teacher. "Phillips Brooks' mother," says Dr. W. N. Clarke, "was one of the most religious of the religious, intense, conscientious, self-sacrificing, rapturous. Few men have ever known such mother-love as embraced this son so long as his mother lived." She was a woman of extraordinary piety. She possessed all the fervor of a primitive Methodist, united with the intelligence and keen spiritual perception of the descendant of a long line of the most learned of the New England divines. "She had a deep interior life of the soul whose phases were more real and vital than the phenomena of the passing world. Religion to her was a life in Christ, and her love for Christ and his truth was a passion. She was a diligent student of the Bible and its teaching, that she might better teach her children. In this task of teaching her children religion she was diligent and indefatigable, laboring with a concentrated purpose in season and out of season, never for a moment forgetful of her mission, quick to seize the passing moment which seemed fertile for opportunity, but withal gentle and alluring and making religion attractive."

She showed remarkable wisdom in her religious teaching and effort to win her sons one by one to a personal self-commitment to the Christian life. "She studied her opportunities of approach to the soul," Professor Allen says. She knew when to speak and when to keep silent, careful not to press them, in her zeal, to the point of disgust and repulsion of the subject which she was so earnest to have them consider. To an anxious mother she once said, "There is an age when it is not well to follow or question your boy too closely. Up to that time you may carefully instruct and direct him; as you are his best friend. He is never happy unless the story of the day has been told; you must hear about his friends, his school; all that interests him must be your interest. Suddenly these confidences cease; the affectionate son becomes reserved and silent; he seeks the intimate friendship of other lads; he goes out; he is averse to telling where he is going or how long he will be gone. He comes in and goes silently to his room. All this is a startling change to the mother; but it is also her opportunity to practice wisdom by loving and praying for and absolutely trusting her son. The faithful instruction and careful training during his early years the son can never forget. Therefore trust not only your heavenly Father, but your son. The period of which I speak appears to me to be one in which the boy dies and the man is born; his individuality rises up before him, and he is dazed and almost overwhelmed by his first consciousness of himself. I have always believed that it was then that the

Creator was speaking with my sons, and that it was good for their souls to be left alone with him, while I, their mother, stood trembling, praying and waiting, knowing that when the man was developed from the boy I should have my sons again and there would be a deeper sympathy than ever between us."

Happily her efforts were warmly assisted by her husband and her pastor, Dr. A. H. Vinton, the minister of St. Paul's Episcopal Church, Boston, which they made their religious home when Phillips was four years old, they having previously attended the First Church (Unitarian).

Upon his graduation from Harvard, Phillips Brooks, then not twenty years old, obtained the appointment of usher, or subordinate teacher, in the Boston Latin School. He had not made any public profession of religion then and had no inclination to become a preacher of the gospel. His plan was, after gaining some experience in teaching in the Latin School, to go abroad for further study and fit himself for a college professorship. But "though man proposes God disposes": never was there a more striking example of this truth. His experiment in teaching proved an utter and most humiliating failure, and he resigned his position in a few months. The cause of his failure was his inability to maintain good order among the unruly, rowdyish set of boys placed under him. He was made of too gentle stuff to cope successfully with those turbulent spirits.

After a season of uncertainty and bewilderment he turned his thoughts to the Christian ministry, and entered the Episcopal Theological School in Alexandria, Va., not yet having received confirmation, by which in the Episcopal Church its adherents publicly profess their faith. This act was delayed until the close of his first year in the seminary, indicating how abruptly he had entered upon his studies for the ministry. He apparently fled (secretly) to the seminary to hide his shame. But though he had made no public profession of faith, we have a signal proof that he was not without faith, in the words preserved for us by Professor Allen, "with which he closed the record of his thoughts on the eve of his departure for Virginia":

"As we pass from some experience to some experiment, from a tried to an untried life, it is as when we turn to a new page in a book we have never read before, but whose author we know and love and trust to give us on every page words of counsel and purity and strengthening virtue."

He did not find the Theological School pleasant or satisfactory. It was a poor, ill-furnished, meagerly equipped institution. Writing to his father soon after his arrival he said: "It is the most shiftless, slipshod place I ever saw. The instruction here is very poor. All that we get in the lecture and recitation-rooms I consider worth just nothing." There was on the Faculty only one man of mark and ability in teaching, Dr. Sparrow, and he "so out of health that we seldom see him and when we do he is too unwell to exert himself at all." The library he describes as "worth just nothing at all, pretty much like all the rest of the seminary, which seems poorer and poorer to me every day." Finally he says near the end of the first year: "I have serious doubts whether it will be worth while for me to come back here for two more years, whether it won't be better to study at home, if this is really the best seminary in the country." He would have found Andover a far better seminary, where was a staff of very able theological instructors and a kind of teaching vastly superior; and near the end of the year he writes to his father: "I am thinking strongly of Andover, please let me know what you think of it." For some inexplicable reason he did not go to Andover, which, in addition to its strong Faculty, on which were Professors Park, Phelps, and Shedd, then in their meridian glory, and a well-furnished library and other inviting conveniences, possessed the additional recommendation of having been established and endowed by his maternal ancestors.

The scheme was not favored it seems by his pastor, Dr. Vinton, or his father, and probably it was quite as well for him to stay in Alexandria. The defects in his seminary curriculum and teaching, says his biographer, "forced him to work for himself, to take his theological education in a measure into his own hand," and this self-education proved better in his case probably than the best teaching he could have received from the ablest theological faculty. It begot in him independence of mind and habits of solitary thought and study, of free investigation and diligent reading that were of the greatest value.

The students of the seminary also, in the lack of competent teachers, gave to themselves a teaching and drill in their clubs and societies that was in some respects superior to anything they could have found in the classroom or private instruction of the best professor. They criticized one another with a freedom and justice and wholesome severity which would have been called harsh and cruel in him. Two examples are given in Professor Allen's life of Brooks: There was among the students a young man of sonorous voice and showy physique, but meagre attainments, who met with small success in his essays at preaching. He asked, "why, with his fine presence and striking elocution, he made no better impression as a preacher?" "Why," answered a classmate, "you don't know enough. You don't study enough. You are too noisy. Perhaps if you'd take more load on your cart, it would not rattle so."

Another example is one where a sermon of Brooks himself was the subject of criticism. It was his first sermon, on the text, "The simplicity that is in Christ," 2 Cor. 11:3. "A cruel classmate's criticism," he says, "was that there was very little simplicity in the sermon and no Christ." He adds, "The sermon was never preached again. It was an attempt to define doctrine instead of to show a man, a God, a Savior."

By his professors and fellow students Mr. Brooks was quickly recognized as a star of first magnitude. "As a classical scholar," says a classmate, "none matched him. The Greek of the New Testament Epistles, as he dealt with it, 'rejoiced like Enoch in being translated.' " ❙ His rare gifts as a writer were

manifest in his earliest essays. The style ha . .
grace of the after-sermons, a nameless quality the
made some of us feel that we must begin over ag es-
The same with the thought. It never seemed lik
yours or what might come in time to be yours.
The only cheering thing about it was that it surprised the professors. There was some comfort in
hearing Dr. Sparrow say: "Mr. Brooks is very
remarkable"; and "that he recognized in him a
pupil who needed none of his instruction." The
late Dr. W. N. Clarke thus briefly sums up the work
done by Phillips Brooks at the theological seminary
in Alexandria: "In the three years that he spent
there his first conscious and well-directed work was
done. The seminary was so little absorbing that
he took his own way and it was the way of reading.
His reading was enormous in amount and very wide
in range. He sought to lay hold upon the best
that the human mind had done, and to make it his
own."*

One practice observed by him in the seminary
preserves the record of his reading and its wide
range, that contributed greatly to his development
of mind. He never was without a note-book, to
record the books he read, to preserve extracts from
them that he deemed especially notable and worth
preserving, and the thoughts of his own suggested
by them. These thoughts are upon every variety
of subject, and possess an originality, a depth, wisdom and value that are most remarkable. Many of
them are equal to the ideas and reflections of his

* See Art. *Huxley and Phillips Brooks.* Bib. Sac., Jan. 1902, Vol. 59.

ays. As an exercise, it was of inestimable
in developing his powers of independent
ught, and training him to the clear and easy
expression of his thought. "One of the most important features of the note-books," Professor Allen
points out, "is the intimations they contain of a
profound conception of the scheme of things,
wrought out by an isolated student in much inward
perturbation with no assistance from his teachers.
When Phillips Brooks left home for the theological
seminary, he provided himself in advance with these
books, in anticipation of the service they would
render. When he reached his new abode, and found
himself among strangers, in an inconvenient room,
with a bed too short for him, with no 'arm chair'
or any of the comforts and conveniences of life,
with only the light afforded by a tallow candle,
he sat down at the earliest moment to his self-imposed
task and continued the work of registering his
thoughts. He divided his note-book in two equal
parts, the first for holding remarks of others worth
copying, hints and suggestions from his reading,
stray bits of information, all the items in short for
a miscellaneous commonplace-book. In the second
half he wrote down the thoughts which were his
own. It is worth mentioning that he filled out the
second half of the book long before the first, and
went back to fill the empty pages with the ideas
that were coming thick and fast."

"The first thing which impresses one in turning
over these note-books is the capacity shown for
high scholarship. Greek and Latin were no longer

dead languages, but were at his disposal. . . . Thus in the first few months after he reached the seminary, we find him reading Herodotus and Aeschylus, and among Latin writers, Plautus, Lucretius, and Lucan; of ecclesiastical writers, Augustine, Tertullian and the venerable Bede. Tertullian attracted with him a singular charm, as though he found in that vehement, passionate soul something akin to his own moods. From all these writers he was making extracts, sometimes in the original, or translating as an exercise for the mastery of the language. Schiller's 'Wallenstein' also attracted him and he kept up his French by reading Saint Pierre's 'Etudes de la Nature.' He had special qualifications for such work in his gift for languages.

"Next to the study of the classics and early ecclesiastical writers comes his devotion to English literature. He was reading so many books during his first year in the seminary that one marvels how he found time for the required tasks of daily recitations." Professor Allen names thirty-four English authors "into whom he is dipping at will, from whom also he is making extracts in his note-books. The quotations he copies reveal the character of his mind; and there is disclosed here a veritable hunger to know the best thought of the world."

"The note-books indicate that in his reading he kept his eye upon one incidental object, the accumulation of ideas, of pithy phrases, or epigrammatic statements, and above all of similes and comparisons. These he puts down in condensed form as so much material for future use. There are many hundreds of similes collected here, which afterwards reappeared in his preaching."

His biographer states that in all his reading and thinking he had one particular aim of supreme importance. It was "to trace the connection between ideas and principles of conduct, between theological dogmas and the actual life of the soul, to show how they ministered to the growth of a man in righteousness of character. Confronted as he was with doctrines and dogmas, whose acceptance was regarded as important, he asked for their *nexus* with the human will, or with the reason and the feeling that led as motives to the action of the will." If he found no connection he called them "theological dry rot." "There was another thought," says Professor Allen, "much in his mind and finding frequent expression, which was to become one of his ruling ideas—that truth had many aspects, that what failed to bring one man strength or consolation might to another be the source of joy and peace. To condemn another man's belief or to sneer at it was madness": "Poor feeble creatures in a feeble world, we each must catch what is most comfort to his feebleness. Believe in mine for me, I will believe in yours for you. Surely we each have quite enough to do to hold our own, without this cruel folly of saying to another, 'Your comfort is a cheat, your hope a heresy, the earnest life you are living a lie.'"

"Now and then," says Dr. Allen, "but rarely, he jots down in his note-book some item gained from his teachers. Whatever help by way of suggestion and inspiration was afforded by Dr. Sparrow, yet the ultimate solution of theological problems was made by Phillips Brooks himself in his own distinctive manner."

Examples from his note-books of the first year in the seminary (he was then only twenty-one) are: "We must learn the infinite capacity of truth to speak to every human mind, and of every human mind to hear, and more or less completely understand the truth that speaks. . . . Let us then reverence our neighbor's way of finding truth. If by his life and faith we can clearly see that he is finding it indeed, let us not turn away because he hears it in another tongue than ours. The speaker is the same. If he can read in a stormy sky, or a sunny landscape, lessons for which we must go to books and sermons so much the better for him."

"A noble principle or thought, like the widow's barrel and cruse is never dry. We draw on it for our daily life, we drink of its power in our weakness, and taste its power in our despair; but God's blessing is on it and the fulness of his truth is filling it, and so it never fails. We come back to it in our next weakness or our next despondency, and find it thoughtful and hopeful as ever, till the famine is over, and, kept alive and nurtured by its strength, we come forth to gather new harvests of great thoughts."

Like almost all successful preachers, he began to preach while a student in the seminary. In his senior year he and another member of his class took charge of a small mission at Sharon, three miles distant. This is the best way to learn to preach. Thus only can the powers that are used in preaching, especially extempore preaching, be developed. He is said to have made a total failure on his first attempt, receiving as his only encouragement the advice to "try again." This he did, and with such promising success, that he soon after wrote to his brother, "Though no orator as Brutus is, it goes pretty glib." Better evidence than this is found in the fact that two strangers toward the end of the year were seen in his congregation, who after the sermon sought an interview with him, and so favorably impressed had they been with his sermon, invited him in the name of their church, whose committee they were, to become the pastor of the Church of the Advent, Philadelphia. He accepted the call and entered upon his work on Sunday, July 10, 1859, at the age of twenty-three and one-half years.

Ten years he labored in Philadelphia, two and one-half years as minister of the Church of the Advent, seven and one-half as minister of the Church of the Holy Trinity. Twenty-two years he labored in Boston as minister of Trinity Church, and for a year and a half he served his Church as the Bishop of Massachusetts.

His development in pulpit power as a preacher of the gospel was rapid, almost astonishing, and his reputation as a remarkable preacher soon became established and wide-spread. Of course he did not at once attain the acme of his power. This had its stages of growth, like that of lesser men, and it did not reach its culmination until he went to Boston and was midway in his ministry there, but the chief qualities that characterized his preaching in the fulness and maturity of his glorious manhood, were developed and manifested in those years of his early ministry spent in Philadelphia. "Later years," says Dr. Brastow, "may have witnessed in many respects more important service for the church and the world, but none were marked by greater intellectual brilliancy or more popular effectiveness than those years of the Philadelphia ministry."

What then were the chief characteristics of his preaching? What qualities distinguished this great man, who for a full generation, upward of thirty-three years, was to stand before the American people in two of their chief cities and proclaim to them with most convincing and impressive powers the everlasting gospel of Christ?

(1) He was a magnificent specimen of physical manhood. Tall of stature—six feet four inches—of stalwart, symmetrical form, which was surmounted by a large, shapely head with dark, kindly eyes and noble features, expressive mouth and chin, unconcealed by any beard, the very appearance of the man drew attention.

(2) An agreeable voice, which Dr. Brastow describes (in "Representative Modern Preachers") as "a full, strong voice, not well-managed, but full of feeling and force." It was "not well-managed," because, unlike Beecher, he never tried to improve it by judicious elocutionary training; he "despised elocution as begetting self-consciousness, at war with naturalness and simplicity." In his case, his agree-

able sympathetic voice with its unspoiled naturalness joined to his unconscious earnestness was
probably an advantage, in spite of the torrent-like
rapidity of his utterance.

(3) He was a very thoughtful preacher. In the
natural opulence and productiveness of his mind
he resembled Beecher. But he greatly surpassed
Beecher as a scholar and in the extent of his reading
and literary culture. He laid under tribute nearly
the whole realm of good literature. And so there
was in his sermons, as Professor Allen says, "an
indescribable flavor of the world's richest literature."
They possess also a greater literary value than
Beecher's as sermon literature, because of the superior training in English received by him in the Latin
School and at Harvard, and his constant practice
of careful writing in his note-books as well as of his
sermons. He inherited from his father a talent for
clear, exact expression, with which there was united
an imaginative charm which arrested attention and
held it spellbound.

(4) He possessed an extraordinary capacity for
feeling and especially religious feeling. "It was this
element," says Professor Allen, "that formed one
large constituent in the secret of his strength. His
capacity for deep feeling was like the ocean in its
majesty; ideas, experiences, the forces of life that
appealed to him, roused him as a whirlwind, in
waves of inevitable power, and feeling became a
torrent until it had found expression. But this
feeling found its freest expression in the pulpit,
going forth to the great congregation." In this

capacity for deep, overwhelming feeling, Brooks and Beecher were alike, and both derived the endowment from their mothers. It is characteristic of all the great preachers and is the chief element of impressive, enthralling eloquence.

(5) He was possessed of a rich and fertile imagination, which gave color to all his preaching. He habitually looked at truth through the revealing or transfiguring light of imagination. "This habit of looking at truth through the imagination, which, Dr. Brastow thinks, was in part at least the result of his study of Alexandrian philosophy and the Church Fathers, Tertullian, Cyprian and Augustine, was prominent in his preaching throughout his career" ("Representative Preachers"). His mind was analogical and was quick to discover resemblances. It found in outward things attractive and instructive images of divine truth. His sermon, "The Candle of the Lord," is an interesting example. How skilfully he uses the candle and its relation to the fire that kindles it into a blaze and makes it subservient to its uses, as an analogue of man's spirit and its relation to God!

Through his imagination, Phillips Brooks was an able and most interesting interpreter of truth. By it also he glorified truth and so commended it to men, that they suddenly found it attractive who previously had discovered no beauty or compelling charm in it.

(6) His vision of things unseen and eternal was most clear, constant and real. "That vision of soul, that sense of the invisible and eternal," says

Dr. Brastow, "was one of his choicest gifts and it
was nourished by all the choicest sources of his
culture and all the great experiences of his life." He
inherited this also from his mother. It grew and
expanded his horizon with the advancing years.
He lived habitually in two worlds, this mundane
world and the heavenly world. "In the realm that
to Huxley was non-existent for want of evidence,"
says Dr. W. N. Clarke, "Brooks lived and moved
and had his being. Hear the voice of one who finds
it most real, and dwells at home in its spiritual
atmosphere. Quotation is the quickest way to
show what Phillips Brooks found there: 'I knew
all about God before you told me,' said little blind,
deaf, dumb Helen Keller to me one day, 'only I did
not know His name.' It was a perfect expression
of the innateness of the divine idea in the human
mind, of the belonging of the human soul to God."
In a more personal strain, he says again: "Less
and less, I think, grows the consciousness of seeking
God. Greater and greater grows the certainty that
he is seeking us and giving himself to us to the complete measure of our present capacity. 'That is
love, not that we loved him, but that he loved us.'
There is such a thing as putting ourselves in the way
of God's overflowing love and letting it break upon
us till the response of love comes, not by struggle,
not even by deliberation, but by necessity, as the
echo comes when the sound strikes the rock." What
language is this, for affirmation of infinite but tangi-
ble realities discovered in that world which Huxley
found blank and bare! In this region moved year

after year the thought and utterance of the man, and the action of his life. There he found a splendid freedom, and his ample powers struck out in generous activity. He did not look into religion and into God as a bird may look from its nest into the open sky. He rose into religion and into God, and was there sustained.

A beautiful illustration of the truth of Dr. Clarke's representation here of the operation of the religious faculty, in the case of Phillips Brooks and of all whom he inspired with like faith, has been given the writer of this "study," while at work upon it. On the piazza of our summer cottage, some little wrens have built their nest and reared their young. The time-having come for their young to leave their nest and launch themselves upon the air in flight, it seemed marvelous, that with no experience in flying, they boldly flung themselves upon the air, as their instinct prompted, and found themselves equipped with the needful wings that carried them safely in it; and that, in a little while, these wings being strengthened and developed by exercise, they found flying a joy and the air their natural element. So let a human soul commit itself to the religious life as taught by Christ, and its faith will be justified that this life is the life for which it was intended.

"To Phillips Brooks," says Dr. Clarke, "God was the greatest and most certain of realities. Christ has revealed God, and shown what manner of God he is, and to this man Christ stood for God: Christ in the infinite beauty and power of his character meant the meaning of God to him. God meant Christ, and Christ meant God; and under either name he had before him the reality which he felt to be the glory of this world and of all worlds. /Accordingly his keywords were such as God, Christ, the soul, personality, love, life. The keyword of his later ministry was life. In those glorious years of spiritual power he used to say that he had only one text and one sermon, and the one text was, I am come that they might have life, and have it more abundantly. The soul's experience of inexhaustible, overflowing life in fellowship with the living God, this was his own theme, and this experience he helped multitudes to make their own."* He might have truly said, with the apostle: "My citizenship is in heaven. I have directed my mind to things above where Christ sitteth on the right hand of God." He walked with God; he conversed with Christ as his most intimate friend. He loved his earthly friends and fondly sought and lingered in their society, but for none of them had he such attachment as for Christ. Him he knew better and from him received an influence more potent, real and palpable than from any other. His mother's exhortations: "Keep close to your Savior, Philly," "Preach Christ faithfully," he carefully observed.

(7) He possessed an independent mind. Though he studied the works of the great men of the past and of his own time, and appreciated them, the works of the Christian Fathers, of Bacon, Robertson, Bossuet, Goethe, yet he owned none of them as

* Article, *Huxley and Phillips Brooks.* Bib. Sac., Vol. LIX, pp. 14-15.

master. He weighed the thoughts and opinions of each in the balance of his own mind and accepted what in his judgment was true. He did not give an unquestioning, blind assent even to the greatest. Furthermore, he was not willing to accept another's opinion of a book or author; he wanted to read him for himself. The practice of review reading as a substitute for one's personal examination of books, he condemned as unprofitable. "To read merely what some one has said about a book," he says (see "Essays and Addresses," *Courage*) "is probably as unstimulating, as unfertilizing a process as the human mind can submit to. Read books themselves. To read a book is to make a friend; if it is worth your reading you meet a man; if there is anything in you, he will quicken it."

(8) He magnified Christ out of a rich and *ever deepening personal experience* of his grace. His preaching, like that of the apostles, was largely a personal testimony, a speaking of things which he has seen and heard. Quite as much as Beecher, he aimed to hold up and commend Christ to his great congregation, rather than discourse to them upon abstract theological dogmas and abstruse themes. Among his published sermons, there are four or five upon the single text, John 8:12: "I am the Light of the World, he that followeth me, etc." We recommend to our readers to read the particular one which furnishes the title to the fifth series of his sermons, "The Light of the World." In it, he represents Christ as doing for the individual soul and the world of humanity, what the sun does

for the physical world; as waking it up from its previous darkness, torpidity and sterile state to a state of transforming light and life, beauty and fruitfulness. Christ and the soul were meant for each other as the sun and the earth. And as the quickening sun in the morning and in the spring-time, calls to the drowsy and frost-blighted earth, to awake and array itself in its beautiful garments, and in doing this to come on to its true self, so the Christ in like manner calls to man to put off his sin and misery and enter upon his true life and fulfill his high destiny. It is a message that appeals to the best that is in man and encourages him to attempt for himself what is best. It is a gospel of redemption from sin and death.

(9) He possessed a power of universal sympathy, the power of entering into the lives of people of every class, and inspiring them "to the elevation of high strung feeling and purposes." "Marvelously," says a distinguished Methodist preacher,* "did he bring out of that wonderful gospel teachings which appeal to the profound and the learned, and plain lessons which also help the unlettered." The scholar said, "He is of us," and the unlettered, "He is of us." The poor said, "He is of us," and the rich said, "He is of us." To the young he was full of buoyancy; to the troubled he was a man deeply acquainted with grief. All men, of all classes and conditions claimed him because in his magnificent heart and sympathy he seemed to enter into their trials, disappointments and successes,

* Vol. 2, p. 812 of Professor Allen's Life.

and had power to heal the soreness of heart which was common to them all.

(10) He was unmistakably a great man in every respect, physically, mentally, morally and in heart. "I have known," says Dr. Weir Mitchell, "a number of the men we call great—poets, statesmen, soldiers— but Phillips Brooks was the only one I ever knew who seemed to me entirely great." His was that genuine greatness which made itself quickly felt in spite of every obstacle. Personal prejudices, theological differences and antagonisms, sectarian bitterness and worldly-mindedness, pride of intellect—each and all were swept away; men were made captives to his will, and glad to have it so.

Whatever he did was greatly done. There was the stamp of his great heart and soul upon it. A remarkable example: When still a young man of only twenty-nine, scarcely known outside of Philadelphia, he was given the signal honor of making the prayer at the commemorative service of Harvard in honor of its soldier dead, who had fallen in the war. "Why should such a part have been given to so young a man on such an important occasion?" many asked, and in asking they implied their displeasure and disposition not to be satisfied with any service he might render in performing the difficult function. But with the first sentence their attention was caught and they listened breathless. When the prayer was over the people turned and looked at one another and said: "What a prayer!" "It was the most impressive utterance," says President Eliot, "of a proud and happy day. Even

Lowell's 'Commemoration Ode' did not at the moment so touch the hearts of his hearers."

His eloquence was unique, entirely unlike that of any other preacher. It owed little or nothing, as we have said, to his elocution or grace of delivery. It was an eloquence entirely of thought and feeling, "a stream of liquid fire, hurrying on in a careless monotone so swiftly as to tease and half baffle the most watchful ear, until the great throng in painful, eager silence became entranced and ecstatic under its influence." This was true of his written sermons closely read, as he stood impassive, almost statuesque before his audience. He possessed, however, another kind of eloquence, that of the extempore speaker, which was even more wonderful. "As an extempore speaker he was simply matchless," Dr. Weir Mitchell says. This mode of speaking he practiced from the beginning. In Philadelphia he had regularly a Wednesday evening service, at which he usually spoke in this way, and as Dr. Weir Mitchell thought, the most impressively. "There and thus, you got all the impressible sympathy his noble sturdiness (of person) gave to the torrent of speech, which at first had some hesitancy, and then rolled on, easy, fluent and strong." He prepared himself for preaching with the greatest care. His method of preparation is fully described in the fourth chapter of the second volume of Professor Allen's "Life." It is well worth careful study for its homiletic value. It offers the best example of the art of sermon-making we know of.

The first step was to jot down in his "note-book"

(some kind of note-book was his inseparable companion) the idea of his sermon, as it occurred to him in his thinking or Bible study. Carrying constantly in mind the thought of his ministry, he was always on the lookout for sermon topics, and was quick to catch any hint that might give him a sermon and made haste to write it down with the related suggestions that might come with it.

Here are two examples:

John 1:46 "Come and see."

"The proper appeal that may be made to a sceptic to come and test Christianity. (1) The truth of the Bible. (2) The phenomenon of Christ. (3) The Christian History. (4) The religious experience, by putting himself into the power of what he did hold."

Acts 3:3 "Silver and gold have I none, but such as I have give I thee."

"There is something better for us to *have* than money. So there must be something better to *give*. The greatest benefactors have not given money—Christ. So of those who have helped you most. Do not make anything I say an excuse for not giving money. What we can give besides; ideas, inspiration, comfort, and above all access to God for what He alone can give—forgiveness and grace. A man must really possess, himself, before he can really give."

A multitude of germinal ideas and embryo sketches of this kind are found in his note-books. He thus never lacked subjects to preach upon.

Usually he had settled upon his text by Monday

noon for the next Sunday morning, and he gave Mondays and Tuesdays to the collection of materials for it, "bringing together in his note-book or on scraps of paper the thoughts which were cognate to his leading thought, or necessary for its illustration and expansion." Wednesday forenoon he devoted entirely to writing out the plan he would follow. The hardest part of his work was then believed to be done. Thursday forenoon and Friday forenoon were devoted to writing the sermon. "He wrote with rapidity and ease, rarely making a correction, and in a large, legible handwriting."

In a similar way he prepared his plans for his extempore sermons. He never trusted to the time of preaching to give him what he wanted to say. He previously fixed upon his topic and outlined his course of thought.

In reading Dr. Allen's description of his plan-making, you get the impression that there was something mechanical about this work, and wonder how he could make those dry bones live, or clothe these skeletons with such strength and beauty. But that was the work of his genius, quickened by his religious faith and supported by his unflagging labor in thinking, reading, and observation of life, through which abundant materials were supplied.

"He first opened his soul to the influence of the truth which was to constitute his message, devising the most forcible method in order to make it appeal to his own heart, and then under the influence of his own conviction he wrote and preached his sermon. This process kept him natural, sincere and unaffected, preserving his personality in all and free from the dangers of conventionalism and artificiality." Two impressions were paramount in his preaching, as especially characteristic of his eloquence: They were its inexhaustible affluence of thought and feeling, and its genuine life. Professor A. B. Bruce, of Glasgow, after hearing him three times with growing admiration said: "Our great preachers (of England and Scotland) take into the pulpit a bucket full, or half full, of the word of God and then by the force of personal mechanism they attempt to convey it to the congregation. But this man is just a great water-main attached to the everlasting reservoir of God's truth and grace and love, and streams of *life* pour through him to refresh every weary soul." "*Life*," says Professor Allen, "was a word running through all his sermons. This ever recurring word is expressive of the man."

Whenever he rose to address the great congregations that were attracted to his preaching, his heart kindled at the sight, and he was eager to communicate the truth which he believed to be divinely adapted to human need. It was a living message that came from his lips.

At the outbreak of the Civil War in 1861, the second year of his Philadelphia ministry, he threw himself with patriotic fervor into the various questions of emancipation and reconstruction, and his eloquence, like Beecher's, was raised to its highest pitch by their influence. It was a time of mighty inspirations, and he was touched and deeply moved by them. "It awakened and evoked the greatness

of Phillips Brooks." His patriotic sermons and
platform addresses then mightily stirred men. He
was reckoned among the foremost of the advocates
of moral and political reform.

The Episcopal Church, prior to the war, and even
after its beginning, was very conservative and
silent upon the subject of slavery, and disposed to
frown upon any utterance condemnatory of it, as
"political preaching" unsuitable to her pulpits and
unbecoming her ministers; but through Brooks'
influence this reactionary attitude of his Church was
changed, and she was brought into full sympathy
with the government in its struggle with the rebel-
lious states trying to maintain that great iniquity.

When the assassin Booth, inspired by its spirit,
killed Lincoln, Brooks' voice was among the most
eloquent to deplore his death and eulogize his great
virtues and service. Among his published addresses
this eulogy holds a notable place. Its appreciation
of Lincoln is a measure of his own greatness as well
as of Lincoln's. Only a great soul can so worthily
estimate, and so eloquently speak the praises of
another great soul.

Another influence, second only in importance to
that of the Civil War, which contributed to his development in Philadelphia was that of his friendships.
He was a sociable man, whose heart craved the society of congenial friends, and whose mind expanded
and appeared at its best under the stimulus of their
presence and conversation, Included in the circle
were his brother ministers, W. W. Newton and
C. A. Richards, and some eminent laymen.

PHILLIPS BROOKS

I have spoken of Dr. Weir Mitchell's estimate of his greatness and eloquence. He became the pastor of Dr. Mitchell in Holy Trinity and formed with him and his invalid sister, Elizabeth, a most intimate friendship. "Always once, and usually twice a week, he dined with us," says Dr. Mitchell, "and five evenings out of seven he was in the habit of dropping in about ten o'clock for a talk before the fire in my library. The friendship thus formed matured with years. How dear it was to me I like to think. . . . With my sister it was as close a tie. She was by nature fond of books and her reading was wide and various. In many directions she became singularly learned, especially in all biblical literature and the history of the Church. Witty, quick of tongue, picturesque and often quaint in statement, her talk was full of pleasant surprises. He said to me once, that no one had so influenced his opinions as this remarkable woman."

We speak of his friendship with her and her gifted brother, to indicate that he was no recluse, either in Philadelphia or in Boston, though he never married. As a matter of fact he was one of the most genial and companionable of men and he had in full development all the social virtues. This is one secret of his large-hearted, universal sympathy with men and of the attraction he exercised over them. He was entirely unspoiled by his great success and widespread fame. He never put on airs, or exhibited anything like personal vanity or arrogance: modest and seemingly unconscious of his indisputable claims to consideration, he was courteous and friendly to all, manifesting the meekness and gentleness of Christ, with whom he lived in spirit.

There never was a pastor who enjoyed more of the love and confidence of his people. When he entered upon his ministry in Boston, as pastor of Trinity Church, October 31, 1869, he was not quite thirty-four years old. In his service of twenty-two years with this church, it steadily grew in strength and influence, until it became, through the attractiveness of Mr. Brooks' preaching, one of the most notable churches in the land. His congregations were variously composed of strangers from abroad, the élite of the city, large numbers of young men and women, and the poor; and it attests the largeness and kindness of his heart, that the humblest class received as much of his notice as the highest, and as keenly enjoyed his message. His sermons increased in spirituality and heart-power, and sounded an ever-deepening note with the advancing years; and their unfailing, unwaning interest for the great throng which hung upon his lips, year after year, proved that he had unmistakably "the true genius of the preacher, which consists in the power of so uttering spiritual truth that it shall be effective in influencing the hearts of men."

During his lifetime, he published five volumes of sermons, which had a very large sale; thirty thousand, twenty-five thousand, twenty thousand; and since his death the number of volumes has grown to twelve. They are among the choicest in homiletic literature. In those first volumes only five of his Philadelphia sermons were published. As compared with his later sermons, "they are," Professor Allen thinks, "more poetic and imaginative, with a higher literary finish. The traces of work are more manifest in them." Example: The seventh sermon of the First Series, "All Saints Day," "perhaps the most beautiful of all," Professor Allen says. "In his later preaching the contagion of a great conviction, into which with growing clearness he had come, was manifest." On the power of this the preacher most relies for the propagation of the truth.

In Boston his fame became not only national but international. He now had the honor of preaching repeatedly in Westminster Abbey and before the Queen of England; and his preaching across the sea made as profound impression as in his own country. Sermons preached in Westminster Abbey: "Symbol and Reality," sixteenth of First Series: "The Candle of the Lord," first of Second Series. With both of these Dean Stanley was greatly pleased. Sermon before the Queen, "A Pillar in God's Temple," fourth in Second Series.

Three notable things during his Boston ministry are especially worth attention for their relation to his expanding influence and ministerial powers:

His preaching in Huntington Hall.

His "Lectures on Preaching" before the Yale Divinity School.

His ministry to the students of Harvard College.

He preached for four years in Huntington Hall because of the destruction of his own church in the great Boston fire, in November, 1872. Those four years mark a distinct epoch in his ministry. The

location of the Hall, on Boylston Street, was more
convenient, its accommodations more ample, and
its novelty as a place of worship especially attractive
to many, though its secular character and associations, made it objectionable to many churchgoing
people. Immediately the great Hall became a
center of interest and attraction. It was soon filled,
thronged beyond its utmost capacity, morning and
afternoon. "No courses of lectures on literature,
art, or science with which the Hall was associated
ever witnessed a greater audience. This was the
case Sunday after Sunday, till people became accustomed to it as to the gifts of God and hardly won-
dered at the munificence of the feast." There,
Principal Tulloch, of the University of Aberdeen,
Scotland, heard him, in the spring of '74, preach the
sermon entitled "The Opening of the Eyes," (published in the Fifth Series) and sitting down to write
home to his wife, he said, "I never heard preaching
like it. So much thought and so much life combined;
such a reach of mind and such a depth and insight
of soul. I was electrified. I could have got up and
shouted."

His lectures to the students of the Yale Divinity
School were given in 1877 upon the Lyman Beecher
lectureship, and form the most precious volume in
the whole series. We recommend to all divinity
students to procure the book, "Lectures on Preaching," and to read it once a year for five years, until
their minds are fully possessed of and enriched by
its ideas upon the subject discussed. A more stimulating and instructive volume upon the general

subject of the Christian ministry we never have met. "It abounded in sentences which linger in the mind." Brooks was then forty-two years old, and in those lectures he gave to the theological students and the younger clergy the ripe results of twenty years experience and thought. "They constitute the autobiography of Phillips Brooks, the confessions of a great preacher." Besides their literary charm and personal flavor, they have the additional merit of presenting to the ministry the noblest and most inspiring ideal of the preacher's work and character. We reckon it the most precious of his writings. It has had a mighty influence in moulding the characters and shaping the work of the ministry in the last generation. It was republished in English and translated into the French and read by ministers of every denomination. The good it has done can not be estimated.

His ministry to the students of Harvard College may be said to have begun almost with his coming from Philadelphia to Boston. His voice was often heard, in sermon and address, in Appleton Chapel and in the Episcopal Theological School of Cambridge. They thronged to hear him whenever he was advertised to speak, and they went over to Boston in large numbers to hear him Sunday afternoon. When the college adopted the plan of having a body of temporary Chaplains, who should severally serve a number of Sabbaths, as preacher and pastor, in place of one college preacher to minister to the students, he was foremost among those selected, and he was repeatedly chosen to serve the college in this way. Of all the preachers whom the students heard, he was the most enthusiastically admired and loved. It was fitting, in view of this love and the great influence that he had exerted over them, that when he died his body should be borne to and from Trinity Church, where the funeral services were held, on the shoulders of Harvard students. He had been their best counsellor and friend. He, more than any other man, had delivered the college from its former reproach of being a godless place, and made its atmosphere religious and wholesome, so that the last time he preached in Appleton Chapel at the beginning of the college year he could truly say, "If there is any man of whom this place makes a sceptic or a profligate, what can we sadly say but this: 'He was not worthy of the place to which he came, he was not up to Harvard College.' The man with true soul cannot be ruined here. Coming here humbly, bravely, he shall meet his Christ. Here he shall come into the fuller presence of the Christ whom he had known and loved in the dear Christian home, and know and love Him more than ever."

No higher or harder test of a preacher's character and power can be found than to win the respect and love of such a body of young men. He who does it must be pure gold. They are keen to detect any counterfeit, and merciless in their contempt for it.

He died in the early morning of Monday, January 23, 1893, in the fifty-seventh year of his age. He had preached on Tuesday evening of the preceding week his last sermon at the Visitation service given as bishop of the diocese to the Church of the Good Shepherd in Boston. The subject of his sermon was, *Christ Feeding the Multitude in the Desert,* a subject that lay close to his heart and which may be said to have embodied the principal theme of his ministry. The announcement of his death, unheralded by any previous notice of his illness, produced a great shock of surprise and of wide-spread sorrow. By his death Boston felt that it had lost its greatest citizen. The popular sentiment demanded that a bronze statue, to perpetuate his imposing form and noble face, should be erected to his memory. The eminent sculptor, St. Gaudens, executed it among his last works, and it now stands in front of Trinity Church. It gives a good idea of the superb manhood of its subject.

Among the substantial tributes given to his memory is "The Phillips Brooks House" at Harvard College, a noble building erected for religious purposes to perpetuate in the college the Christian atmosphere which he did so much to create there. The fund for it was started by the class of 1855, his own class, and it was swollen by large contributions made by English friends and admirers. On the tablet in the central hall is this inscription:

"A preacher of righteousness and hope, majestic in stature, impetuous in utterances, rejoicing in the truth, unhampered by bonds of church or station, he brought by his life and doctrine fresh faith to a people, fresh meaning to ancient creeds; to this University he gave constant love, large service, high example."

Thank God for such a character, for such a ministry, for such a life, in which the aspiration expressed in his own words was fulfilled:

> "—a life that men shall love to know
> Has once been lived on this degenerate earth,
> And sing it like some tale of long ago
> In ballad-sweetness round their household hearth."

BIBLIOGRAPHY

The Interest and Value of Ministerial Biography as illustrated in:
The History of Christian Preaching. By Prof. T. H. Pattison. American Baptist Publication Society. Philadelphia, 1903.

The Outlook. November 12, 1910. Reminiscences of Edward Everett Hale.

Autobiography of Lyman Beecher. Edited by his son. 2 vols. Harper & Brothers, 1871.

Life and Times of Saint John Chrysostom. By W. R. W. Stephens. London. John Murray, 1883.

Historical Sketches. By John Henry Newman of The Oratory. 2 vols. London. Basil Montague Pickering, 1876.

John of Antioch in Orations and Addresses. By R. S. Storrs, D. D. Boston. Pilgrim Press.

Ben Hur. By Gen. Lew Wallace. New York. Harper's, 1880.

Bernard of Clairveaux. The Times, the Man, and His Work. By Richard S. Storrs. New York. Chas. Scribner's Sons, 1892.

Church History of Britain. By Thomas Fuller. Encyclopedia Brittanica. Article, "Monarchism."

Life of John Bunyan. By Rev. John Brown. Bunyan's Grace Abounding. Pilgrim's Progress. Bunyan's Sermons: Come and Welcome to Jesus Christ. Bunyan's The Barren Fig-Tree. The Jerusalem Sinner Saved. Life of Dean A. P. Stanley. Inauguration of Bunyan's Statue at Bedford. Bunyan's Sermon: The Heavenly Footman.

Life and Times of Richard Baxter. 2 vols. By William Orme, Bishop Gilbert Burnet's History of His own Times. Baxter's Saints' Rest, and The Reformed Pastor. Reliquiae Baxterianae: or, Baxter's History of his own Life and Times.

Address at the Inauguration of the Statue of Richard Baxter in Kidderminster. By Dean A. P. Stanley. Littell's Living Age, vol. 127.

Bossuet: Orator Études Critiques sur les Sermons. Par Eugene Gandar. Paris. Errin et Cie, 1888.

Occasional Papers. By Dean R. W. Church. Vol. 1: No. 14. Bossuet's Oraison Funébres. Paris. Garnier Fréres.

BIBLIOGRAPHY

Life and Letters of Frederick W. Robertson. By Stopford A. Brooke. New York. Harper & Brothers, 1878.

The Sermons of F. W. Robertson. Complete in One volume. New York. Harper's, 1878.

Representative Modern Preachers. By L. O. Brastow, D. D. New York. The MacMillan Co., 1904.

The Life of Alexander McLaren. By Miss E. T. McLaren. Hodder & Stoughton. London.

Sermons Preached in Manchester. 3 vols. MacMillan & Co.

The Secret of Power. MacMillan & Co.

Life of Henry Ward Beecher, the Shakespeare of the Pulpit. By John Henry Barrows, D. D.

Henry Ward Beecher. By Lyman Abbott.

Autobiography and Correspondence of Lyman Beecher, D. D. Edited by his son.

Six Sermons upon Intemperance. By L. Beecher.

Sermon against Duelling. By L. Beecher.

Life of Phillips Brooks. By Prof. Alexander V. G. Allen. 2 vols. New York E. P. Dutton & Co., 1900.

Bibliotheca Sacra, for January, 1902. Vol. 59. Article, Huxley and Phillips Brooks. By Dr. W. N. Clarke.

Sermons, 1st, 2d, and 3d Series.

Yale Lectures on Preaching. By Phillips Brooks. E. P. Dutton, New York, 1877.

Yale Lectures on Puritan Preachers and Preaching. By Dr John Brown, D. D.

INDEX

INDEX

vain attempts made over King's Declaration to reconcile religious differences 134–140; declined the bishopric of Hereford, 140; attends the Savoy
Conference, 140–142; deprived of his charge in Kidderminster; his offense;
therefore ever an object of bitter persecution by Bishop Morley and
others, 143–145; his marriage and devoted wife, 145. His pen busy in
spite of poor health, "Dying Thoughts," "Narrative of His Life," 145–
146. His unfortunate, offensive manner of attacking opponents; the
comparison his biographer, Orme, makes between his manner and that
of Dr. Owen, 146–147; controversey with Edward Bagshaw, its sad ending
and his regret over it, 147–148. Notable change wrought in his last years
from contentiousness to tolerance, his motto for toleration, 148–149.
His own record of changes in his own mind and opinion, "since the
unriper times of his youth,"—Dean Stanley's estimate of its value, 150.
"Counsels of Moderation," 151–157; monument to his memory dedicated
July 28, 1875,—significance of it, 157–158. In Judge Jeffries Court—
imprisonment—closing years and death, 159–161.

Henry Ward Beecher, parentage, early home environment, 325–328;
boyhood in Boston—attends Latin School—desires to go to sea—diverted
from this by father's wisdom, 329; Mt. Pleasant School, good teachers
and revival turn his thoughts toward the ministry, 329, 330; enters
Amherst College, habits of study, college standing, 330; at Lane Seminary, 331; profitable study of New Testament under Prof. C. E. Stowe,
but neglects Systematic Theology—never had much knowledge of it,
331–332; the Seminary then a storm center of theological controversy,
from which his father suffered to the disgust and perplexity of Henry
Ward, 332; has a remarkable revelation of God's truth, 333–334; effect
of this upon him, 335; call to Lawrenceburg, marriage and early house-
keeping, 335; ideas as to conditions of success, favorable impression soon
made by his sermons, large congregations, the theology in his preaching,
335–336; his widening influence, call to Indianapolis, crudeness of the
place of that time, 336; impression made by his preaching there; where
he got his ideas of the aim and right method of preaching; his indebted-
ness to the Book of Acts and writings of St. Paul; his preaching evangelistic and productive of revivals, lectures to "Young Men," 337–338;
pictorial style of preaching, illustrations fresh, original and profuse, 338–
339; extended reputation, call to Plymouth Church, Brooklyn, N. Y.,
ill health of his wife, Plymouth Church's growth under his ministry, 339;
his equipment and capital for the business of the ministry, 340–347;
his remarkable voice, not natural but result of careful culture and training, 342; his pulpit prayers, remark of a gifted lady, 346–347; his good
sense, 347; summary of his theology, 348; after 6 months, Plymouth
Church crowded, 348; policeman's direction to strangers; "Follow the

his contempt of critics and opponents, 104; the father of modern rationalism, 104; Bernard's opinion of him, 104–105; the two men represented
"colliding tendencies," 105; they join issue at Council of Sens, 105;
Abelard's conduct there inexplicable—a puzzle of history, 107; Bernard's
insistence that the Council condemn him unjust, 707; alleged danger of
his teaching not a good reason, 107; Abelard finds a refuge at Clugni,
108; character of Peter the Venerable, its abbot, 108; Abelard's "History
of Calamities," 108; his reconciliation with Bernard and peaceful end;
his life not a failure, 109; Dr. Storrs' summary, 110.

Bible biographies, 6, 7.

Binney, Dr. Thomas, 310.

Biographies, Ministerial, spiritually beneficial, 6; entertaining, 10;
inspiring to the discouraged, 12; suggestive of good method, 14; give
ideals, 25.

Bossuet, most celebrated preacher in reign of Louis XIV, 165; M.
Gandar's careful study of Bossuet, 165; dedicated by pious parents to the
Catholic priesthood, 166; educated for it in Dijon, his native city, and at
College of Navarre, Paris, 166; youthful precocity exhibited in Salon of
Marquise de Rambouillet, 167; tribute to Nicolas Cornet, 166; unspoiled
by early admiration, 167; the "fatal gift" of fluency, Lord Russell quoted,
168; from things required of a good preacher, 169; Bossuet's six years in
Metz, 169; incident in French history about Cardinal de Bouillon, 170;
the things emphasized by Bossuet reveal his own method, 170; the two
most essential things, 170; primary purpose of study of the Scriptures,
171; value of Church Fathers; much accomplished by little regular
persevering study, 171; remark of Lamartine, 172; accent of authority
derived from Scripture, 172; his lighter diet, 172; a grand style natural to
him; things learned later, 173; two remarkable powers, 173; unfettered
freedom, 173; benefit of previous writing, 174; reputation in Metz, 174;
Dr. John Brown quoted, 174; Mr. Gandar; Dr. Horace Bushnell on the
"talent of growth," 175; two means of self-improvement used, 176;
benefits from a year in Paris, 177; influence of Pascal, 178; Dean Church
quoted, 179; these efforts commendable, 179; preaches before Anne of
Austria, Queen Mother, 180; invited to preach Lenten Sermons of the
Louvre, 180; in constant request from 1660 to 1670; his audiences, 180;
funeral orations, 181–182; remark of Guisot, 182; culmination of career,
183; always a learner, 183; not of blameless life or flawless character,
183; approved of Revocation of Edict of Nantes, 183; absurd laudation
of Louis XIV, 184; Guizot's opinion of Bossuet, and the estimate of Mr.
Gandar, 184: "Golden Age of the French Pulpit," fruitless, 184; its preaching compared with that of Baxter and the Wesleys, 185; reasons for its
ineffectiveness.

INDEX

Boswell, James, biographer of Samuel Johnson, 130.

Boyd, Rev. Archibald, 245.

Brainard, David, 242.

Brastow, Prof. L. O., quoted, 255, 272, 278, 361, 377, 379, 380.

Breda, 134

Brooks, Phillips, his parents and birthplace, 361-363; education at Latin School and Harvard College, 364, 365; spiritual and religious development, his mother's wisdom in it, 365-367; Dr. W. N. Clarke quoted, 365; not successful as a teacher, 367; theological school in Alexandria, Va., 368-371; notebooks, 371-375; first attempts at preaching, 375-376; called to Church of the Advent, Philadelphia, 376; ministry in Philadelphia, 376-377; personal qualities, 377-385; Dr. Weir Mitchell quoted, 385, 386, 391; Commemoration Day at Harvard, 385; President Eliot's remark, 385-386; Brooks' eloquence, 386; made of preparation for preaching, 386-388; affluence of thought and feeling,—Professor A. B. Bruce quoted, 389; influence of the outbreak of the Civil War, 389-390; Eulogy of Lincoln, 390; his friends, 390-391; ministry in Boston, 392; published sermons, 392-393; preaches in Westminster Abbey and before the Queen, 393; preaching in Huntington Hall, testimony of Principal Tulloch, 394; "Lectures on Preaching," 394; ministry to students of Harvard College, 395-396; his death, body borne to and from Trinity Church by students, 396; his last sermon on the main theme of his ministry, 397; his statue by St. Gaudens, 397; the Phillip's Brooks House at Harvard, 397; the Inscription in Central Hall, 397; his aspiration fulfilled, 398.

Brooks, William Gray, father of Phillips, 361-363.

Brown, Dr. John, quoted, 174, 212, 213, 224, 227, 296, 299, 300.

Bruce, Prof. A. B. Bruce, 389.

Bunny's Resolution, 113.

Bunyan, John, Dr. Thomas Arnold's estimate of him, 191; birth and parentage, 191,193, a great genius trained in the school of Providence, 192; Epictetus and Marcus Aurelius, 192; "Grace Abounding," 192; living in the Age of Cromwell and the Civil War he scarcely refers to its events, 193; account of himself as boy and young man, 194, 195; opinions of Macaulay and Froude, 195; a soldier, 195; his marriage, wife's dowry and good influence, 196; three providential agencies that shaped him, 197; the poor Bedford women, 198; Mr. Gifford their pastor, 200, 206; began to read the Bible as never before, 201, 215; examples of enlightenment from the Bible, 202-203; the harm from introspection, 204; temptations of Satan, 204, 205; preserved from madness by soothing influence of the Bible, 205; his dialogues with Satan like Luther's, 206; Bunyan's beliefs and doctrine those of the Reformer, 206; relief given by Luther's Commentary on Galatians, 206; Bunyan's use of Scriptures, 207; the

INDEX

"law work" upon Bunyan's soul, 207; benefit resulting from it, 208; ordained for the ministry at twenty seven, 208; Froude's estimate of him as a preacher, 208; his fame reached to London, 209; Dr. John Owen's remark to the king about his preaching, 209; qualities that distinguished him as a preacher, 210; his remarkable style, 211, 223; on "Christ as our Advocate," 212; Dr. John Brown quoted, 212, 213, 224; examples of use of his imagination, 213; productiveness of his mind in religious subjects, 214; the value of the Bible as a fertilizer of the mind, 215; his sermons as examples of homiletic skill, 216; use of the dialogue, 217; the use of it by Prof. E. A. Park, 217; imprisonment for preaching, 217–218; the two jails of Bedford, 218; John Howard's name and work associated with them, 218; imprisonment of Bunyan and Quakers cost of liberty, 219; Froude's lame defense of the government, 220; Bunyan's wife to the judges, 220; his employment in prison, 220; his treatises, "Grace Abounding," "Christian Behavior," "The Holy City" and "Pilgrim's Progress" composed in prison, 218, 221, 222; his style, 223; Dean Stanley upon the "Pilgrim's Progress," 225–226; his last words from the pulpit, and death in London, 228; "Bunhill Fields" his burial place, 228; his Memorial Window in Westminster Abbey, 229.

Burke, Edmund, 5.

Burnet, Bishop Gilbert, 134, 142.

Bushnell, Dr. Horace, 175.

Butler, Rev. Daniel, 12.

Calvin, John, the Reformer, 91

Charleton, Margaret, wife of Richard Baxter, 145.

Chapman, Dr. J. W. 9.

Chrysostom, John of Antioch,—Dr. R. S. Storrs' estimate of him as a preacher, 21, 58; birth, parents, 31; Antioch in the Fourth Century, A.D., 32; twofold environment, local and imperial, 32–35; "Ben Hur" story of Lew Wallace, 32–33; the decaying Roman empire, 34; the peril attending Imperial dignity, 35; instability of the government, 35; general apprehension of ruin, 35; the remarkable men and women of this time, 36; precocity of Chrysostom, his teacher Libanius, 36; enters on the practice of law,—but soon abandons it to study for the ministry, 37; his friendship for Basil, 37–38; influence of Meletius, bishop of Antioch, 38; of Diodorus, the teacher of Bible, 39; the two friends shun episcopal dignity, 39; the broken promise, 39; Chrysostom's justification of himself, 40; his mother's death permits the longed for retirement to monastery and hermit's cell, 40; ordained deacon by Meletius, and served under Flavian, 40; duties of this office, 40–41; Chrysostom's personal qualities, 41; Cardinal Newman's estimate, 41–42; ordained presbyter by Flavian in his fortieth year, 42; his preparatory training of fifteen years needed for his work, 42; at once rose to the zenith of fame as preacher in Antioch; his eloquence, personal appearance, and oratorical ability, 42–46; has a rational theology, 46–49; "Riot of the Statues," 49–50; Treasonable Acts of the Mob—revulsion of terror, 50; the Emperor's vengeance feared, 51; advantage taken of the situation by Chrysostom, and calming effect of his preaching, 51; Bishop Flavian's winter journey to Constantinople, 51; wonders wrought by Chrysostom in his absence, 52; extracts from his reported sermons, 52–58; their enduring vitality and interest, 59; eloquence of Chrysostom attracts the notice of Eutropius, who desires to make him Archbishop of Constantinople, an honor which he shuns, 59–60; strategem used to kidnap him and carry him off, 60; the dignity not a bed of roses, 60; differing ideas of Eutropius and Chrysostom in regard to its obligations, 60; at first everything seemed fair through popularity of Chrysostum's preaching, 61; torch-light pilgrimage to martyr's shrine, and natural admiration of preacher and empress, 61–62; a change to hostility, 62; rebuke of the sins of the great, 62–63; his austerity distasteful to the great, 63; downfall of Eutropius, 64; asylum of St. Sophia given him; Empress Eudoxia offended and furious, 65; plots for Chrysostum's destruction, 65; condemned and deposed by the "Synod of the Oak," 66; exiled and recalled, 66; exiled a second time, 66; his death and last words, 67; his relics brought back to Constantinople by Eudoxia's son, who kneeling above them implored forgiveness for the sins of his parents, 68; but few in the history of the world more deserving of honor, 68.

INDEX

Eutropius, 59–60, 64–65.

Finney, Rev. Charles, G., 9.

Flavian, 40, 42, 51.

Fox, Charles J., distinguished British Orator, 20.

Fox's "Book of Martyrs," 139.

Gandar, M. Eug., 165, 175, 177, 184.

Gibbon, Edward, historian, 41.

Goodell, Dr. C. L., 23, 24.

Guisot, French historian, 182, 184.

Guthrie, Dr. Thomas, Scotch preacher, 16–18.

Hadley, S. H., 9.

Hale, Dr. Edward Everett, 10.

Hale, Sir Matthew, English Judge, 145.

Hall, Dr. Newman, 21.

Hall, Robert, 59.

Hamilton, Alexander, 174.

Henrietta, duchess of Orleans, 181.

Hodge, Dr. Charles, 37.

Hooker, Richard, 115.

Hyde, Chancellor, Earl of Clarendon, 134, 136, 138.

Jeffries, the infamous English Judge, 159.

Johnson, Dr. Samuel, 130.

Jowett, Professor Benjamin, Oxford University, VII, 143.

Jowett, Dr. J. H., Clergyman, quoted 261, 262.

Judson, Dr. Adoniram, Missionary, 9.

Keble, John, author of the "Christian Year," 239.

Knox, Alexander, 295.

Knox, John, Scottish Reformer, 13, 139.

Lamartine, 172.

Lenten Sermons of Bossuet, in 1662, 181.

Libanius, teacher of Chrysostom, 36–37, Liddon, 59.

Louis XIV, King of France, 181, 186–187.

Lowell, James Russell, 28.

Luther, the Reformer, 13, 277.

Mather, Cotton, 161.

McChene, 24.

McLaren, Alexander: his name 283; birthplace and parents, 283–284; a scholar in Glasgow High School and University, 284; enters Baptist College at Stepney, Rev. Benjamin Davis, Principal, 285; religious development, influence of Rev. David Rusell, 285; "had to be" a minister, 286; called to preach at Portland Chapel, Southampton, at age of twenty, 286; benefits of his early ministry there of twelve years, 286; conception

INDEX

INDEX

harm of desultory reading; the mischief of "careless multifarious" reading, 240;—his reading of Classic and standard English writers, 241; his ministry in four places, 241; in Winchester, as curate—his rector, Mr. Nicholson, 241; life and work at Winchester, Brainard's Life; his sermons, 243; ordered to Switzerland for his health; health improved by change; valuable acquaintances in Geneva; Cesar Malan and Helen Denys, whom he marries, 245; given a curacy in Cheltenham; happy in his rector, Rev. Archibald Boyd, 245; his inspiring preaching in Cheltenham, brilliancy as a talker, 245–246; three things greatly affected him there: friends, the social atmosphere, and books, 247; influence of the social atmosphere baneful, other two good; Cheltenham, a fashionable watering place, frequented by intolerant religious people, 248; Robertson estranged from the Evangelical School by the harsh, untruthful utterances of the *Record* and *Guardian;* hasty and unjust in his judgment of this School, 249; The break with them gradual, 250; his reading of Tennyson's "In Memoriam," Carlyle, Guizot, Nicbuhr, Dante expanded and enriched his mind, 251; other profitable reading; neglect of exercise,252; Wordsworth quoted, 253; determines to sever connection with Evangelical School, 253; goes to Tyrol and Innsbruck, 254; Spiritual Crisis, 254; Professor Brastow quoted, 255; given charge of St. Ebbe's Oxford, by Bishop Wilberforce, 256; the attraction of his preaching because of new light received, 256; the principles of his teaching henceforth, 257; Trinity Chapel, Brighton, offered him; enters upon his labors there in his 32nd year, 257; Brighton as a fashionable watering-place, 257–258; expository lectures on 1st Samuel, 258; accused of political preaching, 259; charged with Socialism, 260; the *Record* attacks him, 260; his reply, 261; Dr. J. H. Jewett quoted, 261, 262; Robertson's intense sensitiveness; his preaching in Trinity Chapel, 263–267; mode of preparing sermons, 264; their enduring interest, 265; contemporary conditions: a time of transition in theology, 268; of transition in politics, 269; of transition in style of preaching, 271; shattered health, 272–273; chronic morbidness of mind, 273–274; laid upon himself unnecessary crushing burdens, ex: writing out his sermons after delivery, 275; the world's profit from this sacrifice of friendship and the fame thus won scarcely a compensation for the misery it cost him, 275; symptoms of distress and breakdown, 276; premature death in middle of 38th year, 276; Luther's remark, 277; Robertson's repugnance to hearing commendation of his sermons, 277; a *seer* as well as an eloquent preacher, 278; his wholesome modernism, 278; the shifting of emphasis from theological dogmas to ethical precepts of the New Testament and the example and spirit of Christ largely due to him, 279.

Richards, Rev. C. A., 390.
Russell, Rev. David, 285.

INDEX

Lightning Source UK Ltd.
Milton Keynes UK
UKHW021936180219
337529UK00011B/773/P